I0127205

Ali Abu AK-AWAR

Parus aux éditions G.S.P

- Daniel JOAQUIM, *Jugement eschatologique selon Matthieu 25 :31-46 : approche théologique et philosophique*, Guérin Scholar's Press, Montréal, 2019.
- Dr. Samson N'Taadjèl KAGMATCHÉ, ***Chérubins bibliques : Tradition chrétienne et L'Art de la Renaissance,*** Guérin Scholar's Press, Montréal, 2019.
- Dr. Jean KOULAGNA, *Exégèse et Kérygme : Une introduction pratique à l'exégèse biblique au service de la prédication,* Guérin Scholar's Press, Montréal, 2018.
- Dr. Samson N'Taadjèl KAGMATCHÉ, ***Les ennemis et adversaires dans la Bible****: ruses et tactiques,* Guérin Scholar's Press, Montréal, 2018.
- Dr. Samson N'Taadjèl KAGMATCHÉ, ***The Lamassu and the Cherubim: Two Hybrid genii.*** *How did the Cherubim become Angels?* © Guérin Scholar's Press, Montreal, 2017.
- Dr. Samson N'Taadjèl KAGMATCHÉ, ***The God of Mount Carmel: The Contending views associated to the Biblical Mount Carmel,*** Guérin Scholar's Press, Montreal, 2017.

À paraître:

* Oulandja TADOURÉ, *Colonisation et Chefferie en pays Konkomba de 1897 à 1960.*

Dr. Ali Abu Al-Awar

ISRAELI – PALESTINIAN CONFLICT ON AL- HARAM AL- SHARIF

Pious Palestinian Women Supporting the Religious and Political Role of al-Haram al-Sharif

Montréal, Canada

435 rue St-Roch, CP: H3N 1K2; # 4, Montreal,
Canada
www.guerinscholarspress.com
info@guerinscholarspress.com
ISBN: 978-1-999-0-982-2-3

Ali Abu AK-AWAR

ISRAELI – PALESTINIAN CONFLICT ON AL- HARAM AL- SHARIF

Pious Palestinian Women Supporting the Religious and Political Role of al-Haram al-Sharif

ACKNOWLEDGMENT

I am so grateful to my wife, Eman, and my children who supported and believed in me throughout the preparation of this thesis.

Sincere thanks go to my advisers, Prof. Ruth Roded and Prof. Yitzhak Reiter, for their guidance, encouragements, discussions and faith in me and my project. My PhD would never have taken the shape it did without their support.

Special thanks also to Prof. Lihi Ben Shitrit, Prof. Meir Hatina, Dr. Yael Bedra, Prof. Gili Drori, EranTzidkiyahu, Dr. Nir Boms, Dr. Uzi Rabi, Tova Gottesman and Authority Research Students at Hebrew University of Jerusalem For their encouragement.

My thanks go to the editors Kevin Daromar and Chelsi Muller for their excellent editing of my study. I would like to thank Prof. Noah Feldman and Mr. Menachem Butler, for their hospitality in Cambridge, MA during November 2017, when I delivered portions of this thesis at an international conference that they hosted at the Harvard Law School that explored various perspectives of the Temple Mount/Haram al-Sharif. I look forward to our continued friendship and work together in the years ahead.

Thanks to all my friends who patiently stood by me as I worked hard with this project: Bashar Moulem. I am also especially grateful to all those I met/ or interviewed over the work of my fieldwork in Al-Haram al-Sharif, Jerusalem, West Bank and Gaza Strip- thank you for your time, patience and willingness to share.

Thank you to Al-Bierh Public Library and all the employees who helped me in the references and documents.

Finally, I would like to thank the former Mufti of Palestine and Al-Aqsa Mosque Preacher, Sheikh Ikrima Sabri, the leaders of Murabitat and Murabiteen. I am deeply grateful that you trusted me enough to allow me to take a glimpse into your lives and homes, and I am immeasurably indebted that you spoke with me frankly and without fear.

Ali Abu Al-Awar
Jerusalem, Old City
January 2018

ABSTRACT

Al-Haram al-Sharif is the third most sacred place in the Muslim World, and the most holy Muslim site in Jerusalem as well as the holiest site in Judaism (and also a Christian holy place). Since the 1920s it serves as a nexus of political, cultural, religious, and social activities among Palestinians and Israelis, and since 1948 also to Arabs citizens of Israel.

Moreover, Al-Aqsa Mosque was and still is the focal point of Palestinian struggle against the Jewish Israelis and it serves as a barometer of tensions in the Israeli-Palestinian arena. Therefore, it is not surprising that pious Palestinian women visit the site regularly and take part in activities there; particularly when they feel it is under attack by Jewish Israelis.

Palestinian women began to play significant social and political roles in the early 20th century, similar to those played by women in Arab countries that were colonized such as Egypt, Iraq, and Syria. Their activities included establishing associations, centers, and unions. Their focus was on national rights; usually with a secular orientation but occasionally with a religious underpinning.

The role of Palestinian Muslim women on the political stage is not a new phenomenon. One of the most important social and political trends in Palestine and in the Arab countries in the early days of the twentieth century was the involvement of Palestinian women's movements in the social and political sphere, particularly in matters which related to education. Pious Palestinian women were active alongside their "secular sisters" in the national movement at least since the British Mandate period. Beginning in the 1970s, the pious women's social and educational activities prepared them for prominent political roles in the first intifada beginning in December 1987. In the late 1980s and throughout the 1990s, pious Muslim women played a prominent role in supporting the Islamist movements in Palestine, especially Hamas, and advocating for and carrying out political actions in mosques, charities and Islamic schools. They played a major part in the victory of Hamas in the 2006 elections, in which Hamas women assumed six seats in the Legislative Council, one of them, Mariam Salah, served as the minister of Women's Affairs in Hamas' government in 2006.

The leadership of the Palestinian women's movement 1920's-1948 was from the social elite with some middle class participation. Lower class rural women did, however, participate in the Qassam movement and in the 1936-1939 Arab Revolt. As the women's movement evolved, its membership shifted from the hands of the upper and upper middle class to lower class women and from urban to rural women. The first intifada was a major turning point in women political activism because of the extensive participation of women of all backgrounds and the involvement of the Palestinian Islamist movement in the armed resistance.

By the end of the 1990s, the Islamic Movement headed by Sheikh Ra'ed Salah became active in Jerusalem. Salah conducted activities that emphasized the Islamic identity of Jerusalem and Al-Haram al-Sharif. One of the activities, which came in response to Jewish visitors to Al-Haram al-Sharif, and in light of the increasing number of Jewish religious an ideological groups visiting Har HaBayit/Al-Haram al-Sharif in the last decade, including organized Jewish women, the Islamic Movement decided, to establish study circles of *Murabitin* (male defenders), and later *murabitat* (female defenders), in order to have the largest possible number of Muslim men and women at the site. This step was the continuation of what Women for Al-Aqsa (*Nisa min ajl al-Aqsa*), a branch of the Islamic Movement in Israel, had started. It was particularly aimed at facing Jewish religious women visiting al-Haram al-Sharif for ideological purposes. Jewish female activists at the Temple Mount, and Muslim women at the Haram al-Sharif, have similar religious belief that the site is the closest point to God. The two groups are very much aware of each other, are influenced by each other's actions, and devise their work largely as a reaction to each other.

In 2010, the northern branch of the Islamic Movement in Israel began organizing study circles (*masateb al-i'lm, halaqat dirasyieh* in Arabic) for women in Islamic law or Shari'a,

Islamic doctrine (*fiqh*), and Qur᾿an. The study circles were held under the trees of al-Haram al-Sharif. They were led by prominent female and male teachers from Palestinian universities. The participants received monthly stipends from the Islamic Movement in Israel, increasing the groups' membership. These Israeli Muslim women joined pious Muslim women from the Jerusalem area who came to al-Haram al-Sharif to pray and study. They became known as the *murabitat*. The *murabitat* emerged against the background of almost a century of Palestinian women's political activism.

This study documents how contemporary Palestinian Muslim women, both the *murabitat* as well as other female worshippers, who come to al-Haram al-Sharif, have had a hand in strengthening the role of this site in the Palestine and the Muslim World and in Arab and Islamic politics in general. They participate in study circles and religious celebrations and conduct activities which they view as defending al-Aqsa against Jewish plans. They see their participation as being influential in the Palestinian society by taking on a political role in the struggle against Israeli occupation particularly in Jerusalem, by gaining honor for these actions, by being close to God, and by enhancing their image among the Palestinian religious and political leadership.

The study explores the various activities of pious Palestinian women at the Haram al-Sharif, particularly through the Murabitat program established by the Islamic Movement in Israel. It is based on first-hand observations on al-Haram al-

Sharif, as well as interviews with women who visit there regularly and interviews with female and male religious and political leaders. Special attention has been paid to researcher-participant relations along the lines of ethnicity, gender, and class. Like the activists on al-Haram al-Sharif, I am a Palestinian Muslim man. My personal identity was a key factor which facilitated access to the site and to those I interviewed.

The study analyzes the religious and political role of women on al-Haram al-Sharif by surveying Muslim women who visit the site regularly. It also discusses the impact of the Islamic Movement in Israel and the Jewish Temple Mount organizations for women on the motivation and scope of *Murabitat's* activities.

Murabitat encompass three categories including teachers, leaders and rank and file Murabitat, who constituted the majority of the Murabitat. The rank and file of the *murabitat* interviewed in this study are unique in that they belong to the middle class, they are not highly educated and most are over 40 years of age. They originate from the Old City and other neighborhoods of Jerusalem (which were villages in the not too distant past). They carry Israeli identity cards. The *Murabitat's* members do not seem to fit the common profile of Palestinian female activists. The female *Murabitat's* teachers, however, are highly-educated, upper middle class women who have worked outside the home, are related to prominent men, and come from villages and cities outside of Jerusalem – such as Hebron and Abu Dis.

They fit the common profile of Palestinian activist women.

In this study I am addressing five major topics: The first issue addresses the **ties** between the women of the Islamic Movement in Israel who come to al-Aqsa and work on its behalf, and the Muslim women and girls from the Palestinian territories who participate in the activities on al-Haram al-Sharif. My findings show that the women in the Islamic Movement in Israel coordinate connections between the *Murabitat's* leaders and the leaders of the Islamic Movement in Israel. Consequently, Murabitat got financial support and other kinds of support from the Islamic Movement in Israel.

Second, the **motivation** of the religious, political, and social activities of Muslim women in al-Haram al-Sharif and their views. My conclusion is that Murabitat fear of Jewish activities that aim to divide al-Aqsa Mosque between Jews and Muslims and the destruction of the Mosque. Although they may initially come to the Haram al-Sharif to pray or study, the political aims - the *Murabitat's* rank and file members are mobilized for political activities–include protecting al-Haram al-Sharif from Jewish Temple Mount activists.

The third topic elaborates on the **relationships between the female leaders and the male leaders** of the Islamic movements on al-Haram al-Sharif and the attitude of the female leaders and the male leaders toward Muslim women's activism on al-Haram al-Sharif. The research concludes that

Hamas leaders supported the Murabitat and encouraged their female siblings to join the Murabitat. On the other hand, the Salafi leaders rejected the Murabitat movement and their activities. The Salafi leaders stated that the Murabitat were a threat to Al-Aqsa Mosque because the provoked an increase in the number of Jewish visitors to Al-Haram al-Sharif. The leaders of Hizb al-Tahrir refrained from taking sides.

The fourth topic is the **role of the girls' school** and college within al-Haram al-Sharif in gaining more female participation at the Haram. This study found that when the Israeli police prevent students from going to their school, a number of the girls join the *murabitat* outside al-Haram al-Sharif and shout *Allahu Akbar* with them in the faces of the Jewish visitors.

The fifth issue explores the personal identities, family statuses, and geographic, social and political **profiles** of the women who participate in activities on al-Haram al-Sharif.

Few women expressed the idea that women's activism demonstrated their competence or their independent thought and action. Some leaders and teachers, however, use the term "women rights "and feel that women are capable of leadership roles in Palestinian society. Most of the *murabitat* do not seem to have gender consciousness. The majority of the *Murabitat* have adopted the concept of "women's rights" from feminism, applying it to the Shari'a, and the notion of "respect" for women in place of "agency."

The significance of this study is underscored by ongoing events in the Israeli-Palestinian arena–since, in fact, it was the activities of the *murabitat* that contributed to the "Al-Quds intifada" in October 2015. The study also shows how the Palestinian society respect and appreciate the role of the murabitat in preventing the Jewish groups from taking over Al-Haram al-Sharif, Moreover, the study shows the involvement of Jewish women in the Jewish groups' activities.

CONTENTS

Introduction

There have been many studies about Al-Haram al-Sharif, including its religious importance and its political significance. However, I have decided to conduct a study about Al-Haram al-Sharif because its political significance has developed into a bloody conflict between Palestinians and Israeli (Jew. Muslim), leading to fatalities among innocent civilians on both sides. The source of the conflict is that both sides claim ownership of the site.

Henceforth, the study aims to explore the background of the conflict, the Muslim and Jewish traditions leading to claiming ownership of the site, and to recognize the actors who conduct activities on the site and those behind them. The actors include grassroots organizations, government agencies, and religious movements.

Another reason for selecting the site is that during recent years Jewish groups have been seeking to alter the status quo at the site of Al-Haram al-Sharif. In response to that, the Islamic Movement in Israel and Islamic leaders in Jerusalem created the Murabitat movement to confront the activities of the Jewish groups on the site, which has been another reason for my selection of this site. The conflict created by these groups has escalated the conflict and made the study worthwhile.

On the issue of theoretical and conceptual framework – the study relies on two conceptual frameworks, the first deals with the history of the Israeli-Palestinian struggle (Jewish-Muslim) and on Jerusalem and the Temple Mount (Quds and Al Aqsa) and focuses on the changing role of women in this struggle. In the past, when Palestinian women participated in national struggles, however, they came mainly from the elite, middle-class and secular circles. The Murabitat struggle brings a new dimension to this issue: religious women of lower ranks with national religious-agenda that is not separating between the "religious" and "national". In front of us is a unique case since, for the very first time, we see women participating in a struggle of religious nature in a sacred place. Moreover, for the first time religious women are granted legitimacy and support from the men in the family to participate in this religious struggle and even gain respect and admiration from the men regarding the results of this campaign. This is a significant expression of changing gender relations and empowerment of women.

The second conceptual framework relates to gender and feminist literature. The theoretical and empirical literature overview shows different approaches to women's struggles in the Arab and Muslim Worlds from which I build my research: The literature focuses on a number of theories: a clear feminist theory; Agency; Women activism and "Gender Jihad." As Mahmud writes – promoting Islamic gender norms. I am examining the study whether the activity of the Murabitat is compatible with the theories of agency and to other frameworks dealing with women rights struggles. I have found that there is certainly an aspect of agency although it is directed towards the political-religious-national dimension, rather than towards women's rights. The Murabitat rejects the feminist approach despite the fact that their struggle ultimately promoted the status of women inside the family, the neighborhood and Arab Muslim society at large. These insights were now added to the introduction of the work.

Additionally, the Murabitat and their activities and their financial support show that the Murabitat movement is an agency and that the Murabitat demand political rights such as having a political role in the Islamic movement.

The selection of pious Palestinian Muslim women is due to the fact that previous relevant studies failed to dwell on the direct involvement of pious women in protests, da'wah, coordination with male religious leaders, and direct confrontation between pious women and Israeli police leading to detention, house arrest, physical abused, and other forms of punishment.

These activities by pious Palestinian Muslim women are new to the conservative Palestinian society. The study is about a key question; **what is the role of the Murabitat?** The study answers this question using research methods, which will discussed in another part of the study. The following statement by Amal, one of the Murabitat, explains briefly the role of the Murabitat:

"I am here to preserve the Islamic identity of al-Aqsa Mosque, to stop the Jews from taking it over, and to triumph over the Jews and say to them that al-Aqsa Mosque belongs [only] to the Palestinians and the Muslims. I am connected to this place by something sacred." (Amal from Isawiya, one of the *murabitat* of al-Aqsa Mosque, interview, July 9, 2015).

Amal's opinion and activity reflect a one-sided narrative and ignore early Islamic accounts narrating the tradition according to which the site was identified with the Temple of Solomon. Al-Haram al-Sharif is the third most sacred place in the Muslim world, and the most holy Muslim site in Jerusalem and Palestine. It serves as a nexus of religious, political, cultural and social activities among Palestinians, including Arab citizens of Israel. This thesis focuses on Islamist activities that take place on al-Haram al-Sharif, and the activities of pious Muslim women in particular. Pious Palestinian women visit the site regularly and take part in activities there, particularly when they feel it is under attack by Jewish Israelis. This thesis will examine the phenomenon of pious women's activism on al-Haram al-Sharif and will provide details about their beliefs and their activities. All in all, this study aims to show the ways in which these pious women play a major role in the politicization of al-Haram al-Sharif.

Jerusalem is the holiest city for three monotheistic religions, Judaism, Christianity and Islam. The city's religious character has generated its political importance, as well as its symbolic impact, but its religious position has also been at the root of a considerable controversy. This controversy focuses on who has the greater attachment and entitlement to the city, and for whom Jerusalem has the greatest religious, cultural, historical and political importance.

Al-Haram al-Sharif for Muslims and the Temple Mount for Jews, is a holy site for both, but al-Haram al-Sharif or al-Aqsa Mosque identified it its current location since the 7th century AD in Muslim Tradition (Qur᾽an and Sunnah) (Ju'be, 2009) is also a site of Muslim practice today. The Israelite Temple was built and destroyed twice throughout history, and was finally destroyed by the Romans some 2,000 years ago. Nevertheless, Jews around the world have prayed to the East where the Holy Temple existed, and often had pictures of the "Wailing Wall" or the Dome of the Rock in their homes to remind them of the location of the Temple.

Early Islamic traditions also acknowledge that Solomon's Temple existed where the Dome of the Rock was built by the Umayyad Caliph Abd al-Malik in the late 7th century. A modern Palestinian historian of Jerusalem, Aref al-'Aref, mentioned this fact in his book titled "The Concise History of Jerusalem" (1986: 14). Aref al-'Aref wrote in *Al-Mufassal fi Ta'rikh al-Quds* (A Detailed History of Jerusalem) that the stones of the Temple Mount were taken from Jerusalem from the area on the right side of Damascus Gate. Al-'Aref added that King David started the construction of the Temple and King Solomon completed it. He brought stones from a quarry which is present to this day and is located on the right hand side upon exiting from Bab al-Amud (the Damascus Gate). To this day this quarry is referred to as the quarry of King Solomon because he took from it the stones for the building of the Temple (Al-'Aref 1986: 14).

On the other hand, Jewish Israelis believe that Temple Mount is the holiest site in Judaism. To the Jews it is known as Har haMoriyah where Abraham sacrificed his son Isaac and Har haBayit or the Temple Mount where the Jewish Temple once stood. For the Jews the Temple Mount contains the holiest place where the "holy of holies" resides. The "holy of holies" refers to the place where the high priest used to enter on the Day of Atonement to atone for the sins of Israel" (Shragai, 2014). Hence, the sacred compound is contested and disputed between Jewish Israelis and Palestinian and other Muslims. So tense became this conflict that Palestinian women were recruited to become "defenders" of Al-Aqsa Mosque compound.

In addition to the religious significance of Jerusalem and al-Aqsa Mosque, the Palestinian-Israeli conflict granted Jerusalem an increased scope of activities and colored the struggle with religious dimensions. Consequently, the increased presence of Muslims in Jerusalem prompted many Palestinian religious groups to carry out innumerable undertakings to compete over control of al-Aqsa Mosque.

Since the 1920s al-Haram al-Sharif has served as a rallying point for consolidating political support for the Palestinian national movement as well as for recruiting the Muslim world for the Palestinian cause. During the 1920s and 1930s the Grand Mufti of Palestine, Haj Amin al-Husayni, employed al-Haram al-Sharif as a focal point of struggle; particularly during the Western Wall Riots of 1929 (Porath, 1977); (Kupferschmidt, 1987); (Jbara, 1998); (Reiter, 1996); (Cohen, 2013). Al-Husayni also used the site for the interment of pan-Islamic leaders (Azaryahu and Reiter, 2014). Al-Haram al-Sharif lost its profound status during Jordanian rule between 1948 and 1967, though the assassination of King Abdullah I that took place at al-Aqsa Mosque in July 1951 (Ju`be, 2009); (Reiter, 1997). In other words, al-Haram al-Sharif is continually being produced, reproduced and transformed by the constant dynamics and activities found at the intersections of religious, political and national controversies (Luz, 2004).

After June 1967, when Israel occupied East Jerusalem - Jerusalem, including al-Haram al-Sharif, became known as an occupied city as defined by the international law and UN decisions and UNESCO decision (October 18, 2016), which consider Israel as an occupying power of Jerusalem, Israel imposed its jurisdiction over it, al-Haram al-Sharif was again turned into a major site of religious and political activity. This began with the fire set to al-Aqsa Mosque in August 1969 (Reiter, 2008). The challenge posed by Jewish religious nationalists who venerated the Temple Mount/ al-Haram al-Sharif started in 1967. However, in 1980, the activities of Jewish groups escalated the tensions around this compound. The site became again a rallying point of demonstrations and violent clashes culminating in the outbreak of the first intifada in December 1987 (Klein, 2001); (Shragai, 1995); (Luz, 2004); (Tal, 2011); (Reiter, 2011).

Though the first intifada had a secular nature, holy sites were employed to gain the support of Muslim countries and to compete with Palestinian Islamic groups such as the Islamic Jihad and the Muslim Brotherhood - later Hamas. The conflict between the Israelis and the Palestinians in regard to al-Haram al-Sharif continues since both parties claim ownership of the place. Moreover, Muslims deny any historical, cultural or religious claims of the Jews to the holy site.

Several historians describe how both Israelis and Palestinians have created "facts on the ground" in order to claim their holy places. Klein (2001) describes the competing claims of both Israelis and Palestinians regarding Jerusalem and its holy places. He shows how Palestinian national institutions have operated clandestinely since the Israelis occupied the eastern half of the city, and how the Israelis have tried to suppress them. Dumper (2014) discusses the scattered borders of holiness between Israeli and Palestinian in Jerusalem, terming the situation as "Hebronization," meaning an Israeli attempt to divide al-Haram al-Sharif by gradually creating facts on the ground.

Following the opening of the Western Wall Tunnel in September 1996 and the violent clashes between Israelis and

Palestinians, the northern branch of the Islamic Movement launched a political campaign titled "Al-Aqsa is in Danger" and was involved in construction projects at al-Haram al-Sharif and other activities contributing to the increase of tensions at this compound (Luz, 2004; Reiter, 2011).

In 1996 the northern branch of the Islamic Movement began mobilizing women for the *shad al-rihal ila al-Aqsa* project (fasten the saddles [for a pilgrimage] to al-Aqsa). This project drew its inspiration from the al-Bukhari and Muslim *hadiths*: "Do not set out on a journey except for three mosques, i.e. Al-Masjid al-Haram, the Mosque of Allah's Apostle, and the Mosque of al-Aqsa (in Jerusalem)" (Sahih Bukhari, trans. M. Mushsin Khan, Vol. 2, Book 21, No. 281). "The saddles should be tied to three mosques: The sacred mosque of Mecca, this mosque of mine (al-Medina), and al-Aqsa Mosque. (Muslim, trans. Abd al-Hamid Siddiqui, Book 7, No. 3099).

The demonstrative visit of Ariel Sharon, the Likud leader, to the Temple Mount/ al-Haram al-Sharif on 28 September 2000 instigated the second intifada, named "Al-Aqsa intifada." The Palestinians perceived the visit as a provocation and a challenge to their sovereignty and control of the holy site. Since then, Palestinian activity aimed at demonstrating their hold on al-Haram al-Sharif and opposing Jewish actions has increased dramatically (Klein, 2004). The Palestinian activity is varied: it includes increasing their presence on al-Haram al-Sharif during the entire day using the traditional term of *ribat* (defense) as well as organizing study circles (*masatib al-l'ilm*) inside al-Haram al-Sharif. Part of this strategy involved the inclusion of large number of women in activities on al-Haram al-Sharif and their assumption of a prominent role in harassing the Jewish visitors who visit the site (Tal, 2011). These women were conceived of as *murabitat.* The word *murabitat* is derived from the word *ribat,* which in classical Islam refers to a land that has been conquered by the armies of Islam and where a garrison (*murabit*) has been stationed in order to defend the Islamic frontier against the enemies. In a similar way the *murabitat* of al-Haram al-Sharif see themselves as defending this holy site against the Jewish invaders. Hereafter the word *murabitat* in this thesis refers to the Islamist women who see themselves as the defenders of al-Haram al-Sharif.

The role of Palestinian Muslim women in the political play is not a new phenomenon. Pious Palestinian women were active alongside their "secular" sisters in the national movement at least since the period of the British Mandate (Budiri, 1994:12).

We cannot separate Palestinian secularism and Islamist women's activism. Islam was and still is one of the principal elements of Palestinian identity, particularly within the occupied territories. The Islamist movement in Palestine has represented and encompassed nationalist discourse since the beginning of the Mandate period. It is truly difficult to draw a dividing line between Islamists and their nationalist opponents (Budiri, 1994:12).

Other historians believe that there have been rises and falls in the degree of Islam in the Palestinian national movement. Beginning in the 1970s, the pious women's social and educational activities prepared them for political roles in the first intifada beginning in December 1987 (Abdulhadi, 1998); (Nad'a, interview, 2014). The political activities of pious Muslim women were heightened by the entry of Hamas into the resistance movement in 1988 and the official definition of women's roles in the Hamas Covenant of 1988 (Hroub, 1996); (Bajes, 2012); (Lahlouh, 2010); (Jad 2010).

Mariam Saleh, (Professor of Shariʿa at al-Quds University and the first female Hamas minister for women's affairs,) contends that in the late 1980s and 1990s, pious Muslim women played a prominent role in supporting the Islamist movements in Palestine, especially Hamas, advocating for and carrying out political actions in mosques, charities and Islamic schools. The involvement of women in the religious-political play in Jerusalem began before the 2006 elections to the Palestinian National Council (PNC) while many of them supported Islamic movements (Mariam Saleh, Interview, 2014). They played a major part in the victory of Hamas in the 2006 elections in which Hamas women assumed six seats in the Palestinian Legislative Council and one minister headed the Ministry of Women's Affairs (Salah, 2014). Mariam Saleh described the Islamist women's activism in the West Bank and Jerusalem by saying "Palestinian Muslim women played a prominent role in supporting the Muslim movement in Palestine, especially Hamas in the late 1980s.

In 2010, the northern branch of the Islamic Movement in Israel organized study circles (*masatib al-' i lm, halaqat dirasiyya*) for women in Islamic law (Shariʿa), Islamic doctrine (*fiqh*), and Qurʾan at al-Haram al-Sharif. The study circles were held under trees and inside al-Aqsa Mosque. They were led by outstanding female and male teachers from Palestinian universities. The participants received monthly stipends from the Islamic Movement in Israel increasing the groups' number of members. These Israeli Muslim women joined pious Muslim women from the Jerusalem area who came to al-Haram al-Sharif to pray and study. They became known as the *murabitat.* Thus, the *murabitat* emerged against the background of almost a century of Palestinian women's political activism.

The *murabitat* movement on al-Haram al-Sharif was established with the aim of mobilizing women for *ribat al-Aqsa* (defense of al-Aqsa Mosque). This is based on the above mentioned *hadith* or oral tradition attributed to Prophet Muhammad according to which every Muslim is commanded to visit al-Aqsa Mosque in addition to the pilgrimage to the mosques of Mecca and Medina (Tal 2011). The purpose of this endeavor was to strengthen the hold of Muslims on al-Haram al-Sharif, to combat the movement of Israeli Jewish women and men ascending the Temple Mount by shouting *Allahu Akbar* (Allah is greater), *Khaybar Khaybar ya Yahud jaysh*

Muhammad qad ya'ud (Oh Jews, remember the Battle of Khaybar - the army of Muhammad will return) and *Allah ya'khudhum* (literally: may Allah take them [I hope they die]), and to confront the Israeli police that protected them. The women in the *murabitat* movement came from East Jerusalem as well as from Israel proper.

Goals of the Study

This study aims to document how Palestinian Muslim women (*murabitat* as well as other female worshippers) who come to al-Haram al-Sharif have had a hand in strengthening the role of this central religious site for political ends. This study describes and analyzes Muslim women who visit the site regularly, as well as their participation in prayer, study, *da'wa* (proselytizing), and defense of al-Aqsa against the Jews. The study attempts to understand what the women's participation means to them. The study also discusses the impact of the Islamic Movement in Israel and of the Jewish women in the Temple Mount organizations on the motivation and scope of the *murabitat's* activities.

Literature Review and a Theoretical Challenge

There is a growing body of literature discussing various aspects of religiosity and politics in Jerusalem that concentrates mostly on the changes in Israeli and Palestinian understanding of the place, the importance of the conflict and the contemporary changes in the cultural landscape of the site and its environ (Dumper, 2009, 2002, 2014); (Reiter, 2001, 2010); (Cohen, 2007, 2013); (Luz 2004, 2014); (Inbari, 2009); (Tal, 2011); (Ben Shitrit, 2016).

Yitzhak Reiter, for example, discusses in *Jerusalem and Its Role in Islamic Solidarity* the elevation in sanctity and the dynamic sanctity and importance of al-Aqsa Mosque and Jerusalem in the Palestinian national struggle for Jerusalem and Palestine by claiming that they are one and the same (Reiter, 2008). He examines the way al-Haram al-Sharif/ the Temple Mount is used to fuel political, territorial, and religious tension between Muslims and Jews, and between Palestinians and Israelis by radical Islamic and Jewish groups. He also makes a comparison between the historic and religious foundations of the Muslim and Jewish claims to Jerusalem/ al-Quds and al-Haram al-Sharif/ the Temple Mount. Reiter also discusses the inherent connection between politics and holiness with a special focus on the process of elevating the sacredness of al-Aqsa Mosque and the process of denial or denigration of the other party's attachment to the site. He explains the post-1967 Islamic ethos toward Jerusalem and the affinity between this religious ethos and the political aspirations of the Palestinian people. Perhaps the most interesting part of Reiter's book is his analysis of religions concepts (Judaism and Islam) as barriers to arriving to a solution to the Israel-Arab conflict.

The most important study in the area of al-Haram al-Sharif and the Islamic activities is a study by Luz (2004), titled: *Al-Haram al-Sharif in the Arab- Palestinian Public Discourse in Israel: Identity, Collective Memory and Social Construction.* This study outlines the role of the Islamic Movement in Israel, headed by Sheikh Ra'ed Salah, which provided an excellent example of the social, religious and political activities on al-Haram al-Sharif. The Movement held a number of festivals for women to raise public awareness about what was perceived as dangerous Israeli measures against al-Aqsa Mosque and also to alert Muslim women to the religious and national significance of Al-Aqsa Mosque as an Islamic landmark. Although Luz does not focus on women's activities, this study helped to situate my research within the larger framework of Palestinian and Jewish attitudes toward and activities related to al-Haram al-Sharif.

Other scholars have delved into the presence of Muslim women in Jerusalem and their activities therein. In her book *Women in the Mosque*, Katz provides an **historical** narrative of Muslim women's physical presence at mosques for the purpose of worship, including mosques in Jerusalem and al-Haram al-Sharif. Katz argues that Muslim women have visited mosques throughout the history of Islam. However, the number of Muslim women who visit mosques is on the rise. Katz also talks about the physical arrangement of rows of men and women during prayer at mosques and the viewpoints of the various Islamic groups concerning women's worshipping at mosques.

Ellen Fleischmann (2000) narrates an **historical** account of the development of women's organizations in Jerusalem during the British Mandate in her article *Jerusalem Women's Organizations during the British Mandate 1920s-1930s.* Fleischmann dwells on the connections between women's and men's movements and the influence male leaders had on women's activism. The writer argues that feminism and support for women's rights were not among the objectives of the Palestinian women's activism during the British Mandate.

In *Hamas' Social Agenda* (in Arabic), Ala'a Lahlouh (2010) examines Hamas' viewpoints concerning women and civic rights as well as other issues. The writer examines the extent to which Hamas, as a Muslim Brotherhood offshoot, succeeded to enforce its social agenda through preaching and utilization of mosques and charitable organizations. Lahlouh examines Hamas' position concerning women's rights. He says that Hamas agrees to reform laws that better women's rights; however, women's rights must be consistent with Islamic Shari'a. Hamas believes that the home is the place for women where they have children and look after them. Alternatively, Hamas does not oppose women's involvement in public affairs as long as it is in line with Islamic teachings. The writer examines Hamas's conundrum concerning allowing women to occupy senior political positions. Hamas believes that women are too emotional to make important decisions, however, the movement gave ministerial positions to women in its 2006 government.

From the 1990s, studies have included or focused on the actual activities and views of pious women in the Arab world. Badran's groundbreaking study (1994) of the activities and views of prominent women in Egypt was based on interviews and included interviews with Islamist women. Badran coined the term "gender activism" as a more neutral phrase for Islamist women who rejected the term "feminism" but promoted women's rights. The Palestinian situation is very different from the Egyptian case because the Palestinians are involved in a national and religious struggle against Israel which occupies the West Bank so the women's rights are demoted to second or third place at best. Egyptian women can combine their feminist or women's rights efforts with their opposition to the regime.

Alternatively, the Murabitat have a different purpose, which is to defend Al-Haram al-Sharif against the visiting Jewish groups. The Murabitat had not demanded any women's rights since they considered the safeguarding of Al-Haram al-Sharif of paramount importance that prevailed over and demand for women's rights. Moreover, the Murabitat refrained from being labeled with feminism. According to Khadija Khweis, a Murabitat leader, "feminist" is for Western women and for the women's activities and rights in Western Culture.

The Murabitat activities have Islamic nature and they call themselves Islamists.

Abdulhadi's innovative study (1998) also focuses on secular Palestinian activist women, but did not ignore the undertakings and opinions of pious women. Her study of nongovernmental Palestinian women's associations in the early 1990s, based on interviews and fieldwork, revealed a multiplicity of views.

Dalal Bajes (2003) examines the political involvement of women in the Islamist movements of the Arab world in *Al-Nisa' aal-Islamiyyat fi al-'Alamal-'Arabi* (*Islamist Women in the Arab World*). Bajes found, like Fleischman, that Arab women give and sacrifice so much but get less than the minimum rights, especially political rights **Islamic women's activism**. The concept of Islamic women's activism is used to describe women activists and political leaders who do the actual work. Bajes says that Islamist women and secular women fail to recognize each other. She also narrates the development of views - based on the Qur'an and Sunnah - concerning Muslim women and the rhetoric used to support allowing women more involvement in the various aspects of public life.

Mahmoud's influential study (2005) of the urban women's mosque movement in Cairo, based on field research and interviews conducted during 1995-1997, documents the work of female preachers (*da' iyyat*) and mosque lessons. She concluded that the idea of "human agency," used by feminists, limits our ability to understand the actual activities of all women, and suggested that the pious women she studied have "agency" through cultivation and performance of gendered Islam. Mahmoud also pointed out that mosque lessons in Egypt helped recruit women for social and political activities against the secular Egyptian government. In that respect, Mahmoud's work is very relevant to the current study because lessons for women at al-Haram al-Sharif led to their social and political activism.

Deeb's valuable ethnography (2006) of publicly pious Shia women in the southern suburb (*dahiyya*) of Beirut, based on fieldwork from 1999-2001, describes social services run by pious individuals and *jam'iyyat* or associations, including those affiliated with Hezbollah. Many of the social services described by Deeb bear a similarity to those carried out by the *murabitat* of al-Haram al-Sharif and help increase the popularity of political Islamist movements. Unlike the pious Shia women of the *dahiyya* of Beirut, however, the *murabitat* of al-Haram al-Sharif may actually participate in the fight against Israelis, which Hezbollah does not permit. In view of the similar role of the Islamic resistance movements against Israel, Hezbollah and Hamas, and the comparable suffering of the population on account of Israeli attacks, it is interesting to compare their awareness of being discriminated against as women and their challenge to the male leadership.

Jad (2010) concentrates on Hamas's ideology regarding women, as well as the actual experiences of Islamist women in the political ranks of Hamas during the years 1997-2003. She found that Islamist women created space for the activities of women's groups, who were thus bestowed with an air of moral legitimacy in public life.

Tal's study (2011, 2016) of women in the Islamic Movement in Israel, based on an extremely wide variety of primary sources, shows the development of the movement from providing social and educational services to participating in political activities, as well as the important contributions of women, including mobilizing voters during elections. The detailed descriptions of contemporary undertakings are excellent points of departure for evaluating activities of the *murabitat* of al-Haram al-Sharif. Tal briefly mentions the accomplishments of the Israeli Islamic movements on al-Haram al-Sharif, but this is not the focus of her work. The movements of Islamic women in Israel are sister movements to the West Bank pious women, it is interesting to determine how similar they are.

Lihi Ben Shitrit devoted an article and a full volume's paper (2013) to the roles women play in the conflicts caused by multi-religious groups' claims over the Temple Mount/al-Haram al-Sharif, and the involvement of women in conservative religious Jewish and Muslim movements in the politics of the Middle East. Ben Shitrit's interesting analysis of such involvement of women is focused on how the boundaries of conservative religious movements that are built around women collapse to allow for limited activism to serve national or proselytizing purposes. Her findings are not very relevant to the focus of my study, since women affiliated with the southern branch of the Islamic Movement in Israel come to pray on al-Haram al-Sharif but do not make as much of a social and political contribution as the women of the northern branch. Moreover, the southern branch deals only with religious *da'wa*, not with political activism.

Ben Shitrit's *Righteous Transgressions* (2016) shows that women engage in types of activism that seem to transgress or overstep their movements' restrictive positions on gender roles. "Frames of Exception" temporarily suspended, rather than challenged, some of the limiting aspects of their movement's gender ideology in favor of broader goals. This analysis is extremely relevant to the activities of the *murabitat.*

Studies regarding the role of al-Haram al-Sharif in the Israeli-Palestinian conflict underline the nexus between religious and national activities. However, almost no research exists regarding the role of Muslim Palestinian women in the political activities on al-Haram al-Sharif. This research aims to fill this gap.

Research Questions

The research seeks to answer the following questions:

1. How did the historical, religious and political conflict between Muslims and Jews over the meaning of al-Haram al-Sharif lead up to the founding of the *murabitat*?
2. How do the *murabitat* differ from other Palestinian women's movements? To what extent were they similar to pious women's movements in other Arab countries?
3. what is the role of the Murabitat?
4. What types of women participate in activities on al-Haram al-Sharif?
5. What kind of religious, social and political activities do they engage in? How do the girls' schools at al-Haram al-Sharif support the religious, social and political roles of this site?
6. What motivates women to visit al-Haram al-Sharif and what do they feel they gain from the religious, social and political activities they participate in?
7. To what extent do the attitudes of the women and the men toward Muslim women's activism at al-Haram al-Sharif differ? What did the women learn about Jews at al-Haram al-Sharif? Do the *murabitat* exhibit "agency" as did their Palestinian pious activist predecessors in the 1990s and their sisters in other Arab countries? If not, why?
8. What are the ties between the Muslim women activists from the Jerusalem area, and the women and men of the Islamic Movement in Israel who come to al-Aqsa Mosque and work on its behalf?

9. How does the participation of Jewish women in the Temple Mount organizations influence the participation and presence of Muslim women on al-Haram al-Sharif?

Research Methods

The current study is based on research and fieldwork conducted on al-Haram al-Sharif. The primary sources of the proposed study are participation in the activities thereon and first-hand, observations of what took place there. It also draws extensively upon interviews with women who visit there regularly, and interviews with female and male religious and political leaders. Haram, so there are many activities from Muslim Palestinian both men and women.

The study extensively focuses on Muslim women; especially pious women, the way they are organized, the activities they perform, and the ideology they express through the ideas they believe in. Moreover, the study focuses on the social class, geography, education and the relationship between these Muslim women and the Islamic movements of wide grassroots support such as Hamas and the Islamic Movement in Israel.

This dissertation is based on observation of actual activities on the ground at the site, as well as interviews with women leaders and participants, whose voices are rarely heard in the scholarship. In addition, the decision to give a fair amount of space in the dissertation to the voices of these women interlocutors is very commendable both ethically and in relations to usefulness for future researchers interested in these voices.

The study extensively focuses on Muslim women; especially pious women, the way they are organized, the activities they perform, and the ideology they express through the ideas they believe in. Moreover, the study focuses on the social class, geography, education and the relationship between these Muslim women and the Islamic movements of wide grassroots support such as Hamas and the Islamic Movement in Israel. All these important issues that I raise were supported by interviews and direct observations as well as direct involvement in the daily activities of these women such as the circle lessons and their full commitment to them. Murabitat come every day in the morning from 7:30 in the morning to 2 o'clock in the afternoon. I observed their activities and took part in them for more than ten months. These aspects make my study different and distinguished from other studies, which rely on interviews with leaderships with political agenda and ignored the real active and history-making elements.

Therefore, and due to the nature of the study, my research strategy combines two methods: The first method includes conducting interviews. Consequently, I have interviewed fifty rank and file girls and women, five female Murabitat leaders, five male Murabiteen leaders, the previous Mufti and current preacher of Al-Aqsa, as well as leaders of other Islamic movements (Salafis and Hizb al-Tahrir), and Jewish activists.

The selection of the two methods combined gives the study validity since relying on just one of the methods means that the outcome would be lacking. For instance, adopting the interviews method alone means that observation would be missing and the questions would lack inclusive coverage. Observation means informed questions; hence, the two methods produced a fully informative study.

The interviews method (see the Appendix A- List of Interviews – Names and Dates) involves face-to-face talks with Murabitat. The Murabitat are divided into three groups; leaders, teachers, and rank and file. The questions asked in the interviews cover personal information such as (age, function, marital status, dependents, education, and place of residence). There are other questions asked covering date of ribat, religious interest, political interest, method of ribat, and measure taken by Israeli police against the Murabitat).

The protocol of the interviews involves questions on different levels depending on the group of the interviewees. The questions addressed to the rank and file Murabitat are direct questions seeking direct response such as the reason behind being involved in the Murabitat. Questions addressed to leaders and teachers are of political nature that may require in-depth and analytical responses (i.e. Are you a political power? Are you affiliated to a political religious movement? Do you demand women's rights?) The interviews are held on site at Al-Haram al-Sharif. These interviews mainly are with rank and file Murabitat. Interviews are also held in the area outside the fates of Al-Haram al-Sharif. These interviews are with the Murabitat who are banned from the site (blacklisted Murabitat). There are also interviews held at the houses of Murabitat under house arrest.

The second method is the first-hand observation involved daily visits to al-Haram al-Sharif for ten months (January to October 2015). The daily visits came to a halt from the start of the al-Quds intifada and became weekly visits conducted on Fridays for at least six months in order to evaluate women's activities there. In addition, I participated in all the festivals that took place on al-Haram al-Sharif and recorded the degree of women's participation.

I have used observer participation, which gives me the opportunity to know and discuss and ask more questions about every detail of their actions. My observation stared at 7:30 AM as Jewish groups entered al-Haram al-Sharif. The observation continued until the last visiting Jewish group leaves the site at 2:30 PM. The observation includes all the activities conducted by the Jewish visiting groups and the Murabitat. Though the creation of the Murabitat movement is linked to political objective, the Murabitat have no quarrel with the Jews for being Jews. The Murabitat are not against visits to the Al-Aqsa by Jews; however, they fear that extremist Jewish groups may take control over the al-Haram al-Sharif and the Jewish groups would have religious rights in al-Haram al-Sharif and they fear the destruction of the Al-Aqsa and the Dome of the Rock and the construction of the Third Temple.

Also I took pictures and videos of evolving events, which helped me remember all the actions and the reactions from both sides. This also helped me retrieve pictures of the body language and words. I also jotted down the words chanted and written on banners. The observation also took notes of the way Murabitat are dressed (hijab, niqab, and Murabitat leaders' uniform).

The other component of the methodology involves a review of historical studies on al-Haram al-Sharif and the way it is depicted and understood in Islamic scriptures and chronicles as well as the way the site (Har haBayit) is treated by Jewish tradition.

I have used open-ended, in-depth interviews and observer participation, which gives me the opportunity to know and discuss and ask more questions about every detail of their actions (Shikedi, 2003) also known as women's narratives, as employed by Mernissi (1988) in Morocco, Sayigh (1996) in Palestinian refugee camps in Lebanon, and Abdulhadi (1998) in the Palestinian territories, as well as qualitative research (Shikedi 2003) juxtaposed with quantitative methods. Snowball interviews sampling is employed.

Challenges and solutions:

As a male scholar, I have encountered a number of challenges while conducting the study. The challenges include the gender challenge. The study involves working with female activists belonging to a conservative Muslim society operating in an atmosphere of a religiously revered site. These women come from religious families that traditionally prohibit contacts females and male strangers.

To overcome this challenge, I involved both professional and family ties (my wife's links to a well-known family from the Old City of Jerusalem). Hence, I managed to gain the trust of the Murabitat. The fact that I am a Muslim resident of the Old City of Jerusalem means that I am privileged with access to the Al-Haram al-Sharif, which facilitates contact with the Murabitat. Participating in the events and activities of the Murabitat gained me further trust from them. This is important because trust meant obtaining accurate information about the murabitat from the murabitat themselves. Conducting interviews at the homes of the murabitat meant that a mutual feeling of trust and closeness was established and fears were overcome.

Moreover, I have social ties with one of the Murabitat's leaders who introduced me to other women. My experience as a journalist who had written articles about the murabitat in the Palestinian press made me welcome among them, and I was even detained and interrogated by the Israeli police on suspicion of being one of them. This enhanced my Palestinian nationalist credentials. An indication of my acceptance by the murabitat women was that they invited me to eat with them, and I also visited them in their homes. Conducting interviews at the homes of the murabitat meant that a mutual feeling of trust and closeness was established and fears were overcome. I have paid special attention to researcher-participant relations along the lines of ethnicity, gender, and class. As Muhanna points out (2013) in Agency and Gender in Gaza: Masculinity, Femininity, and Family during the Second Intifada, the socio-economic distance between the researcher and the interviewees is an important factor for the accuracy of the information. In my case, I come from an authentic family from the Old City of Jerusalem. Since I am educated, there is some distinction between me and some of the participants, but in the course of time I developed a relationship that overcame hierarchical barriers, as witnessed by the fact that I referred to them as "sisters" (akhawat) and they called me "brother" (akh).

What makes my study different from other studies is that I got involved with women who had been active all the time but had never had their voice heard. I managed to establish social relationships with the rank and file Murabitat as well as the leader Murabitat. These relationships developed and became more than just a researcher and an interviewee relationship. They involved social visits to their homes, which enriched the study and developed it beyond traditional norms.

The other challenge is the Israeli police measures at the Al-Haram al-Sharif including restricting entry of men to the site during visits of Jewish groups. This, of course, had not facilitated my study. To overcome this, I used to arrive to the site at 06:00 AM and conduct interviews and other tasks.

Discussion between the reseracher and the murabitat

Structure of the Study

Chapter one provides a religious and political background to the emergence of the *murabitat* movement and their activities. It describes the importance of al-Haram al-Sharif for Muslims and Jews. The chapter includes an analysis of the competing stories of the Jews and the Muslims concerning the site. The chapter then dwells on the concept of *ribat* and the development of the *murabitat* movement.

Chapter two explains the foundation of the Islamic Movement in Israel in 1970s and traces it through four developmental stages. It also assesses the role of Sheikh Ra'ed Salah in Jerusalem. The chapter explains the goals of the Jewish organizations and their ideology (Jewish fundamentalism and the Temple Mount). There is an historical background for entering and praying on al-Haram al-Sharif and the role of Jewish faithful organization on al-Haram al-Sharif especially when they plan to rebuild the Third Temple, which caused tension in 1990 leading to the killing of 21 Palestinians by the Israeli police (Israeli sources speak on killing of 17). The chapter reflects the opinions of the rabbis in Israel towards Jews' entry to al-Haram al-Sharif. The rabbis have two opinions in this regard: the first rejects and prohibits entry and the second supports entry and worshipping on the site. Finally, the chapter discusses current circumstances at the site.

Chapter three introduces the role of Palestinian women in the making of the history of Palestine leading up to the period covered by the study; the development of the Palestinian women's movement, and a description of how it coped with the British Mandate and the activities of the Zionist movement in Palestine. The period in history covered in this chapter is 1920 to 2010 when the Islamic Movement in Israel founded the *murabitat* movement. The second part of this chapter deals with concept of "agency," described by other researchers of pious women's activism in the Arab countries, and assesses the extent to which their case studies and analyses are relevant to the *murabitat*.

Chapter four provides information on the age and marital status of the *murabitat*, their numbers, their geographic and socio-economic backgrounds, their education and their political affiliation.

Chapter five focuses on women's prayer on al-Haram al-Sharif. It provides a brief historical description of women's worship on al-Haram al-Sharif from the early days of the 10th century until our present time. There is a description of praying arrangements and gender separation at the site: The chapter introduces the study circles including their timing and the topics they discuss. The chapter concludes with a description of the Shariʿa girls and boys schools located inside al-Haram al-Sharif, how the society views the students of the Shariʿa schools, and a brief history of the development of education in Palestine.

Chapter six is on *daʿwa* (proselytizing) as it is used by Islamist movements to recruit supporters and promote their view of Islam. The *Murabitat* utilizes *daʿwa* to recruit family members and neighbors to the movement. This chapter also reflects on Hamas's view of women based on an analysis of Hamas's views of women's activism, as well as Hamas women's role in *daʿwa* at Palestinian universities, mosques, and homes. The chapter describes the *daʿwa* activities of the women activists in the Islamic Movement in Israel and the *daʿwa* practiced by the *murabitun* and *murabitat* at the study circles or *masatib al-ʿilm*. The chapter also deals with how *murabitat* are mobilized for political activities at al-Haram al-Sharif. The chapter looks at how regular *murabitat*, who come to pray and study at al-Haram al-Sharif, are mobilized for political activities to protect al-Aqsa Mosque from the Jews and prevent them from taking it over or dividing al-Haram al-Sharif.

Chapter seven examines the views of the *murabitat's* rank and file concerning the personal development of the *murabitat* movement, the achievements of the movement, the value of the *murabitat's* political activism, the gender consciousness of the *murabitat*, as well as a description of their views on feminism and secular women's movements. The chapter shows how the *murabitat* identify with the *sahabiyyat* (female companions of the Prophet) and what they do to contest Jewish visitors to al-Haram al-Sharif. The chapter focuses on the political orientation of the *murabitat*, its gender consciousness, and its teachers' religious and political roles, it describes what they teach the *murabitat*, and it also describes what the Islamic movements and secular female leaders think of the *murabitat*. Finally, the chapter reflects on the *murabitat's* self-perception and compares it to how its leaders perceive the group. The concluding chapter addressess the major research questions.

1. Al-Haram al-Sharif and Its Defenders

al-Aqsa Mosque – al-Haram al-Sharif
(144,000 square meters) (Waqf Department)

The phenomenon of female defenders of al-Aqsa Mosque emanates from the conflict of Jewish and Muslim narratives regarding the sanctity of Jerusalem. Al-Aqsa Mosque/ al-Haram al-Sharif/ the Temple Mount symbolizes the Jewish-Arab and Palestinian-Israeli conflicts and as such it has served as a rallying point for different parties to employ the site as a religious symbol for their causes. This chapter seeks to shed light on the religious background of the *murabitat* and their activity. It begins with describing the religious importance of Jerusalem for both Muslims and Jews and analyzes their contesting narratives. This is followed by a description of the role of the sacred Temple Mount/ al-Haram al-Sharif compound for contemporary political mobilization. Then it sheds light on the Islamic concept of *ribat* and the development of the *murabitat* movement.

Jerusalem as a holy city has drawn the continued attention of the world community, especially among the adherents of the three monotheistic religions: Judaism, Christianity and Islam. Some of the most sacred places for each of these religions are found in Jerusalem, al-Haram al-Sharif for Muslims, the Temple Mount and the Western Wall for Jews, and the Church of the Holy Sepulcher for Christians. The city's religious centrality has generated its historical and political importance, as well as its symbolic impact, but its religious role has also been at the root of a considerable controversy.

Jerusalem and the Temple Mount in Jewish Tradition

The significance of the Temple Mount in Jewish tradition requires little elaboration. Its paramount importance is reflected in Jewish law, prayer and holiday traditions. However, since its destruction, the Temple has remained largely symbolic–an object of longing, deferred to a seemingly unattainable future era, and framed by a system of restrictions and rituals that moderate preoccupation with the question of its reconstruction. It is precisely because of the sanctity of the Temple Mount complex–the site of the First and Second

Temples–that there is a halachic prohibition of Israel's Chief Rabbinate against visiting the Mount, as differentiated from the case of the ritual sacrifice service, which found a substitute in public prayer in synagogues (Be'er, 2013).

This halachic ruling has been challenged by hundreds of rabbis as will be discussed later.

The Jewish people are inextricably bound to the city of Jerusalem. "No other city has played such a dominant role in the history, politics, culture, religion, national life and consciousness of a people as has Jerusalem in the life of Jewry and Judaism (Teddy Kolleck, 1990)." Since King David established the city as the capital of the Jewish state c. 1,000 BCE, it has served as the symbol and most profound expression of the Jewish people's identity as a nation (Ma'oz and Nusseibeh, 2000). For Jews, the holiness of Jerusalem underlines 3,000 years of continuous Jewish connection to the city of Jerusalem, from its establishment as the holy city during the time of the biblical figure of King David to the present day. One example of this narrative is the 1995 Israeli governmental announcement regarding preparation to celebrate 3,000 years to the city of David and the postal stamp that was issued to honor this event (Benvenisti, City of Stone: 1).

The Israeli-Jewish narrative of Jerusalem is based on both the biblical and rabbinic texts (the traditions of the Mishna and Talmud, and the broader corpus of the writings of Chazal), as well as on other historical writings about the ancient world, including works of the historian Josephus Flavius. In addition to referring to these traditional texts, Jewish scholars draw on recent archaeological findings. Particularly in rabbinic texts, Jerusalem is often referred to as "Zion", which is the mountain where King David's fortress was said to be built and where, according to legend, David was buried. Although there are different Jewish historical interpretations and narratives one can highlight a meta-narrative stressing the centrality of Jerusalem to Judaism and the Jewish people that is accepted by the majority of the Jewish people and by most Israelis at both the official and the grass root strata of society (Reiter, 2008).

For Jews, Temple Mount is the site of the first and second Jewish temples. According to the Talmud, the world was created from a foundation stone in the temple mount. It is also the site where Abraham offered his son in sacrifice to God (Stewart, 2009). The First Temple existed for 374 years until it was destroyed in 586 BC and the Hebrew elite were expelled to Babylon. It was there that the psalm "By the Waters of Babylon" was believed to have been composed: "If I forget thee, Oh Jerusalem, may my right hand lose its cunning." Following the defeat of the Babylonian Empire by Cyrus the Great of Persia, the Jews were allowed to return to Jerusalem 48 years after their expulsion, in 538 BC. Twenty-two years later, in 519 BCE, the building of the Second Temple was completed by Governor Zerubavel and the Hebrew returnees from Babylon... The

Second Temple survived some 589 years, and the two temples' combined lifetime was 963 years. The presence of the Hebrews in the Holy Land from the thirteenth century BCE until their expulsion by the Roman general Titus in 70 CE lasted about 1,400 years. Judea survived as a Hebrew province under the Persian, Ptolemaic, and Seleucid Empires. For about one century between 152 and 63 BCE, Judea enjoyed self-rule under the Hashmoneans. After Herod's death in 4 BCE, the Romans took over direct rule of the colony of Judea, with the Jews undertaking two great revolts against their oppressive rule, in 67-73 CE and 132–135 CE. The second revolt of Bar Kochba against the Romans ended in a disastrous defeat in 135 CE. The Jews, counting approximately 1.3 million people in Palestine before the revolt, lost half of its population. Hadrian changed the name of the province of Judea to Syria-Palestina–a place that was later on known as Palestine and in Arabic: Filastin. In addition, Hadrian rebuilt Jerusalem as a pagan city, renaming it Aelia Capitolina and forbidding Jews to enter except on Tisha B'Av, the Ninth of Av, the date commemorating the destruction of the two temples... The Israeli ethos maintains that Jerusalem is the only capital of the Jewish people throughout their history, and is considered as the holiest city in Judaism. The Jewish meta-narrative tells of the yearning and longing of Jews in exile for 2,000 years to return to Zion, to rebuild Jewish Jerusalem, and to resurrect the Jewish Temple. The narrative highlights that the Jewish connection to Palestine remained consistently steadfast throughout the ages, with ongoing efforts to return, even if it was only to die and be buried on the Mount of Olives. All Jews, both in the Holy Land and in Diaspora, pray in the direction of Jerusalem, they mention its name constantly in their prayers and end the Passover service with the words: "Next year in Jerusalem." The return and rebuilding of Jerusalem is mentioned at least four times in the blessings recited at the end of each meal (Reiter, 2008).

Below the Temple Mount/al-Haram al-Sharif lies the Western Wall. It is also known as the Wailing Wall. This retaining wall dates to the time of the second Jewish temple, and since 1967 functions as a large outdoor synagogue, with segregated areas to allow male and female worshipers to pray" (Stewart, 2009). Since 1967 the Western Wall became the central place of worship for Judaism representing the Temple Mount and substituting it in practice.

Al-Quds and al-Haram al-Sharif in Islamic Tradition

"Al-Aqsa is a responsibility you have been entrusted with. Al-Aqsa is [only] for Muslims." Shaheed (martyr) Musbah Abu-Sbeih, who carried out an operation against Israeli military on October 9, 2016, posted on his Facebook on October 7, 2016 a statement showing his longing for the holy site. Abu Sbeih was a well-known figure at al-Aqsa Mosque. He was banned from entering the site for several months" (www.ma'annews.net).

The sanctity of Jerusalem in Islamic tradition is based on being the first direction of prayer (*qibla*) before the Kaaba became the *qibla* for Muslims; therefore, it is referred to as "the first of the two directions of prayer" (*ula al-qiblatayn*). Jerusalem is also mentioned in the Quran in the description of Prophet Muhammad's Night Journey (*isra'*) from Mecca to Jerusalem and ascension to heaven. This gives Islamic scholars such as Sheikh Yusuf al-Qaradawi ground to connect between al-Aqsa and the Kaaba. This link between the two mosques conveys the message that whoever abandons al-Aqsa Mosque will soon abandon the sacred mosque of Mecca" (Reiter, 2008).

According to a recent interpretation, in al-Aqsa Prophet Muhammad "led other prophets in a prayer at both sites; both shrines are mentioned in one verse of the Quran, both were blessed by God, both hosted the angels, the Prophet called upon God in both places, a single prayer at both is equivalent to many prayers in other mosques, any harm to one of them is much more injurious than a mal-action in any other mosque, sins are to be forgiven at both shrines, a pilgrimage to Mecca beginning at al-Aqsa is favored, both are pilgrimage destinations both are destinations of encouraged emigration as conquered by Islam and serve to defend its territory, both are protected from the antichrist (Dajjal), both were favored by the prophet; both are located in a non-cultivated topographic area, both are neighboring fertile agricultural areas, both have holy springs (Zamzam and Silwan - Siloam), both have a rock that was blessed by God, both were conquered by jihad, the Prophet's muezzin called to pray at both mosques, both have to be respected by attendees' manners, both have many names (Barzaq, 2003: 15-80). This message is also given by the former Palestinian Authority (PA) Waqf minister Sheikh Yusuf Salama, who wrote 'Allah connected the Sacred Mosque [in Mecca] with al-Aqsa so that Muslims would not make a distinction between the two mosques or belittle either of them, since if one is belittled then the other is belittled as well' (Reiter, 2008: 29).

A similar context appears in the work of another Palestinian commentator (one who, based on his writing style, belongs to an Islamist stream) who claims in his 1993 book on Jerusalem that the Isra' (nocturnal journey) was intended to connect all of Palestine with *Dar al-Islam* (the territory under Islamic control) even before it was conquered by the Muslims (Al-Nahawi, 1993: 19). Another example is taken from Reiter's work:

"One visual expression of the elevation of al-Aqsa's and Jerusalem's importance in the contemporary Muslim consciousness is an illustration that appears on Islamic websites, one that presents the two holy sites next to the Isra' verse, with the Dome of the Rock building, representing al-Aqsa, standing taller than the Kaaba Mosque in Mecca. This illustration accompanied Sheikh Yusuf al-Qaradawi's sermon marking al-Isra' and al-Mi'raj Day in September 2004, in which he stated, among other things, that this event symbolizes the duty to recognize 'the greatest problem faced by Muslims today–the problem of Jerusalem and the problem of al-Aqsa Mosque and the problem of Palestine as a whole'" (Reiter, 2008).

Jerusalem and al-Aqsa are also central in many prophetic traditions (*hadith*). The most important of them is the *shad al-rihal* tradition, according to which the Prophet recommended the visit to three mosques of which the third after Mecca and Medina is al-Aqsa (Bukhari and Muslim, 1996, hadith no. 1397).

Since late medieval times, Al-Aqsa Mosque compound was also referred to as the Noble Sanctuary (al-Haram al- Sharif) to qualify the high status of Haram as Mecca and Medina. In modern times, however, al-Aqsa Mosque is described as the third most holy site in comparison with Mecca and Medina.

Other traditions from the Muslim literature are also being used in praise of Jerusalem (*Fada'il Bayt-al-Maqdis*). According to these traditions, a single prayer at al-Aqsa is regarded as the equivalent of 500 prayers (in another tradition, 1,000 prayers) at other mosques (Al-Muqaddasi, 1994); (Al-Qadoumi, 1994).

The Role of al-Haram al-Sharif in Contemporary Palestinian Muslim Politics

The claim that Jerusalem in particular and Palestine in general are an Islamic endowment (*waqf*) was first invented in 1988 by the Islamic Resistance Movement – Hamas. Azzam al-Khatib, director of the Jerusalem Islamic Waqf and Al-Aqsa Affairs explains that a "waqf, according to Islamic law, is property that may not be sold or change in any way; it follows, say those who promote this view of Palestine's status as waqf, that such property may not be relinquished" (Al-Khatib, interview, 2014). Hamas believes that "Palestine is an Islamic waqf given to all generations of Muslims until the Day of Resurrection" (Article 11, *Hamas Charter*, 1988). "Indeed, Jerusalem's multifaceted meaning stands behind the interest of Muslims all over the world in the land of Palestine as a whole. The city has strong evocative and emotional associations and has its own place in the hearts of Muslims" (Abu-Amr, 1995).

Jerusalem holds significant importance to the Islamic world beyond just the Palestinian-Israeli conflict. Its disposition resonates deeply with the average Muslim, and it ties the Islamic world on a personal level to the plight of the Palestinians unlike any other issue. For Palestinians this connection adds an important dimension to their negotiation strategy, as a protector of Jerusalem for the Islamic people because of its sensitivity and importance (Stewart, 2009).

Al-Haram al-Sharif is considered today not only the most sacred Islamic place in Palestine, but also the focus of most Palestinian national aspirations for an independent state. Many Palestinian groups "stress the Islamic character of the city and Muslim entitlement to it, and their attachment to Jerusalem constitutes part of their doctrinal views of the city (Abu-Amr, 1995)." For example, the northern branch of the Islamic Movement in Israel is promoting the status of the city by launching a public campaign branded: *Al-Aqsa fi khatar* (Al-Aqsa is in danger) (Luz, 2004; Reiter, 2008).

The Islamic Movement in Israel focuses its activities on al-Aqsa Mosque to produce and reproduce their dynamics and activities at the intersections of political and social networks in Jerusalem between Arab Muslims in Israel and Palestinians in the West Bank including Jerusalem. This is done by using various methods: daily use of local and national media, targeted efforts such as organized public renovations on site, and a transportation system that brought thousands of devotees from all around Israel for prayers (Luz, 2004). Thus, al-Haram al-Sharif is gradually becoming the most sacred and revered national symbol of Arab-Palestinian Israelis, and Palestinian people in the West Bank and the Gaza Strip.

In sum, the Temple Mount/al-Haram al-Sharif served as a symbol of pride and struggle for Jews and Muslims as well as Israelis and Palestinians. Since 1996, dynamics in this holy esplanade intensified and escalations continued until recent years. One event that caused tension was the Israeli government's pronouncement of the northern branch of the Islamic Movement as illegal. This movement, headed by Sheikh Ra'ed Salah, took the lead in the Palestinian struggle for al-Haram al-Sharif (Dumper, 2012).

Al-Aqsa Mosque was and still is the rallying point of the Palestinian struggle. Many of the mass-scale demonstrations and violent actions that have taken place in Palestine were launched from al-Aqsa Mosque; such were the waves of violence in October 2014 and September 2015. Al-Haram al-Sharif is undoubtedly one of the most sensitive and contentious locations in the Holy Land and a barrier in the Israeli-Palestinian negotiations. Moreover, since the Israeli police are absent from the compound during Muslim prayer times, the site has been employed by Palestinian Muslims for political demonstrations, resistance to Israeli policies and for launching clashes. The following section portrays the history of using al-Haram al-Sharif for political mobilization.

The Palestinians have strong social, political and religious relationships with al-Haram al-Sharif. For them, al-Haram al-Sharif is more than a place of worship. The religious figures, such as imams and muftis, address many social and other issues for thousands of worshippers and Jerusalemites. Many people meet there and get to know each other through prayers, worship, workshops and religious tutorials. In addition, the Palestinians hold national and Islamic festivals inside the mosque to voice their rejection for the Israeli occupation and to discuss other religious, social, political and cultural issues. The imams of al-Aqsa Mosque take advantage of the Friday speeches and lessons by addressing the religious, social, and political situation of Jerusalem from a Palestinian point of view. By doing this, they highlight their political position. Many social, religious and political festivals and events are held in al-Haram al-Sharif. Such events and occurrences gain tremendous public popularity due to the large number of worshipers who come from all over the West Bank, Jerusalem and Israel.

Finally, the importance of al-Haram al-Sharif encourages conducting *da'wa* more and more. It encourages worshippers to come to al-Haram al-Sharif especially during Ramadan. For instance, half a million worshippers were present on al-Haram al-Sharif on the occasion of Lailat al-Qadr on August 4, 2013 (Maan news agency). In addition, Muslims conduct the daily five prayers at the site. The numbers increase dramatically during Friday prayers when the Israeli authorities ease restrictions on entry to the site, including on people from the West Bank and the Gaza Strip.

Al-Haram al-Sharif During the British Mandate, 1920-1947

The conflict between Arabs and Jews began in the early 20th century during the British Mandate. It was intensified after the Balfour Declaration. However, during that time, Jews only claimed rights to the Western Wall. Al-Haram al-Sharif was under the control of the Supreme Muslim Council. The British Mandate government kept the status quo that prevailed during the Ottoman rule of the city.

Despite this, the British authorities restricted public access to the Wall during Jewish prayers and allowed some worship accessories, resulting in it gradually turning into a "Jewish site" - Many (Palestinian) Muslims saw this as a precedent of a growing Jewish presence threatening their holy site (PASSIA, 2015).

Al-Haram al-Sharif under Jordanian Rule, 1948-1967

Although Article VIII of the April 1949 Armistice Agreement between Jordan and Israel provides for arrangements to be made with regard to "free access to the

Holy Places, "the Jordanians failed to make any arrangements to safeguard Israeli Jewish access to the Western Wall and the Jewish cemetery on the Mount of Olives" (Reiter, 2008). Also, "Jordan decided not to elevate Jerusalem as the Hashemite United Kingdom's capital and actually favored Amman over Jerusalem in almost every aspect" (Reiter, 2008).

One of the senior Muslim clerics under Jordan during the 1960s was Sheikh Ikrima Sabri, former Mufti of Palestine and today a preacher at al-Aqsa Mosque and Head of the Supreme Islamic Authority. Sabri informed me in an interview that even prior to 1967 there were religious and political activities inside al-Aqsa Mosque, particularly two great demonstrations: the first, when the Palestinian populace welcomed Ahmad al-Shuqayri who was the head of the PLO in 1964, the second, was a demonstration against the Israeli military attack (or massacre according to the Palestinians) on Al-Samo'a village near Hebron (Sabri, interview 2-11-2015). Al-Shuqayri, backed by Egyptian President Gamal Abdul Nasser, was in 1964 considered the last hope for liberation and the return of the refugees to their pre-1948 villages and towns. Thousands of worshipers participated in these demonstrations. The most important aspect of these political demonstrations inside al-Aqsa Mosque was that the national movement was able to instigate them and all the slogans and cries inside al-Aqsa

Mosque were heavily supportive of Egyptian leader Gamal Abdel Nasser. It is important to note that there was no women's participation in any of these political demonstrations (Sabri, interview, 2015).

Al-Haram al-Sharif After the 1967 War

In July 1967, Israel extended Israeli law to East Jerusalem, including the Old City and al-Haram al-Sharif, which came under Israeli sovereignty. However, as the State Departent Annual Report on Religious Freedom described:

> "In a statement at the Western Wall, Minister of Defense Moshe Dayan indicated Israel's peaceful intent and pledged to preserve religious freedom for all faiths in Jerusalem: '. . .I hereby promise faithfully that their full freedom and all their religious rights will be preserved. We did not come to Jerusalem to conquer the Holy Places of others' Defense Minister Dayan immediately ceded internal administrative control of the Temple Mount compound to the Jordanian Waqf (Islamic trust) while overall security control of the area was maintained by Israel. Dayan announced that the Jews would be allowed to visit the Temple Mount, but not to hold religious services there" (sixdaywar.org).

It went on to say,

> "Although the Israeli High Court of Justice ruled that the right of access of Jews to al-Haram al-Sharif includes their right of worship, the Israeli government, as a matter of stated policy and practice has prevented non-Muslims from worshipping at al-Haram al-Sharif since 1967. Waqf officials contend that the Israeli police, in contravention of their stated policy and the religious status quo, have allowed members of radical Jews groups to worship at the site . . . In 2003, the Israel Police detained four guards employed by the Waqf on charges that they harassed Jewish visitors to al-Haram al-Sharif and banned the four from returning to the compound for 2 months. Waqf officials insisted, however, that the guards in actuality were detained in retaliation for protesting cases of Jewish visitors praying at the site" (State Department, Annual Report on International Religious Freedom, 2004: 557).

Al-Haram al-Sharif: The Period of Quiet Understandings, 1967-1996

The period of quiet understandings is most important, given that it continued for 30 years and both sides agreed to it, and, consequently, this period formed the status-quo, at least in the eyes of the Palestinian Authority and the Jordanian government. The Israeli recognition of the responsibility of the waqf in managing al-Haram al-Sharif, while security remained in the hands of the Israelis forced both sides to communicate and coordinate with each other. With time there was a routine of meetings between the waqf, the Israeli police and the Jerusalem municipality, in which "quiet understandings" were reached, with the agreement of the Israeli and Jordanian governments (Shragai, 1995; Reiter, 2016).

The ability to contain various violent events during the three decades that followed 1967 was due to these quiet understandings. Over the next decades the status quo held, despite occasional attacks and escalations. The security services foiled over a dozen attempts to blow up al-Aqsa Mosque. The period between 1967 and 1996 was witness to a number of violent clashes on al-Haram al-Sharif. On the morning of August 21, 1969 an Australian messianic tourist, Michael Denis Rohan, entered al-Aqsa Mosque and set fire to the mosque including the 800 year old Nur al-Din pulpit (*minbar*) destroying the old priceless wood and ivory pulpit sent from Aleppo by the Muslim ruler Saladin and part of the ceiling (Shragai, 2014). In 1982, an Israel soldier opened fire in the Dome of the Rock, killing a waqf official and injuring Muslim worshippers. With the first intifada (1987-1993), violence spread to al-Aqsa Mosque, as Palestinians sometimes pelted Jews worshipping at the Western Wall. Another tensed issue was the Israeli digging of the Western Wall tunnel and particularly when in August 1981 the excavators dug eastbound beneath al-Haram al-Sharif.

A notable example to the Muslim view that al-Aqsa Mosque is a *ribat* that must be defended is the tumultuous demonstration which took place in al-Haram al-Sharif on October 8, 1990. The demonstration broke out following a report that “Temple Mount Faithful” or *Ne'emaney Har haBayit*, a Jewish movement headed by Gershon Solomon, were intending to lay the foundation stone for the third temple close to the Dung Gate. The year 1990 witnessed the beginning of the first-Gulf-war events, which served to rekindle the first intifada, on the one hand, and to spark Messianic sentiments among certain Jews, on the other. In addition, in that year, the Fatah and Hamas movements reached an agreement for cooperation between them; the activity of young Palestinians, which till then was nationalistic, henceforward became religious (Shragai, 1995: 355).

Despite the announcement by the police that they would not allow the Temple loyalists to near the city gates, the Waqf officials called the masses to arrive ahead of time and prevent the Jewish attempt to take over the site. The police took care to defend members of the group rather than secure the Temple Mount, and therefore was not prepared in the proper manner. On the morning of August, 10, ten thousand Jews gathered in the area of the Wailing Wall, for the annual “Priests blessing” (*birkat hacohanim*). On al-Haram al-Sharif itself, Muslims had already gathered stones in preparation. After a few hours, they began throwing them at policemen. Schools canceled their classes and urged students to go to al- Haram al-Sharif, where the preachers incited the worshippers. Eventually, the police stormed al- Haram al-Sharif, killing 17 Muslim worshippers and wounding over a hundred, due to their fear that two policemen, who had been surrounded by Muslim protestors, would be killed. This was the bloodiest event on the Temple Mount since 1967 (Israel's Report of the Commission of Inquiry, 1990).

I interviewed Jihad al-Yasini (68) from the Old City, who took part in the protests and lost his 16-year-old son, Izz al-Din al-Yasini, in the protests. Al-Yasini said in the interview:

"Al-Aqsa is part of our conviction *(aqidah)*. There is holy relationship that connects us to al-Aqsa. It is the place where Prophet Muhammad ascended to Heaven. We will not allow Jewish groups to take over it. We are here as *murabitun.* A week before the protests, which led to a massacre on October 8, 1990, the Temple Mount Faithful spread the news that they would lay the foundation of the Third Temple in al-Aqsa. Many people gathered on that day to stop the Temple Mount Faithful. On that day, there were large numbers of Israeli security forces. They opened all gates to al-Haram al-Sharif. Protests broke out and my son was shot in the head and the chest. However, we stopped the Temple Mount Faithful from laying the foundation of the Third Temple. Security forces opened fire at protesters and killed 21 people" (Yasisni, interview).

Martyr Izz al-Din al-Yasini died in the events of October 8, 1990

Al-Haram-al-Sharif after the Opening of the Western Wall Tunnel, 1996- 2014

The attempt by the north branch of the Israeli Islamic Movement, in cooperation with the Waqf, to build an underground praying hall for Muslims in "Solomon's Stables" and the Jewish attempt to open an exit to the Western Wall Tunnel aroused Muslim fears. The Israeli Islamic Movement did much through educational and other means to promote the idea of al-Aqsa Mosque's being in danger. Yasser Arafat, PLO chairman also reacted to the excavation of the ancient tunnel by saying: "This is a crime, a big crime against our religious and holy places" (www.http://edition.cnn.com/).

In reaction to the opening of the northern exit of the Western Wall Tunnel and the ensuing violent incidents that took place between Palestinians and Israelis in September 1996, the northern branch of the Islamic Movement in Israel, headed by Sheikh Ra'id Salah, began to organize mass rallies under the slogan "Al-Aqsa is in danger." This slogan transmitted the message to the Muslim public that Israel is seeking, in a deliberate and systematic way, to destroy al-Aqsa Mosque in order to build the Third Temple in its place. The Islamic Movement in Israel's campaign started already before 1996. As noted above, in the early 1990s, Sheikh Ra'id Salah began interpreting Israeli statements and actions as being intended to bring about al-Aqsa's destruction (Reiter, 2008: 109); (Tal, 2011); (Luz, 2004). According to the vision of Sheikh Ra'ed Salah al-Quds would be the capital of the Islamic Caliphate and al-Haram al-Sharif its center of government (Dumper, 2009).

However, Eran Tzikiyahu (2015: 6) explained that the caliphate Ra'ed Salah described is religious and not political.

> "The Islamic Movement's organizational skills, its success as a champion of Jerusalem, and its placing of al-Aqsa Mosque at the center of Palestinian national-religious consciousness transformed the Movement into one of the city's most dominant forces. According to Sheikh Ra'ed and his deputy Kamal Khatib, the role of the capital of the future Islamic Caliphate is reserved for Jerusalem, although, as Hillel Cohen notes, in contrast to the Liberation Party, Khatib and Salah believe that "yearning for the Caliphate cannot replace political action'" (Tzikiyahu, 2015: 6).

In September 1996, when Israel carried out works to open the Western Wall tunnel clashes erupted between Palestinians and Israeli forces resulting in 63 deaths in Gaza and the West Bank, including Jerusalem (https://staff.najah.edu/sites). The traumatic events heightened tensions regarding al-Haram al-Sharif and its environs and fueled the Israeli-Palestinian conflict with religious fervor. The trust built over 30 years of Israeli-Waqf relationship faded away and al-Haram al-Sharif was turned into a major symbol of the struggle.

At the same time the Israeli permission granted to the Waqf Authorities for maintenance work at "Solomon's Stables" led the way for the Islamic Movement to refocus its funds, volunteers, and media attention on the contested al-Haram al-Sharif/ Temple Mount, challenging both Israeli control of the site and PA and Jordanian compliance (Dumper, 2014).

Another event that ignited the outburst of anger among Palestinian Muslims was the visit of MK Ariel Sharon on al-Haram al-Sharif on September 28, 2000 against the background of the failure of the July 2000 peace talks between Israeli and PA leaders. Sharon's visit was understood, probably as he initially intended it to be, as a clear and imposing statement regarding the dominant power over the site. Until 2000, the entry of Jewish visitors to the Temple Mount was coordinated with the Waqf. As a result of that demonstrative visit the site was closed to all visitors for almost three years until August 2003. Since then the Israel Police have overseen visits by Jewish visitors (Luz, 2004); (Reiter, 2016).

The Islamic movement worked constantly to promote the status of al-Haram al-Sharif. It encouraged Islamic solidarity and the spiritual reconnection of Muslims with al-Haram al-Sharif through its sponsorship of religious seminars, special festivals and social welfare events. It also contributed to what Pullan et. al. describe as the "revival and revitalization of the Islamic *da'wa* among the people of the city of Jerusalem." The Movement also organized the March of Flags of Al Aqsa Mosque.((Pullan et al, 2013: 118).

Dumper and Larkin add that Sheikh Ra'ed Salah led Al-Aqsa is in danger' campaign. The rallies of such campaign drew thousands of supporters and the number of visitors of the holy site increased dramatically. Sheikh Ra'ed Salah was also involved in renovating the Marwani prayer rooms in Al-Haram al-Sharif and establishing the Al-Waqf Foundation.

Ideological visits of Jews to the Temple Mount intensified in 2003, and reached a peak in 2014, when political persona, including ministers and members of the Knesset, habitually visited the Temple Mount. This new situation was interpreted by Muslims as an official Israeli policy, rather than as the actions of private people and groups. On October 30, 2014 a precedent was set: the police closed al-Haram al-Sharif for 24 hours following the attempt to kill Yehuda Glick, a Temple Mount activist. A general strike was declared in East Jerusalem, and Jordan returned its ambassador for consultations (Ben-Ze'ev: 650).

During 2004-5, Palestinians from the West Bank were prevented from entering al-Haram al-Sharif. Young Palestinians from East Jerusalem and Israeli Arabs were similarly prevented from entering al-Haram al-Sharif on various occasions when the police had information regarding protests and unrest. During 2013-14, the number of Fridays in which prayers were restricted to women and men over a certain age (45, 50 and even 55) rose dramatically. This was likewise interpreted as a Jewish attack on al-Haram al-Sharif and al-Aqsa (Reiter, 2016).

At the same time, increasingly frequent visits by Jewish extremists to al-Aqsa compound have been taking place, backed by widespread institutional and governmental support, including from within the Knesset and the security services. Calls by religious nationalists to change the status quo appear to have moved from the political fringe to the mainstream (PASSIA, 2015). In addition, there are voices from within the Israeli government demanding a stronger Jewish presence on the site - from proposals to allocate ritual space and prayer times for Jews (similar to the control imposed by Israel at the Ibrahimi Mosque in Hebron), to calls for equal prayer rights (PASSIA, 2015).

Also, Israel is trying to curtail the activities of the Islamic Movement by arresting its leadership, and closing down its media agencies and charitable bodies. Ra'ed Salah, for instance, was imprisoned between 2004 and 2007 and in 2016 he was serving a nine-month sentence. An example of a media agency that was closed down by the Israeli government was the veteran newspaper, *Sawt al-Haqq wal-Huriyya* (Voice of Truth and Freedom) in 2015. Also Al-Aqsa Foundation was closed down in 2008. Finally, the Islamic Movement was outlawed (http://www.jpost.com/A.I Conflict).

National and religious activities by Jewish settlers groups on al-Haram al-Sharif encouraged Islamic Movement's leader Sheikh Ra'ed Salah to form the *Masatib al-'ilm* (study circles) and *murabitun* and *murabitat* movements on al-Haram al-Sharif to prevent Israeli Jewish groups from taking over al-Aqsa, "We made the Masatib al-'ilm and *murabitun* and *murabitat* in defense of al-Aqsa Mosque." (Al-Khatib, interview, September 15, 2015); (Sabri, interview, 2015).

In sum, since the days of the Grand Mufti Haj Amin al-Husayni in the first half of the twentieth century, and even more so since the Six-Day War and the unification of Jerusalem, the Temple Mount/al-Haram al-Sharif has been more than a place of worship for Muslims. It has become a pan-Islamic religious-national symbol, and a tense place of national and religious conflict between the Jewish world and the State of Israel on the one hand, and the Muslim world, the

Arab states, and the Palestinians on the other. Thus, al-Haram al-Sharif is gradually becoming the most sacred and revered national symbol of the Arab Muslim–Palestinians inside Israel, of the religious and secular Palestinians in the Palestinian territories, and of the Muslim world as a whole. On the other side also, Jewish national and religion groups pay regular visits to al-Haram al-Sharif to claim Jewish rights to the site.

Ribat, Murabitun, and Murabitat

Leaders of the *murabitat* movement as well as political and religious authorities state that the *murabitat* movement was founded in 2010. It began with study groups under the trees of al-Haram al-Sharif to fight the Jews and to defend al-Haram al-Sharif/al-Aqsa (Mufti Sabri, interview, November 2, 2015). In fact, the decision-making process leading to founding of the *murabitun* in 2009 and the *murabitat* in 2010 was more complex in light of ongoing events and multiple actors.

Attempts by Jewish groups to enter the Temple Mount/al-Haram al-Sharif, as we have seen, date back to 1967, when Gershon Salomon founded the Temple Mount and Land of Israel Faithful Movement. Yet these Temple Mount activists were prevented from doing so by the Israeli authorities. In addition to this, most rabbis were of the opinion that Jews should not be allowed to enter the compound since they might inadvertently defile the Holy of Holies of the Temple. In 2000, the *Nashim lema'an haMikdash* (Women for the Temple) movement was first organized with six members, but they faced a problem going up to the Mount (Inbari, 2009: 17). National Religious rabbis issued responses (*piskei halacha*) not only permitting Jews to enter the Temple Mount but requiring them to do so and actively recruited Jews for this purpose (Reiter, 2016).

At the same time, the Israeli Police came under increasing pressure to allow more Jewish groups to enter the Temple Mount. As the perceived danger to al-Haram al-Sharif increased, the northern branch of the Islamic Movement headed by Ra'ed Salah founded, in 2002, *Mu`asasat Muslimat min Ajl al-Aqsa* (Muslim Institutions for al-Aqsa) at the initiative of several women in the movement (Tal, 2011: 71). They organized study groups at al-Aqsa, among other activities. In 2003 the women of the northern branch of the Islamic Movement published information, for the first time, about the existence of the *Nashim lema'an haMikdash* movement in their women's magazine (*Ishraqa* cited by Tal, 2011). But it wasn't until 2006 that Jewish women began going up to the Temple Mount in groups with police protection (Gila Fein, interview, January 24, 2016). Gradually, the situation escalated as the number of Jewish groups entering the compound increased, and Muslims feared that al-Aqsa and al-Haram al-Sharif were in danger.

In 2009, the *murabitun*, a men's group to defend al-Haram al-Sharif, was established. A year later, a parallel group was founded for women. The immediate impetus for the founding of a women's group was the policy of the Israel Police limiting the number of Muslim men who could enter al-Haram al-Sharif as well as their arresting young men, leading to the belief that women would be treated better (which did not necessarily turn out to be true). Moreover, the number of Jewish women entering the compound increased and the situation escalated when they prayed on al-Haram al-Sharif with a torah scroll. The founding of a women's auxiliary of the *murabitun* was not however such an unusual step since every Palestinian political movement since the 1960s had women's associations including the Palestinian Islamist movements (Ben Shitrit, 2016).

The defense of Islam and Islamic soil (*ribat*) was always regarded a religious obligation. The root of the Arabic word *ribat*, r-b-ṭ, is present in the Arabic of the 1st/7th century, in numerous derived forms. It is possible to identify a first stratum of usage, comprising Qurʾan, Qurʾanic usages and those of the early caliphate period. Originally, these usages are linked to tribal warfare. According to the ancient sense of the root should be seen as being provided with horses and weapons and being ready to combat. *Ribat* is perhaps associated with tethering a horse in enemy territory; the performance of garrison duty at the frontiers of Dar-al-Islam (domain of Islam) was viewed as a pious duty from the time of the second caliph Umar Ibn al-Khattab.

According to 10th century historian, Al-Muqaddasi, "*ribat* did not necessarily originate in the context of military establishments. There was a connection between Sufis and the word *ribat*, which is also called *khanqah* or *zawiyya*. These terms were first effectively and regularly applied to groups of mysticists devoting themselves to practices of piety (*`ibada*) in a building to which they had rights of ownership (Chabbi and Rabat, 1997: 493- 506).

Ribat meant places that stood in the face of an invasion. The modern use of *ribat* shows a connection between the battles Muslims had throughout history and the conflict of Palestine (Reiter, 2008).

Jerusalem was gradually upgraded in Islamic discourses to become "Islam's Defensive Stronghold" (*ard al-ribat*) (al-Nakhawi: 213). "Jerusalem as "Islam's Defensive Stronghold" appears in various contexts intended to accentuate its importance to Islam. Thus, for example, the claim is made that the Prophet Muhammad's Companions (*sahaba*) fought in Jerusalem or served and were buried there or in its environs, and that Jerusalem is, therefore, sanctified as the repository of the bones of such personages as Abu `Ubayda ibn al-Jarrah, `Ubada ibn al-Samit, Shaddad ibn Aws, and Tamim al-Dari" (Reiter, 2008).

According to Sheikh Abd al-Aziz Ibn Baz, who was Saudi-Arabia's Mufti,

> "*ribat* means standing in guard of the borderlines, at the places feared to be attacked by the enemies of Islam, and a *murabit* is the person garrisoned there, who has dedicated himself to *jihad* (striving/fighting) in the Cause of Allah and defending religion and his Muslim brothers" (www.ibnbaz.org.sa/node).

The Palestinians have used the term *ribat* in the last two decades to describe the increasing Muslim presence at al-Haram al-Sharif throughout the day, as well as the organization of study circles on al-Haram al-Sharif in order to defend it from Jewish invasion or desecration. Part of this strategy involved women's participation (the *murabitat*) in large numbers, particularly in harassing Jews who visited the site (Tal, 2011).

The purpose of the endeavor of the *murabitat* movement at al-Haram al-Sharif was to strengthen the hold of Muslims on al-Aqsa and to combat the parallel movement of Israeli Jewish women (Tal, 2011). The *murabitat* encounter Jewish groups coming to the site of al-Haram al-Sharif by crying *Allahu Akbar*. Jewish groups that come to Temple Mount/ al-Haram al-Sharif include men and women. They are guarded by around fifty armed Israeli security officers. Individual Jewish woman can occasionally be noticed praying at the site of al-Haram al-Sharif. Their prayer would be interrupted by the *murabitat* once noticed (Gila Fein, interview, January 24, 2016); (Al-Ju'be, interview, September 17, 2015). Israeli security forces usually responded to the *Murabitat's* actions with violence and this was among the reasons for the breakout of the al-Quds intifada of 2015.

Today the Islamic Movement in Israel uses the tradition of *ribat* in a contemporary context. Here are few examples:

> "It is narrated on the authority of Sahl ibn Sa`d (may Allah be pleased with them) that the Messenger of Allah (peace be upon him) said: "*Ribat* in the cause of Allah for one day is better than this world and whatever is on it; and the place occupied by the whip of one of you in paradise is better than this world and whatever is on it; and a morning or an evening's journey that a Servant travels in the cause of Allah is better than this world and whatever is on it" (http://www.alifta.net/Fatawa/FatawaSubjects.aspx).

Another tradition being cited by the Islamic Movement is:

> "The deeds of every deceased person are sealed by their death, except for the one who dies as a *murabit* in the cause of Allah; his deeds will continue to be grown (increased) for him until the Day of Resurrection and he will be safe from the *fitnah* (trial) of the grave" (www.tawheedmovement.com/2012).

Conclusion

Al-Aqsa mosque has long been considered the third most sacred Muslim holy site, yet in more recent years it has become Islam's "first political *qibla.*" This elevation or politicization of the site has been traced by some commentators to former Mufti of Jerusalem, Haj Amin al-Husayni, who made efforts to restore and beautify the holy places of al-Haram al-Sharif and to transform them into pan-Arab and Palestinian nationalist symbols.

Al-Aqsa Mosque was and still is the focal point of the struggle against the Jewish people and it serves as a barometer of tensions in the Israeli-Palestinian arena. Many of the popular uprisings and provocations in Palestine have emanated from events that have taken place at al-Aqsa Mosque. Such were the events of the Buraq Uprising in 1929 (Hebrew: *me'oraot tarpat*) when Jews tried to extend their rights at the Western Wall, the setting fire to al-Aqsa Mosque by an Austrialian tourist in 1969, the events of the opening of the Western Wall Tunnel in 1996, and the provocative visit of Sharon to al-Haram al-Sharif in September 2000 which instigated the second intifada.

The Islamic Movement decided, in light of the increasing number of Jewish groups visiting al-Haram al-Sharif, to establish study circles of *murabitun* in order to have the largest possible number of Muslims at the site. They would stand up against the Jewish groups while they conduct visits to the site and jeopardize any Jewish plans to take control of al-Haram al-Sharif. According to Ikrima Sabri, "the *murabitat* movement was established in 2010 during a meeting of Islamic leaders on al-Haram al-Sharif, to face Jewish women who were part of the visiting Jewish groups." This step was the continuation of what Women for Al-Aqsa (*Nisa min ajl al-Aqsa*) had started. Women for Al-Aqsa was a branch of the Islamic Movement in Israel. This branch coordinated the communication between the *murabitat* and the leaders of the Islamic Movement in Israel. In addition, Tal (2011), documents the role of women in the Islamic Movement in Israel in organizing support for al-Aqsa. He added that the similarities between the present day *murabitat* phenomenon discussed in this study, and the historical national Palestinian women's movement include resistance of Jewish activities in Palestine, such as facing Jewish religious and nationalist groups' presence on al-Haram al-Sharif as of 2010; opposition to turn the Western Wall into a public prayer site and a Zionist symbol; and the attempts to take control over the holy sites (Sabri, interview, 2-11-2015).

The term *ribat* was used for a very long time in Islamic history to describe the defense of the frontiers of the Islamic domain. This religious and historical term was invoked after 1967 to resist Israeli occupation with a special focus on al-Aqsa Mosque. Nowadays Palestinians living in Palestine feel that they are in *ribat* or in defense of the Islamic holy sites in Jerusalem and the West Bank.

The Islamic Movement in Israel, particularly its northern branch, view Israeli actions regarding al-Haram al-Sharif as an attempt of the Jewish groups to take control over al-Aqsa and to rebuild the Jewish and its leaders' reaction was the establishment of the *murabitun* and *murabitat* movement, to defend Al Aqsa Mosque. The undisclosed purpose of establishing the *murabitat* movement was particularly aimed at facing Jewish religious women visiting al-Haram al-Sharif for ideological purposes. The fact that the *murabitun* faced tougher measures from the Israeli police upon entry to al-Haram al-Sharif or even detention was another factor to creating the *murabitat* movement.

2. The Islamic Movement in Israel and Jewish Visitors to al-Haram al-Sharif

The Islamic Movement in Israel

> "Muslim women in Palestinian society are respected. They stand alongside men in the defense of al-Aqsa. We in the Islamic Movement are proud of establishing the study circles, the *murabitat*, and the *murabitun*. The *murabitat* are the Islamic army." (Sheikh Ra'ed Salah, An interview with the Al-Quds satellite channel, September 15, 2015)

The words of the head of the northern branch of the Islamic Movement in Israel reflect the role of the Movement in initiating the *murabitun* and *murabitat* groups in what it sees as the human army to defend al-Aqsa. This chapter addresses the role of the Islamic Movement in initiating and cultivating the activities of the *murabitat* and the trigger of establishing this female "army" in addition to the former male guards (*murabitun*). It also presents the mirror picture of Jewish religious and nationalist women organizations, which triggered the *murabitat* phenomenon by encouraging Jewish women to visit the Temple Mount in organized groups.

Sacred places, such as al-Haram al-Sharif in Jerusalem, are being produced, reproduced and transformed by the constant dynamics and activities found at the intersections of political and social networks. This chapter examines the growing involvement of the Islamic Movement in Israel in Jerusalem, both in terms of rhetorical, political and cultural discourse and specific facts on the ground. It explores how al-Aqsa Mosque has been employed, particularly by Sheikh Ra'ed Salah, as a symbol for political empowerment and a focus for religious renewal.

The Foundation of the Islamic Movement in Israel

A short description of the Islamic Movement is needed for understanding where its activism regarding al-Aqsa emanated from and why a radical Islamist organization operates a women's movement and assigns its members with missions equal to those of men.

The Islamic Movement in Israel (*Al-Haraka al-Islamiyya fi al-Dakhil*) known at its outset as *al-Shabab al-Muslim* (the Muslim Youth), first emerged in the late 1970s under the leadership of Sheikh Abdallah Nimr Darwish Issa from Kafar Qasem. Since June 1967, the Muslim community in Israel, cut off from the rest of the Arab world since 1948, was able to reestablish contacts with the Palestinian population following the Israeli occupation of the West Bank and the Gaza Strip. These renewed exchanges also included access to new religious colleges in the occupied Palestinian territories such as Hebron University's Shariʿa College. The Islamic Movement grew popular among the Israeli Muslim citizens (Ben Shitrit, 2015).

On the eve of the 1996 Israeli general elections the Movement split into two divisions: The northern and southern branches. The division is due to some Islamic Movement members' rejection of participation in the Israeli Knesset elections. "In the late 1980s, the leadership of the movement began to debate the possibility of running in the national elections for the Israeli Parliament, the Knesset, an option that it had previously rejected. In 1996, disagreement over the question reached an impasse, leading to a split along ideological lines. Sheikh Abdallah Nimr Darwish, the spiritual leader of the Movement, supported a pragmatic approach to strengthen the movement and to reflect its unique religious identity by participating in the Israel's state institutions. . ." "In opposition to Sheikh Abdallah, a prominent faction of the Islamic Movement under the leadership of Sheikh Ra'ed Salah and Sheikh Kamal Khatib rejected what they saw as an illegitimate compromise and upheld a rejectionist approach. They insisted that the Islamic Movement should not recognize the legitimacy of Israel State institutions such as the Knesset that constituted a component of the Zionist project" (Ben Shitrit, 2015: 47).

The southern branch is led today (2017) by Sheikh Hamed Abu Da`abes, succeeding Sheikh Ibrahim Sarsour, who represented the Islamic Movement in the Israeli parliament eight years ago. The northern branch, which rejects the participation in the Israeli parliament, is led by Sheikh Ra'ed

Salah. The Islamic Movement was born at the beginning of the 1970s during the rise of political Islam in the Middle East and other countries (Tal, 2011: 1). Tal adds that the Islamic awakening among Arab Israeli citizens was prompted by the defeat of the Arab states in the Israeli-Arab war of June, 1967 and the consequent Israeli control over the West Bank and Gaza Strip and the Golan Heights (Ibid.).

Usrat al-Jihad or the Jihad Family was founded in 1979 by the first Israeli Islamist activists who organized themselves as a secret cell conducting violent and sabotaging actions at Jewish villages and towns. Ideologically, it followed the footsteps of Izz al-Din al-Qassam, who aimed at liberating Palestine from the British and Zionist presence and turn it into an Islamic society in the 1930s (Tal, 2011). In 1980, *Usrat al-Jihad* activists were exposed, then detained and after few years in prison they came out with a new approach of nonviolent nature to draw grassroots support focusing on social and religious services.

Issam Aburaiya (2004) writes about the historic development of the Islamic Movement in Israel. He divides the development of the Movement into five different phases. The first phase discusses the creation of the Islamic Movement in the late 1970s by Sheikhs Abdullah Nimr Darwish, Ra'id Salah, Kamal al-Khatib, and Ibrahim Sarsur. These were graduates of West Bank universities. They had religious devotion and a deep commitment to proselytizing (*da'wa*). The second phase covers the early 1980s. This phase saw the growing popularity of the Islamic Movement in Israel. The Movement had a network of local charities, health clinics, mosques and schools. The third phase covers the mid-1980s to the early 1990s. The Islamic movement expanded its power to local government, winning municipal elections and focusing on regional issues. In the fourth phase (1990-1996), the Movement expanded to reach national levels, including political participation in Knesset elections of the southern branch. The northern branch of the Islamic Movement, led by Sheikh Salah, focused on Palestinian concerns such as re-instituting, renovation and protection of pre-1948 abandoned Islamic religious sites. The Movement also focused on "Al-Quds- the blessed city" and "al-Aqsa – the third holiest Muslim shrine" as unifying religio-national symbols. In the fifth phase (1997-2009) the Islamic Movement focused mainly on the defense of al-Aqsa and Jerusalem. The defense was led by Sheikh Ra'id Salah and was distinguished by local activities in Arab East Jerusalem such as renovations of holy sites, protests and religious festivals on al-Haram al-Sharif. The Islamic Movement in Israel is actively involved in national issues. The Movement is also popular and widely respected. (*Middle East Monitor*, 16 December 2016).

It was a significant surprise when Sheikh Ra'ed Salah ran in the local authority elections in Israel in 1989, and won the mayorship of Umm al-Fahm three times.

Sheikh Ra'ed Salah was born in Umm al-Fahm in 1958. He completed secondary education in the town. He studied Islamic Shariʿa at Hebron University in the West Bank, where he came in contact with the *Kutla Islamiya* (Islamic Coalition, a pro-Muslim Brotherhood movement which became part of Hamas in 1988). He graduated in 1981. Sheikh Ra'ed was among the founders of the Islamic Movement in Israel. He also founded Al-Aqsa Reconstruction Association, which collected donations to renovate al-Aqsa Mosque and other abandoned mosques, saint tombs and Muslim cemeteries inside Israel. The activities of Sheikh Ra'ed Salah in relation to al-Aqsa Mosque gave him religious and national significance. According to Sheikh Ra'ed Salah, his branch' activities regarding what he termed as "defending al-Aqsa Mosque" aimed to safeguard the Islamic, Arab, and Palestinian identity of al-Aqsa compound among the Israeli Arab citizens (https: // www. paldf. net/ forum/ showthread.php).

Moreover, Sheikh Ra'ed Salah became to be known in the Arab and Muslim Worlds as "Sheikh al-Aqsa" signifying the battle to exclude the Israeli Jews from the holy shrine, defend it against Zionist aspirations and liberate it from Israeli control. His activities also made him known for representing the Arab-Islamic battle for Jerusalem in the aftermath of the death of the Jerusalemite Palestinian leader Faisal Al-Husayni.

Under Ra'ed Salah's leadership the Islamic Movement have attempted to Islamize Jerusalem by increasing the number of

Muslims on al-Haram al-Sharif, which would contribute to the revival of the Old City of Jerusalem as a commercial hub. And finally "through media campaigns, protests and Islamist discourse the Islamic Movement sought to project Jerusalem as a future capital of an Islamic Caliphate" (Dumper and Larkin, 2009). The other ideological action taken by the Islamic Movement was to present the idea of an autonomous Islamic society within the State of Israel through establishing social, educational, cultural, and charitable institutions.

Israel considered the ideology of the Islamic autonomous society to be dangerous. Hence, Israeli authorities placed Sheikh Ra'ed Salah under arrest from 2004 to 2007. They also closed down *Sawt al-Haqq wal-Huriyya,* the media outlet of the Islamic Movement, and its charitable institutions, like Al-Aqsa Foundation in 2008. Also in November of 2015, Israeli authorities banned the Islamic Movement and placed the Sheikh under arrest for 9 months (https://naamy.net/news/View/1030). The Islamic Movement in Israel responded to the opening of the tunnel of the Western Wall and the violence that followed by organizing rallies that used "Al-Aqsa is in Danger" as a banner. The message was that Israel sought to destroy al-Aqsa Mosque (Reiter, 2008).

Eran Tzikiyahu wrote about the work of the Islamic Movement in Israel in regard to its transport of Muslim women from Israel proper to al-Aqsa Mosque to oppose Jewish groups visiting the area. He writes: "the Islamic Movement in Israel initiated the *Flag*

Parade after Sharon's visit to the Temple Mount. Its purpose was to bring worshippers to Al-Aqsa. Consequently, thousands of worshippers came to Al-Aqsa especially that the Flag Parade provided free transportation" (Tzikiyahu, 2015).

The Islamic Movement also had impact in other areas. Ben Shitrit notes that Israel outlawed the Movement due to, inter alia, its activities in the virtual arena. The Movement's online activity aimed to spread its ideology and attract followers.

Islamic Women's Associations

The Islamic Movement in Israel had a strategy of establishing social institutions including women's institutions. The *Jam'iyat Sanad li-Isalah al-Usra wal-Mujtama* (Family Support and Society Reform Association) was one of the associations established by the northern branch of the Movement in 2000. The purpose of the Sanad Association was to take care of Arab Muslim families in Israel. The Association was led by women with good public relations and education. It was headed by Sawsan Masarweh from `Ara (Tal, 2011, 2016).

According to Ben Shitrit:

> "The women activists do not confine *da'wa* work and guidance on correct Islamic behavior to small mosque lessons. They also organize public events that draw hundreds of women. Sanad... the northern branch's most influential women's nonprofit organization, leads

> educational conferences across the country on a variety of topics such as good Islamic parenting, proper communication within the family, raising adolescent girls, children and globalization, father's responsibilities in bringing up children and how to discuss the hijab with a young girl. These conferences are very popular, and attendance ranges from 200 to 500 women in each... Sanad's members are highly qualified; among leading staff are women activists with degrees in education, psychology, and social work. Sanad conferences include scientific as well as religious argument" (Ben Shitrit, 2016: 97-98).

The Muslim Women for al-Aqsa Association is another creation of the northern branch of the Islamic Movement in Israel. It was established in 2002. The Association was led by sheikh Ra'ed Salah's wife Umm Amer. Its activities include political and social activities. Members of the Association are from Haifa, the Galilee, Jaffa, Lod, the Negev, Shefa 'Amr, Ar'ara, and Ramla. It was the equivalent of the Muslim Men for al-Aqsa Association (Tal, 2011). The idea of setting up Islamic Women Associations was developed among a group of 35 women, representing different Arab villages and cities in Israel. They met in Umm al-Fahm. Their purpose was to contribute to funding the renovation of al-Aqsa Mosque. They met with Ra'ed Salah, the head of Al-Aqsa Reconstruction Association, which aimed to rehabilitate Islamic endowments (*waqf*), and chose Ala Hijazi as the director for the Islamic Women Associations (Ishraqa, London MB Journal). Ra'ed Salah's wife was among the directors of the Association with more than 1,500 members (Tal, 2011: 71).

It seems that the Women for the Temple organization impacted on the development of the Muslim Women for al-Aqsa Association. Tal writes that in 2003, Women for the Temple was first mentioned in *Ishraqa*, a women's magazine of the Islamic Movement. However, Gila Fine, who visited the Temple Mount/ al-Haram Al-Sharif every day with Jewish religious groups, told me in an interview that groups of Jewish women began going to the Temple Mount/ al-Haram al-Sharif only in 2006 (Fine, interview, 2015).

The Islamic Movement's Activities in Israel

Al-Aqsa fi Khatar (Al-Aqsa is in Danger): The 20th Conference of the Islamic Movement in Israel in Umm Al-Fahm

Ben Shitrit explains that the Islamic Movement's activities include social services and *da'wa* as well as political organizing. The services include financial aid and dealing with problems like drug addiction. The Movement also provided assistance to educational institutions, created sports activities, built mosques, and distributed religious publications. It even ran in local elections and won (Ben Shitrit, 2016).

This decision may have increased the popularity of its members. "Despite being outlawed and having its leader, Ra'ed Salah, jailed, the Northern Branch of the Islamic Movement remains popular and appears to function much as before" (Ben Solomon, 2016). The outlawing of the Islamic Movement and the other measures taken against it increased its popularity. The Israeli authorities' measures against Sheikh Ra'ed Salah made him more popular.

Masirat Albayariq (March of the Banners)

The connection between *Masirat Al-Bayariq* and the *murabitat* is close because they serve the same purpose, which is to protect al-Aqsa Mosque from Jewish groups. Most importantly, the *murabitat* and the women from the Islamic Movement in Israel worked together on developing close social relations and coordination of activities, especially organizing religious festivities such as the *Mawlid al-Nabi* (birthday of the Prophet Mohammad) and Child Day in Support of al-Aqsa (Khadija Khweis and Hanadi al-Halawani, 2015).

Sheikh Ra'ed Salah "flagrantly denies all previous history or geography of the compound prior to the Islamic conquest of the seventh century: 'The Aqsa Mosque is an Islamic, Arab and Palestinian property only! And no one save us, no matter who they are, has any right to the place, no right to the end of days!' Salah adds, 'we will renew our covenant with God and our covenant with al-Aqsa and we will pin our hopes on our Islamic Umma and our Arab world and our Palestinian people and reiterate: we shall redeem you in spirit and blood' (Luz, 2004).

In her September 2016 article, Inbal Tal explains that the websites of the Islamic Movement have links that deal with women's issues as well as publishing posts of well-known Muslim women from old and modern times. Abu Amr adds that this was because the religious relationship between the leaders of the Islamic Movement at the beginning of 1970s started with Sheikh Ahmad Yassin and other Islamic leaders from Gaza Strip and West Bank who adopted the ideology of Muslim Brotherhood (Abu Amr, 1994).

JEWISH ACTIVITIES ON AL-HARAM AL-SHARIF

Historical Background: Jewish Presence on al-Haram al-Sharif Since 1967

Israel occupied East Jerusalem during the June 1967 war. Israeli commander Mordechai Gur made a famous statement when Israel took control of al-Haram Al-Sharif: *Har haBait beyadeinu* (the Temple Mount is in our hands).This symbolized the reawakened hope that one day the Third Temple could be rebuilt. However, then Prime Minister Levi Eshkol and Defense Minister Moshe Dayan understood the need for restraint due to the religious and political consequences from the Islamic World (which meant protecting a good political relation with many Islamic countries like Turkey, India and Jordan) of Jewish control of the holy site and Dayan ordered the Israeli flag to be taken down from the Dome of the Rock. This political reasoning was matched by a halakhic message broadcast by the Chief Rabbis of Israel -Isser Yehuda Unterman and Yitzhak Nissim - warning that Jews were not permitted to enter the holy site. This was acted a few days later by the Chief Rabbinate, which ordered the placement of signs to this effect at the gates leading to al-Haram al-Sharif (PASSIA, 2015).

Jewish political and religious groups started in early 1980s have seen a significant increase in activity, to organize prayers and activities at the Temple Mount/al-Haram al-Sharif. They established organized groups all over Israel. The groups include Temple Mount and Temple agenda is being promoted by organizations, bodies and activists who share a common ideology and goals. However, these groups can be distinguished according to their goals:

- The building of the Third Temple by man: The Temple Institute, The Movement for Temple Renewal, The Temple Treasury Trust, Women for the Temple
- Promotion of the Temple or Temple Mount as the cultural center of Israel: The Temple Mount Faithful, El Har Hamor" (Be'er, 2013).

The Temple Mount Faithful is the oldest of the Temple movements which was established in 1967 (Shargai, 1995: 186-188). Gershon Salomon, the secular Jew who founded the Temple Mount Faithful Movement - the first Temple movement in the post 1967 era argued that after the Six day War, then-defense minister of Israel, Moshe Dayan, made a terrible decision when he turned control of the Temple Mount back to the Muslim authorities of Jerusalem.

Yizhar Be'er writes that members of the Temple Mount Faithful ask the police to let them perform rituals at the Temple Mount on Jewish holidays. Among the rituals they perform is laying the Temple cornerstone (Be'er, 2013).

The movement's motivation is more nationalist than religious. "In the early 1990s, religious members of the movement left to establish the Movement for Temple Renewal. Since then, the movement's influence has begun to wane" (Be'er, 2013).

The Chief Rabbinate of Israel warned ever since that according to *halacha* Jews are not permitted to enter the holy site. "In other words, Jews were to confine themselves to the reintroduction of prayers at the Western Wall" (Inbari, 2009: 22). "From a theological point of view, the reasoning was that Jews might accidentally step on – and thereby desecrate due to their impurity - the place where the Holy of Holies once stood" (Moosa 2016). This place would only be known with the advent of the red heifer (the ashes of which are necessary to fulfill the ritual requirement of cleansing).

Ten days after the war, Moshe Dayan met with the directors of the Islamic Waqf and agreed to respect the status quo, accepting their day-to-day administration of al-Haram al-Sharif that allowed Jews and other non-Muslims to visit it (but not to pray!) (PASSIA, 2015). Inbari explains the efforts of Shlomo Goren, the Chief Rabbi of the IDF, to change the then Prime Minister Menachem Begin's position on Temple Mount prayers failed. Hence, Goren could not issue permits of entry to the Temple Mount. (Inbari, 2009: 23).

From 1967 to 2000, the entry of Jewish visitors to the Temple Mount was coordinated with the waqf. The site was closed to Jews from 2000 until 2003, as the second intifada raged. Since then Israel Police have overseen visits by Jewish visitors (http://www.crisisgroup.org/).

Motivations of Jewish Visitors of al-Haram Al-Sharif

One can summarise the motivations of Jewish vititors to the Temple Mount compound as follows:

- Patriotism: the main reason that motivates Jewish visitors of al-Haram al-Sharif is the belief in creating a Jewish kingdom rather than a democratic state and rebuilding the Third Temple as the heart of the Jewish kingdom (Be'er, 2013).
- Following of the *Halakha*: The *Halakha* calls for the rebuilding of the Third Temple or at least to pray there. For instance, there is "... A group of female devotees who call themselves "Women for the Temple" [who] are diligently toiling in private as well as public forums to realize their dream of a third temple in Jerusalem". (https://www.timesofisrael.com)
- Closeness to God: some rabbis believe that the rebuilding of the Third Temple would bring forth closer relationship with God.
- The Messiah: The rebuilding of the Third Temple will speed up the arrival of the Messiah.

The Israeli government permits Jewish groups that visit al-Haram al-Sharif to conduct activities, which Palestinians view as provocative and as attempts to take control of al-Aqsa Mosque. This has provided Palestinians, especially young Palestinians, with motivations to take action to put an end to such provocation. The 1990 events at al-Aqsa, which led to massive violent confrontations between Palestinian worshippers and the Israeli police and led to the death of 21 Palestinians, stand as proof of this claim.

Jews Religious Visitation as a Trigger to Ribat al-Aqsa

The Islamic Waqf on al-Haram al-Sharif stopped cooperating with the Israeli authorities following the violence caused by the opening of the northern entrance of the Western Wall Tunnel. The Waqf decided to close the site to non-Muslim visitors.

Reiter notes that Jewish ideological groups' attempts to change the situation at Temple Mount by allowing Jews to pray increased in early 21st century. In a letter to Prime Minister Ehud Barak in June 2000, Chief Rabbi Eliyahu Bakshi Doron asked Barak to make arrangements for future protection of Temple Mount. In any case, more frequent Jewish presence in the Temple Mount has led to more confrontations between Jews and Muslims (Reiter, 2008).

Rabbi Dov Lior with Haredi Rabbis on the Temple Mount

(Photo: 'Temple Mount News' website)

On July 27, 2009, the Knesset held a conference titled: "Jewish Sovereignty over the Temple Mount–Processes and Changes," organized by MK Michael Ben-Ari, which declared:

> "The public rose to their feet when Rabbi Yehudah Kreuzer, rabbi of the Mitzpeh Yericho settlement and head of the Yeshiva *HaRa'ayon HaYehudi* was called to the stage to talk about the importance of prayer on the Temple Mount. The Temple Mount is the heavenly gate for Jewish prayer, to which all prayers flow on their way upward to heaven." (Tzidkiyahu, 2015).

Reiter explains that the number of Jewish religious visitors to Temple Mount has increased dramatically since 1990s. Those visitors belong to organizations that receive financial support and conduct activities such as giving the 'Shabbat leaflets' at synagogues throughout Israel. Such leaflets contain contact information on how to arrange a visit to Temple Mount (Reiter, 2008). According to him:

Jewish visitors to al-Haram al-Sharif can be divided into three categories:

- Visitors whose motives are both nationalist and religious alike, mostly from within the ranks of religious-Zionists and whose interests are religious. These visitors seek to pray at the site and hope to build a synagogue or Jewish prayer area at the site;
- Ideological non-religious visitors from 'Im Tirzu' ('If you will it') or similar groups, i.e., Students for the Temple Mount, whose interests are nationalistic;
- Religious visitors who belong to the Temple Movements, whose vision calls for building a Third Temple, in the place where the Dome of the Rock currently stands (Reiter, 2016).

The Israeli police imposed restrictions on Jewish ideological groups' visits to Temple Mount between 2003 and 2012. However, the visits increased later and political pressure was exerted on Israeli police to facilitate entry of Jews into the Temple Mount. (Reiter, 2017:102, 104).

In September 2015, the Temple Mount / al-Haram al-Sharif first opened to Jewish visitors on Yom Kippur and Temple Mount supporters visited there. In the years 2013-2014, many Likud party Knesset members took actions in attempts to enable Jews to ascend the Temple Mount, including several secular members. Reiter notes:

"Government ministers and deputy-ministers ascended to the Temple Mount in increasing numbers, making sure they went to the upper-platform of the Dome of the Rock–a place Jewish Temple advocates previously avoided treading, owing to their reverence for the Temple. Deputy-Minister Gila Gamliel stated: "The Temple Mount is the identity card of the Jewish people," and MK Yariv Levine referred to the Temple Mount as 'the heart of the nation'... The interpretation of the 'status-quo' presented by the sub-committee was that the 1967 status quo continues; however, MK David Tzur himself stated the opposite: 'after the Temple Mount was closed due to riots in October 2000, in 2003 it was opened with certain changes [emphasis added] to the status-quo that had been in place since 1967'" (Reiter, 2017:107, 110).

According to my observations, Jewish groups' visit al-Haram al-Sharif through the Mughrabi Gate, between the hours of 7:30am-11am and from 1:30pm-2:30pm in the summer, with the break in between visiting hours during Muslim afternoon prayers.. Hence, most Palestinians believe that this Jewish policy or arrangement of visits will eventually lead to dividing al-Haram al-Sharif between Jews and Muslims where Jews and Muslims obtain a specific divided space and time for conducting their rituals on the site as in the case of the Ibrahim Mosque (the Tomb of the Patriarch) in Hebron. This prompted the Islamic Movement in Israel to take on action to prevent such a division. The actions included organizing study circles, which amounted to a non-stop Muslim presence on al-Haram al-Sharif.

Jewish Women's Activities on al-Haram al-Sharif

There are groups of Jewish women that have been established in Israel on political and religious grounds. These groups conduct visits to al-Haram al-Sharif to perform religious rituals even though such action provokes Muslims and violates the understanding between the Israeli police and the *awqaf*, which prevents any performance of religious rituals by Jewish groups in al-Haram al-Sharif. Lihi Ben Shitrit discusses this issue with respect to Jewish women's activities on al-Haram al-Sharif. She argues that Women for the Temple, which is made up of a core of 25 dedicated activists, have been involved since 2000 in activities in the Temple Mount, which involved ascending the Mount in the name of religious freedom and being close to the divine. They want to pray and conduct ceremonies such as *bat mitzvah* without provoking Muslims or the Israeli police The official mission of the Women for the Temple Mount is to: "strengthen the connection to

Temple Mt. and the awareness of the Temple's absence in the public and private lives of the People of Israel, raising Temple Mt.-awareness among women specifically, and among the People of Israel in general" (Ben Shitrit, 2016).

Moreover, Ben Shitrit writes about one of the Jewish women Temple activists (Rachel). According to Rachel, the activities revolving around the Temple Mount need to be divided between men and women. Men would focus on, *inter alia,* tasks like training *Cohanim* (priests), Temple construction, and political and legal advocacy. Women, on the other hand, need to focus on "traditional" work such as sewing, weaving, and dying of the priests' clothes or the *parochet.* Women can also work on event organizing, PR, outreach, tour guiding, coordination, public speaking, political lobbying, teaching, and religious guidance (2017:10).

Contacts and Influences on One Another

Ben Shitrit argues that Jewish female activists for the Temple Mount and Muslim women activists for al-Aqsa are very much aware of each other. They are influenced by each other's actions, and devise their work largely as a reaction to each other. My observations have led to the understanding that the influence of both parties on each other is due to the similar religious belief among both parties that the site is the closest point to God.

Members of Women for the Temple
visit the Temple Mount (Facebook photo)

Conclusion

The death of Faisal al-Husseini in 2001, a nationalist leader in Jerusalem, created a political vacuum, which gave Sheikh Ra'ed Salah and the Islamic Movement, the chance to initiate activities to strengthen the Islamic identity in Jerusalem. Sheikh Ra'ed Salah viewed himself as a pan-Islamic leader and envisioned Jerusalem as the capital of a future Islamic caliphate. In addition to conducting activities of the nature of the Islamic Movement such as the *Masirat Al-Bayariq,* which aimed, inter alia, to revive the economy of Jerusalem where visitors would not only worship on al-Haram al-Sharif but also shop in Jerusalem Arab stores of the Old City.

During 2010 the Islamic Movement realized that an increasing number of organized Jewish women's groups were visiting the Temple Mount/ al-Haram al-Sharif. This was a factor that helped to prompt the Islamic Movement to establish the *murabitat* movement and to take part in the religious and social events and to coordinate between the *murabitat* and women of the Islamic Movement.

The strengthening of the Islamic identity of Jerusalem by the Islamic Movement continued through assisting impoverished Jerusalemite families in renovating their homes. The Movement also established social relationships with Jerusalemite dignitaries. This was achieved through the participation of Sheikh Ra'ed Salah in social events such as the graduation ceremonies of high school and college students in addition to the organization of study circles on al-Haram al-Sharif. The renovation and cleaning of *al-*

Musala al-Marwani (formerly known as Solomons' Stables) from the debris and transforming the site into a functioning mosque where worshippers can pray largely advanced the status of Sheikh Ra'ed Salah and the Islamic Movement in Israel.

The Islamic Movement was persistent in raising awareness among people and in the media about the dangers of the Israeli excavations under al-Aqsa Mosque and the building of synagogues below the ground. Hence, the Islamic Movement reacted to confront what it viewed as attempts to take over al-Aqsa Mosque. The Movement used the media to raise alarm about the presence of Jews on al-Haram al-Sharif and to emphasize the necessity of having a Muslim presence to confront the Jewish presence. To this end, the Islamic movement created study circles as well as the *murabitat* to confront the Jewish women who visited the site. However, the role of the *murabitat* was magnified when Israeli police restricted the movement of the *murabitun* (the men).

The Islamic Movement played a critical role in the continuation of the Murabitat and the increase in the number of the Murabitat in Al-Haram al-Sharif. Moreover, the Islamic Movement in Israel covered the financial costs of the Murabitat, including paying monthly salaries to the Murabitat teacher, leaders, and rank and file as well as the legal costs of the measures the Israeli police took against the Murabitat. The women of the Islamic Movement also coordinated activities and communications between the male leaders of the Islamic Movement and the Murabitat leaders (Khadija Khwis, interview, September 2015).

The other impact on the Murabitat came from Jewish women in the groups visiting Al-Haram al-Sharif. The presence of the Jewish women boosted Murabitat efforts and gave them justifications to recruit more Murabitat. In any case, we must not forget that the creation of the Murabitat movement was in response to Jewish women's taking part in the visiting Jewish groups to Al-Haram al-Sharif. Moreover, the rituals performed by Jewish women on the site were shocking for the Murabitat, which made them more adamant in defending Al-Haram al-Sharif. The other impact was that Murabitat started to use social media to lobby Muslim women in Jerusalem against Jewish women whose number multiplied in Jewish religious festivities. (Umm Mohammad, interview, July 2015)

3. Palestinian Women's Activism-The Pious Women's Agency

In his 2014 dissertation about Palestinian women's movements, Ihab Aldaqqaq explains that understanding the Palestinian national movement helps understand the Palestinian women's movement(s). Kuttab (2004) writes that social liberation of women in Palestine is part of women's role in the fight against the colonization of Palestine. Moreover, the Palestinian women's movement(s) developed in parallel to development of women's movements in the region (Aldaqqaq, 2014).

A publication of the Palestine Liberation Organization (PLO) states:

> "The activity of Palestinian women, be it social or political, can best be understood in the context of their national struggle. Palestinian women have not fought for their liberation in isolation from the overall Palestinian struggle for national liberation; on the contrary, through it they have been able to tear down many of the barriers of traditionalism and conservatism that commonly obstruct women in their progress toward total emancipation" (PLO, "The Struggle of Palestinian Women," 1975:5).

Palestinian women have had a significant and indispensable role in political resistance against foreign rule throughout the modern history of Palestine, mainly throughout the period covered by this study, from 1920 to 2014. Hence, this chapter explores, through the use of historical means, and in chronological order, the rise and development of the Palestinian women's movement, their political activities within the national movement of Palestine, the role they played in the resistance of the British Mandate and the activities of the Zionist movement in Palestine throughout the time of the British Mandate for Palestine until the present day; mainly from 1920 to 2010 when the *murabitat* movement was founded.

Palestinian Women's Activism

From the Start of the British Mandate Until the Arab Revolt, 1920-1939

In her article published in 2000, Fleischmann notes:

> "In 1929, Palestinian women inaugurated their involvement in organized political activism with the founding of a women's movement. In October 1933, Arthur Wauchope, the British high commissioner of Palestine, noted a "new and disquieting feature" in violent demonstrations taking place in Jerusalem and Jaffa:"the prominent part taken by women of good family as well as others" (Fleischmann, 2000).

The Palestinian women's movement involving Muslim as well as Christian women, took off in the 1920s with the reform of the Palestinian Women's Union, which built on the 19th century political reform movement; however, the movement progressed during the struggle for liberation from the British Mandate and in protesting against the Zionist movement activities in Palestine (Jad, 2004).

Zionism is the ideology centered on the establishment of a Jewish national home in Palestine. The Zionist movement contributed to the materialization of the Belfour Declaration in Palestine and establishing relations with many Palestinian local leaders by supporting them in agricultural projects. During British mandate, the Zionist movement promoted Jewish migration to Palestine and established Jewish institutions and military movements such as Haganah and Lehi, which carried out attacks on Palestinian villages in early 1948, leading to the creation of the State of Israel. (Cohen, 2008 and Mayamey, 2010)

Another scholar named Julie Peteet (1991) writes in "Gender in Crisis: Women and the Palestinian Resistance Movement" about the Palestinian women's associations in 1920s:

> "The women's associations and societies, Muslim, Christian, and secular -nationalist, that gathered in Jerusalem on 26 October 1929 for the first Palestine Arab women's Congress to consolidate diverse efforts, women were clearly organizing around national issues: the Balfour Declaration, Zionist immigration, land sales, the economy, and national independence. The main topics on the agenda were the current political and social situation and the responsibility of the Mandatory Power" (Peteet, 1991: 46). Peteet adds "These leading women were, for the most part, from elite urban families, and their husbands were often involved in national politics during the Mandate period" (Peteet, 1991: 48).

The Palestinian women's movement represented the aristocratic and elite families where the male figures of the families led the national movements. Hence, the demands of such women's movements were directly linked to the demands of the Palestinian national movements including rejecting Belfour Declaration of 1917 and Jewish migration to Palestine.

Palestinian women's movement did not demand social rights; they demanded only political national rights as well as being part of the Palestinian national movement. They believed that women's social rights would be achieved after the liberation.

The political involvement of women was marked by the creation of a women's movement in Jerusalem and Jaffa in 1920s. The early Palestinian feminist movement "defies easy analysis and has to be situated within the complex interaction of nationalism, feminism and colonialism. Palestinian women did not define themselves solely by gender, nor did they perceive a sharp break between nationalism and feminism" (Fleischmann, 2000). Additionally, women actively participated in life outside the home by taking active part in the nationalist movement, which protested against the Balfour Declaration and Zionist immigration (Al- Wahidi, 1986). Among Jerusalem's female activists was Emilia al-Sakakini, who was among the first women to establish the first Arab Women's Association in the 1920s. The Association organized protests against the policy of the British Mandate facilitating a national homeland for the Jewish people and against Zionists' activities. Also it demanded the abolition of the Balfour Declaration, which would lead to the creation of a Jewish homeland in Palestine (Al-Khalili, 1977:78).

In short, Peteet writes:

> "in Jerusalem in 1921, a group of urban, educated, and upper class women, led by Emilia al-Sakakini and Zlikhah Ishaq al-Shahabi, formed the Palestinian

> Women's Union (PWU), the first women's political organization, which activists today refer to as the precursor of the current GUPW. The PWU's interests were welfare activities designed to improve the standard of living of the poor and to organize women around national activities" (Peteet, 1991:44).

A major Arab violent resistance to Zionism in Palestine occurred in August 1929 (termed by Hillel Cohen as the *year zero* of the Arab-Jewish conflict). Clashes broke out between Palestinians and Jews over access to the Western Wall (viewed by Muslims as al-Buraq Wall) in what became known as the Buraq Revolt (*Thawrat al-Buraq*) known by the Jews as *Me'ora`ot Tarpat* (the 1929 riots).

In the same year Palestinian women launched a women's movement, whose inaugural event convened in Jerusalem and was named the Palestine Arab Women's Congress (Fleischmann, 1995). More than 300 women from key Palestinian cities attended the congress, which was held in Jerusalem at *al-Karam al-Mufti* (the mufti's property in Sheikh Jarrah). The congress was headed by Tarab Abd al-Hadi (Al-Hute, 1986).

> "The opening session of the congress was followed by a women's delegation to the High Commissioner for Palestine, Sir John Chancellor and his wife at Government House, where the women delivered the Congress's resolutions. These were protests against: the Balfour Declaration, Zionist (sic) immigration...[and]

the mistreatment of Arab prisoners by police" (Fleischmann, 1995).

The Congress also organized a session in which an Arab Women's Executive Committee was elected to execute and administer the Congress's resolutions.

The Congress Executive Committee (CEC) consisted of 14 women primarily from notable Jerusalem families such as Abd al-Hadi, al-Husayni, al-`Alami, al-Nashashibi, Shihabi, and Budeiri (Fleischmann, 1995: 23); (Abd al-Hadi, 2015). Among the well-known members of the CEC were Nimra Tanous, Nahid al-Sajjadi, Sa'ida Jarallah, and Matiel Moghannam. The CEC members were educated and had a good enough command of English to communicate with the British administration and the foreign press (Ibid).

> "It is important to note that the Congress activities were carefully planned in advance, showing the political sophistication of the organizers. . . . Soon after the congress was over the Arab Women's Executive Committee called a meeting to organize the Jerusalem Women's Association as a branch of the Arab Women's Executive Committee. Although affiliates were eventually established in Acre, Gaza, Haifa, Nablus, Nazareth and Ramla, the Jerusalem branch was the dominant one and the semi-official center from which the Arab Women's Executive Committee operated" (Fleischman, 1999-2000).

This can be explained thorugh the creation and development of the Palestinian women's movement.

The bids of Palestinian feminism were visible as early as the 1920s when many Jerusalemite women lived active and public social lives. "Some women from the middle to upper classes were able to slowly begin to challenge traditions that had kept them secluded from public life" (Fleischmann, 1995).

Remarkably, female residents of Jerusalem have played distinguished and unique roles in the *evolution* of Palestinian national and religious women's movements. Jerusalemite women have been among the first to organize activities explicitly for political purposes as opposed to focusing solely on charitable causes. Hence, the leaders of the Jerusalem women's organizations became national leaders in their own right" (Fleischmann, 1995). Fleischman adds:

> "The ten-year period from the movement's inception in 1929 until the end of the Arab Revolt was a turbulent, energetic, and heady era for the women's movement. Through this movement, Palestinian women of the Mandate years provided a kind of training ground for women to enter public activity. Some have argued that the way women organized in this period 'would not have led to substantial gains in women's status in the long run'. I would argue the opposite; it is precisely the legacy of the historical women's movement that set a precedent for and

> enabled contemporary Palestinian women activists to mark a place for themselves in nationalist and feminist politics." (Fleischmann, 2000).

Fleischmann (2000) writes also about the contribution of Palestinian women to the Arab Women's Executive Committee, which was formed on 26 October 1929, to administer the congress's resolutions which had five Palestinian women members - married to prominent figures, which gave the women's movement more power- including Tarab Abd al-Hadi (wife of `Awni Abd al-Hadi who later became prominent in the Istiqlal Party and was active in politics), Na`mati al-Husayni (wife of Jamal al-Husayni who later became secretary to the executive committee of the Palestine Arab Congress and supreme Muslim Council, founder of Palestine Arab Party), Wahida al-Khalidi (wife of Husayn al-Khaldi who was the mayor of Jerusalem from 1934-1937 succeeding Raghib al-Nashashibi, he founded the Reform Party) and Emilia Sakakini (the sister of Khalil Sakakini who was a Palestinian Christian teacher, poet and Arab Nationalist) (Al-Hute, 1986).

Unlike the political role of women from the upper class, the activity of women and men of the poorer classes was focused more on the exigencies of feeding and providing for their families (Fleischmann, 1995: 13).

Fleischmann also writes about the role of Palestinian women in the early 1930s, including women from aristocratic families, when women took part in violent demonstrations, as Arthur Wauchope, the British high commissioner of Palestine noted:

> "Reporting on the demonstrations, which resulted in the shooting deaths by police of twenty-six Palestinians, police protested that the women had assaulted them, kicked at the gates of government offices, and "did all they could to urge the male members of the demonstration to defy Police orders" (Fleischmann, 2000).

The next chapter of Palestinian women's activism took place during the 1936-39 revolution. Women participated in the national struggle sit-ins to protest the British occupation as well as in other forms of demonstrations. They joined young men in the Old City in "surveillance" of the merchants to enforce the boycott of non-national goods, coordinated the collection of relief funds and raised money for weapons by selling their jewelry (Alqam, 2005: 89); (Kawar, 1996). It is interesting to note that the Islamist Al-Qassam movement did not recruit women fighters. But there were exceptions, a number of women who participated in the 1936 riots were killed (and therefore regarded as martyrs).

Unlike urban women, some peasant women actually joined the revolt in a military capacity. For example, one woman who is cited in a number of sources is Fatma Ghazzal, who was killed in the battle of Wadi Azzoun in June, 1936. Another example is Bahiya al-Ahmad from Jenin who fought and was killed in the 1936–39 Arab revolt in Palestine (Alqam, 2005:89); (Fleischmann, 2003: 126). Another source narrating of the involvement of Arab women in the 1936-39 riots is a British police report that warned that women are taking an active part in village affairs and are constantly urging the men to take definite action for the safety of their homeland.

From the start of revolt, peasant women were not hesitant to resort to violence to defend their villages or men folk, resisting searches, raids, and arrests in the villages. Clashes occurred between British Police and women who stoned them from rooftops, such as one incident in the village Kafr Kanna, where a young girl was shot dead and a British constable seriously injured (Fleischmann, 2003: 126). Another source supports the military role of Palestinian women in 1935 against British Mandate (Peteet, 1991). "During 1935 until 1939, less educated rural women became involved in the national endeavor, particularly in the armed rebellion in the countryside" (Peteet, 1991: 52). In struggling to protect their villages and stay on the land, women participated in the rural armed campaign as supporters. Though some did take up arms; a few fought and died, like Fatmeh Ghazzal, who was killed in battle June 26, 1936 in Wadi Azzun. She is the first known Palestinian woman killed in combat (Peteet, 1991:55).

The Eastern Women's Conference held in Cairo between 15 and 18 October, 1938 under the direction of Huda Sha`arawi, an

Egyptian feminist leader, was a major event aiming at Arab women supporting Arab Palestine's cause. Women participants came from Iraq, Iran, Syria, Lebanon, Palestine and Egypt. Of the twelve Palestinian women who delivered speeches (or had them read), five were from Jerusalem. Many more Palestinian women attended. Some of the resolutions of the conference included a demand for the European taking of responsibility for the Palestine problem, since it was a European creation; the abolition of the British Mandate for Palestine; the creation of a constitutional state; the nullification of the Balfour Declaration; the cessation of Jewish immigration; the prohibition of land sales to Jews and foreigners; the rejection of partition and British government policies; and the release of Arab prisoners and detainees (*Al-Mawsu`a al-Filastiniyya,*1984: IV). Yet no statements were made concerning the promotion of women rights.

The Arabs in Palestine were still disorganized, leaders and had not recovered from the loss of their fighting men in the 1936-1939 rebellion that later deteriorated into a lethal feud between the Husseini and Nashashibi camps (Sharfman, 2014).

In "Al-Mar'a al-Filastiniyya wa al-Thawra" (Palestinian Women and Revolution) scholar Ghazi al-Khalili provides support for the assertion that women played a prominent role in the period of 1929-1930 until 1938. He says:

"These incidents show that, despite most historians' dismissive references to Palestinian women's activity during the Mandate period as "bourgeois," politically "unaware," and "passive," these women had established an organized and often militant movement that was actively involved in social, political, and national affairs. Yet while the history of this women's movement remains marginalized -and this at a time when writing on the contemporary political activities of Palestinian women has evolved virtually into a genre all its own, especially since the intifada-it in fact reveals much about Palestinian history in general" (al-Khalili, 1977:80).

Palestinian Delegation to the 1938 Conference in Cairo, Egypt

Shortly after the 1938 conference, Matiel Moghannam, the secretary of the Women's Executive Committee, gave a speech in Bethlehem, in which she heralded the new moment by saying: "The Arab women enter the realm of public politics and work side by side to support men in their national struggle for freedom and independence ... we've left our houses for the arena of public life, opposing these old customs" (Kawar, 1996); (Alqam, 2005).

Looking back to the 1920s one can trace back Palestinian women's activism to the development of education. For women,

> ." . .education played an important role in opening up the world of work, be it paid employment or voluntary, and women began to participate in the political, economic and cultural life of the city." Many of the women of the upper and middle classes worked as teachers Educated women were the ones who tended to have 'more social freedom to organize'... Indeed, the increased education of women was both a subject of controversy as well as a liberalizing influence in Palestinian society" (Fleischmann, 1995).

The first steps of empowering women in Palestine started with education in the first girls school in Jerusalem (founded in 1838) and the Friends Girls' School in Ramallah (founded in 1889) (Dahdah, interview 2015); (Greenberg, 2010). Greenberg described how Muslim families during British mandate for Palestine, particularly from the elite, endorsed education for girls. For example:

> "Sa'ida Jarallah was the first Muslim woman to travel to England on her own to complete her education in 1938. Her father supported his daughter's engaging in various

> activities outside the house, and their not wearing the hijab. Although they incurred some criticism for their free behavior and public activities, they were protected because of his support and stature" (Fleischmann, 1995: 17).

The Christian schools (private or run by missions) were a model to be adopted and the establishment of girls' education motivated the attraction of modernity as well as by the need to reinforce religious and national identities coping with the challenges of British rule and Zionism. Frida Dahdah, a present-day principal of Friends Girls' School in Jerusalem said in an interview that one of the main goals of the school was to educate Palestinian women who contributed to the formation of women's movements and promoted women's rights as well as women's social and political involvement (Dahdah, interview 2015). Yet, as Nashwan (2003) states, the number of educated girls in post-1948 West Bank was relatively small (600 compared to 5,000 boys in 1954), but after 1967 the numbers increased dramatically.

Pious Muslim Palestinian women seem to have engaged primarily in social welfare activities during the British mandate as did their Muslim sisters in Egypt and Syria.

> "On the social level, the AWA [Arab Women's Association] provided support to the families of prisoners and the prisoners themselves, collecting donations of money, clothing and food, and visiting and feeding prisoners. They also visited the wounded and

> families of the martyrs . . . Palestinian women during that generation said that it was difficult for them to think about demanding their rights when the men didn't have any rights. There is a narrow definition of feminism lurking behind these comments, which reflect limited perceptions of equality constituting "political rights" defined primarily as suffrage" (Fleischmann, 1995).

In short, the nucleus of early Palestinian women's movements consisted of spouses and relatives of leaders in the Palestinian nationalist movement in addition to a few other educated women. Both groups of women came mainly from Palestinian elite families, a fact which later on restricted the female leaders' ability to develop a grassroots movement. After 1948, the Palestinian female leadership, which came from elite Palestinian families, became fragmented in Arab countries such as Lebanon and Jordan. Communication among them was very limited. The women's movement then began to take off at refugee camps, which dictated the nature of the work and refugee women became able to receive education at UNRWA schools.

However, most scholars argue that women's activism in that period was spontaneous and was mainly focused on charitable activities. It should also be noted that the early activities led by Palestinian women did not focus on feminism and excluded hard-core political participation (Aldaqqaq, 2014: 69).

From the Arab Revolt Until the 1948 War, 1939-1948

> "The brutal crushing by the British of the Arab Revolt in 1939 almost totally neutralized the Palestinian national movement, while the onset of World War II initiated a period of deceptive calm in Palestine that was to last until the mid-1940s. The women's movement, in keeping with the times, temporarily turned away from political activism and concentrated instead on social and developmental activities-founding medical clinics and schools for girls, as well as sports and literary clubs, and deepening its involvement with the pan-Arab women's movement. But as the Jewish-Arab conflict escalated after the war, the women's movement again found itself drawn into politics. By this time, however, the movement's leadership had become almost institutionalized, using its tighter organization to coordinate more closely with its constituent elements and the male-led movement in the various protests and in organizing medical and financial support for the fighters. With the chaos of the 1948 war, the women's movement, like most other Palestinian institutions, was fragmented and dispersed, as individual women got caught up in family and communal survival" (Fleischmann, 2000).

The political development in the area included the creation of the Arab League. Britain; however, denied Palestinian involvement in the League.

From the 1948 War Until the 1967 War, 1948-1967

Peteet writes that during the battle of 1948, Palestinian women's movement organizations received refugees for three continuous days. They organized committees to care for the injured and those separated from their families especially children, and to collect and distribute food (Peteet, 1991: 60).

The Palestinian *Nakba* occurred in 1948 when the bulk of Palestinian people became refugees. The Nakba, or the Palestinian catastrophe, resulted in the forced migration and displacement of almost (800,000) Palestinians who became refugees within what remained of historic Palestine (the West Bank, the Gaza Strip, and East Jerusalem), neighboring, neighboring Arab countries (Jordan, Syria, and Lebanon), and the Diaspora (UNRWA.org, 2013).

Beginning in the 1950s many Palestinians were inspired by the Arab nationalist movement as well as Nasserism.

Nasserism is a term used to define the nationalist social ideology inspired by the thinking of Egyptian president Gamal Abdul Nasser. Nasser's ideology was embedded in a leftist, nationalist, socialist anti-imperialist background. He mobilized the Egyptian public as well as the Arab masses to endorse Pan-Arabism. He advocated the idea of one Arab nation, which was also the slogan of Arab nationalism and Ba'th parties in both Syria and Iraq. It is worth noting that the expression Nasserisim emerged after the passing of President Nasser in 1970. Nasserism continues to have a significant resonance throughout the Arab World until present day (Aldaqqaq, 2014: 21-22, n. 28).

Thus Palestinian men and women became active members of Arab nationalist political parties such as the *Qawmiyyun*, the Socialist and the Jordanian Communist Parties (Dajani, 1992: 34). Palestinians also founded their own nationalistic movements. However, these movements were fragmented and weak (Al-Khalili, 1977). They mainly functioned within the countries the Palestinian people fled to. It was not until the 1960s that a Palestinian resistance movement emerged with the participation of women.

As said, in 1948 the West Bank came under Jordanian rule until 1967. Palestinian women took on a political role during this period to support Nasserism in the face of colonialism and the Hashemite policy. Women of the West Bank and al-Quds participated in major protests in al-Quds (Arab ruled Jerusalem) in 1956. A Palestinian female activist named Raja Abu Amsha was killed during the protests against the Baghdad Pact in 1955, a demonstration opposing British involvement in Jordan and Iraq and the Hashemite foreign policy (Dajani, 1992: 34). Aldaqqaq writes:

> "Women's activism, as described above, continued in relatively the same vein until the early 1960s, an era which witnessed the foundation of the Palestinian Liberation Organization (PLO) in 1964. The emergence of the PLO is considered a turning point in the history of the Palestinian

nationalist movement, and therefore, in the Palestinian women's movement. With the establishment of the PLO quickly came the foundation of the General Union of Palestinian Women (GUPW) in 1965, as an official body within the PLO. Accordingly, GUPW is considered, to this day, to be the official representative body for Palestinian women around the world . . .The Palestinian women's movement in the mid-1960s can be characterized briefly as follows. First, the formation of women associations and assemblies was a means for serving needy Palestinian families, which had positive echoes at the national level, but no more than that. Second, the PLO was the main factor behind the creation and, later on, the manipulation of the GUPW. Third, the different political parties did not present women with an equal opportunity to partake in the decision-making process. Yet, despite that lack of attention to women's concerns, women cadres played a leading role in the field – the West Bank, the Gaza Strip and East Jerusalem – in the period following 1967. The involvement of Palestinian women in political parties had a positive impact as it reflected their awareness of the significance of taking part in the political movement. It is worth highlighting that the charitable model continued to be the dominant framework that governed women's activism in the West Bank and Gaza Strip in the decade following the Israeli occupation of the Palestinian territories in 1967" (Aldaqqaq, 2014).

Peteet (1991) concludes that

> "During 1950 and 1960, politically, the tradition of women organizing around charitable issues continued but was eventually to be eclipsed by the entry of peasant, now camp women, and women of an emergent middle class into a political arena previously dominated by men of the landed, mercantile, and clerical elite and the intelligentsia. The political arena was beginning to face a challenge by the middle class and, to a lesser extent, by the poorer peasant strata, a trend that reached its apogee in the 1970s when a considerable proportion of political positions were filled by men and women of the middle class.... As for women's political affiliations during this era, the appearance of pan-Arab nationalist* organizations- al-Ba'th, the Arab National Movement, the Nasserites- and the Communist parties- drew younger middle and lower class Palestinian men to their ranks and a smaller number of women. Commensurate with the often close affinity between kinship and political affiliation among Arab women, these women were usually relatives of male members or students. None of these parties was particularly concerned with mobilizing or addressing the specific problems of women or even in women as a political question. Some middle- class and camp women were entering political parties, portending the future trend of Palestinian

> women in mass- based organizations. The elite women who settled in Lebanon and Jordan soon resumed their organizational work" (Peteet, 1991:60).

In the 1950s and 1960s, in the aftermath of the Nakba, Palestinian women gained some of the social rights such as the rights to education and work; however, women had no direct participation in political parties except through affiliation with national movements which the male family figures supported -women supported the national movements their brothers or spouses supported. In any case, in 1967, Fatah and PFLP recognized women's role and allowed women's membership in their organizations. Palestinian women played decisive role in attacks on Israel. Among those women Dalal Almughrabi (Fatah) who carried out attacks on Israel that involved Israeli fatalities in 1978 and Leila Khaled (PFLP) who was known for hijacking airplanes so that a message is sent that Palestine is under Israeli occupation.

Later on, in 1966, Al-Quds school girls participated in protests against what was termed as the *Samo'a* massacre - an Israeli military retaliatory attack on November 13, 1966 at Samo`a village near Hebron (Alqam, 2005: 138). Palestinian women's reactions to the operation included writing a demand to Arab leaders protect Palestinians from Israel. In their letters they called themselves *murabitat.* They wrote "We are the women of Palestine. We ask you to unite. We are the *murabitat* of Jerusalem; we ask you to support our Palestinian cause" (Al-Khalili, 1977: 141).

However, the *murabitat* of the 1960s were different from the present day *murabitat* who are pious Muslim women defending a holy shrine. The difference can be seen in the attire. For instance, the women who called themselves *murabitat* in the 1960s wore traditional Palestinian dresses and head cover. These are not hijabs as current *murabitat* wear in al-Aqsa compound and elsewhere. The term *murabitat* was only used in the 1960s to invoke the religious feelings among Muslims since it has religious connotation. It was used as rhetorical means to ensure strong and immediate support. "The association was banned by the Jordanian regime in 1966. However, in the late 1960s women became very active - although women's groups consisted of mainly educated middle-class women" (Kazi, 2013).

In any case, prior to 1967, Palestinian women had no political activities at al-Aqsa Mosque, because the mosque was not directly endangered by the Jews who did not dare to demand a foot hole in the mosque compound (their Temple Mount) it was under Jordanian control. However, there were religious activities at al-Aqsa Mosque in the form of study circles (where people sat in circles) for scholars and imams in Qur'an and Hadith; these had no relations to politics. In 1964, Sheikh Asaad Bayud Al-Tamimi, who was nationalist figure, warned of the dangerous of Israeli and Jewish plans to occupy al-Aqsa Mosque (Sabri, interview, 2015).

Within the Palestine Liberation Organization (PLO), 1964

The PLO was founded in 1964 under the chairmanship of Ahmad al-Shuqayri. A year later, the Palestinian National Liberation Movement (Fatah) was launched (on January 1, 1965) under the leadership of Yasser Arafat. Arafat then became the Chairman of the PLO, which had in its membership leftist factions as well as Palestinian women's movement. Hamida After 1948, Palestinians farmers who lost their land had no choice but to enter into wage labor. It was necessary for families to allow women to enter into waged employment, which led to allowing women freedom to move. The Palestinian Women's Association held its first conference in 1965 but was banned by the Jordanian government in the next year. However, women, mainly educated middle-class women, became active in the late 1960s (Kazi, 2013).

Some Palestinian women have been active participants of the PLO activities including membership in its Palestinian National Council (PNC), which held its first meeting in Jerusalem on May 15, 1964. However, the number of female members of the 422 PNC members was only 11. The number of female members of the Palestinian Central Council of the PLO is one. None of the members of the Executive Committee of the PLO during this period were women (Al-Khalili, 1977: 114).

The Palestinian Women's Association was set up after the establishment of the Palestine Liberation Organization in 1964

(Hamida, 2013). The factions of the PLO include Fatah -the mainstream faction, as well as left-wing secular fronts such as the Popular Front for the Liberation of Palestine (PFLP) and the Democratic Front for the Liberation of Palestine (DFLP). The PLO adopted armed resistance (Dajani, 1992). Among the prominent female fighters of the armed resistance of the PLO were Dalal al-Mughrabi of Fatah and Leila Khalid of the PFLP.

The General Union of Palestinian Women (GUPW) was established in 1965 as a new independent body within the PLO to officially represent Palestinian women around the world. It evolved as the umbrella for all women's organizations in Palestine and in diaspora (Kawar, 1996); (Alqam, 2005). The main objective of GUPW was to "involve Palestinian women in the economic, social and political work of the PLO serving the national cause and leading to their own development" (Talhami, 2013: 141). Moreover, GUPW mobilizes women within Palestinian communities to participate in various social, economic and political processes, which contribute to their development. For many years, GUPW has been politically active, supporting Palestinian women at the forefront of the liberation struggle in all its aspects and historical stages, at the national and social levels (Alqam, 2005).

Kuttab writes: The Israeli occupation of the Palestinian territories in 1967 led to a destruction of the political, social and economic infrastructure of the Palestinian society. Therefore, Palestinian people responded with widespread resistance to safeguard their national identity. Among the impacts of such resistance was the democratization of the national struggle (Kuttab, 2009).

Also Lisa Taraki (1991) writes about new political activities, she states:

"The emergence of open frameworks for political, social, and cultural action; the amplification of mass participation in political activities; and most important, the incorporation of new social forces, particularly the less advantaged sectors of society, into Palestinian institutional life" (Taraki, 1991).

Hamida Kazi concludes this period in her article (2013): The first conference for the Palestinian Women's Association was held in 1965. Branches for the Association were opened in the West Bank but the Jordanian government later banned the Association. In any case, there was a shift in women's activities from 1967 to 1972 since the Palestinian national movement adopted armed struggle. Hence, the role of women was more focused on conducting armed attacks rather than just feeding the Palestinian freedom fighters (Feda'yeen)[1]. The most prominent of Palestinian women involved in such fight was Laila Khalid. It is worth noting that most women's groups were educated middle-class women (Kazi, 2013).

Aldaqqaq (2014) concludes that the GUPW became an important body of the PLO and Palestinian women were involved

[1] Feda'yeen are guerilla fighters who are willing to sacrifice their lives executing military operations against enemy targets. The idea of Feda'yeen was inspired by the concept of the Japanese Kamikaze (Aldaqqaq, 2014: 23).

in Palestinian political parties. This involvement made women aware of the necessity of being part of the politics of the national movement, which had a positive impact on women. However, the political involvement of women did not end their participation in charitable activities all the way until 1967 (Aldaqqaq, 2014).

Moreover,

> "From 1967 to 1982, women were freely mobilized. In fact during this period women began to wrestle with the not unique dilemma of reconciling participation in the national struggle and their reproductive role while the continued existence of three and a half million Palestinians dispersed all over the world is under threat, as is the survival of Palestinian culture" (Kazi, 2013).

Taraki notes the following aspects of noticeable changes in women's situation in this period:

> "The emergence of open frameworks for political, social, and cultural action; the amplification of mass participation in political activities; and most important, the incorporation of new social forces, particularly the less advantaged sectors of society, into Palestinian institutional life" (Taraki, 1991).

Members of the General Union of Palestinian Women (GUPW)

Members and activists of the PLO women's organizations are "secular" women. They are mainly supporters of PLO factions, including Fatah, DFLP, PFLP, and the Palestinian Communist Party. They came from the urban and rural middle class in the Jerusalem and Ramallah districts. They are not "pious" women but Muslim, and their themes are patriotic. Their purpose is to organize women in non-violent activities against the Israeli occupation.

Eileen Kuttab explains the situation of the Palestinian women after the establishment of Israel:

"Resistance continues against the British mandate and Jewish immigration to Palestine and was disrupted by the second major event in the history of Palestinian people in general and Palestinian women in particular: the outbreak of 1948 Arab-Israeli War, which created a new reality as a result of the uprooting and dispersion of the Palestinian people. The creation of the Israeli state in the larger part of historical Palestine and the destruction and fragmentation of the Palestinian social networks that represent the basic conditions for sustainability were challenged, which in turn imposed new demands on the women's organizations, and forced them to expand their structures in order to be able to offer relief and social services to needy families" (Kuttab, 2009:105).

Kuttab added:

> "While the Palestinians were still rising from the ruins and coping with the agony of loss from the 1948 war, the 1967 Six-day war erupted resulting in the complete destruction of the political, economic and cultural infrastructure of the Palestinian society, reducing its ability for survival and continuity, which now demanded further solidarity and unity among the people and within the national movement. These events transformed the women's movement to a wide structure of charitable organizations that supported and responded to the needs of the communities" (ibid).

Founding the GUPW in 1965 as an official body of the PLO GUPW's Fourth Conference in 1985

From the 1967 War Until the First Palestinian Intifada, 1967-1987

The PFLP and the DFLP are two major leftist factions of the PLO, led by Yasser Arafat. The PFLP provided women with political roles as well as roles in the armed resistance. Women joined the political committees of the PFLP. Active PFLP female members took part in the strong above-mentioned protests in 1969 and many of them were detained by the Israeli occupation authorities (Al-Khalili, 1977: 125).

The DFLP allowed women greater roles and recruited more women to its politburo compared to Fatah (Dajani, 1992: 41). This is due to the fact that the DFLP (as well as the PFLP) adopt Marxist-Communist ideology which treats men and women equally (Dajani, 1999: 60).

Kuttab writes about the role of Palestinian women in Palestinian territories under occupation post 1967:

> "Following the 1967 war and the Israeli occupation of the West Bank and Gaza strip, structural changes occurred in the Palestinian society that drastically transformed the economic and social lives of its population. The economic displacement of the peasants, through Israeli appropriation of lands, transformed the peasant class into a proletarian workforce for the Israeli labor market, which has put the traditional peasant family at risk. The full control of water resources by the Israelis and the structural distortion of the labor market have transformed the Palestinian economy into an economy fully dependent on the Israeli labor market" (Kuttab 1988).

These changes affected women in general and the women's movement in particular since activities were now centered on preserving the heritage and culture as symbol of the Palestinian identity. This was necessary for the survival of the Palestinian community. Moreover, the role of women in political parties continued and they obtained a new image of militancy. Anyhow, gender and labor considerations continued to prevail (Kuttab, 2009:106).

Fatah female activists first focused their action on helping the families of the Palestinian martyrs. However, Fatah decided in its 1969 Conference to train women to carry guns starting with six of the women's committee members (Al-Khalili, 1977: 117). Fatah gained control of the PLO and Arafat became the chairman of the PLO executive committee in 1969. The PLO of 1964, founded by Abdul Nasser and Ahmad Shukeiri and the PLO Yasser Arafat led were extremely different. The numbers of women in the PNC was increased since more women were allowed to participate in armed struggle against Israel (Kazi, 2013). Moreover, Palestinian women took part in other protests against the Israeli occupation in the West Bank and Gaza Strip in 1967. Some of them were high school girls. Many of them were shot dead by Israeli troops during protests. Palestinian women's activities also included forming groups to distribute food and clothing in the occupied territories to the needy, without the permission of the Israeli authorities.

A number of examples of Palestinian women's activities show women's protests against the Israeli occupation.

"On October 19, 1967, the Israelis arrested Fatima Barnawi on charges of having thrown a bomb into the Zion Cinema in Jerusalem, and affiliation to Fatah as a terrorist organization. The extraordinary courage she displayed during her trial marked her as a pioneer in the struggle of Palestinian women. By 1968 large numbers of Palestinian women had joined the ranks of the resistance and were taking an active part in the armed struggle. In January, 1968, five women were arrested in Nablus for acts of resistance and for giving shelter to Fatah members. In April of the same year 300 Palestinian women demonstrated in Jerusalem in protest the Israeli military parade to be held in the Holy City. Some of the demonstrators were wounded and others arrested by the Israeli police. At the same time, five women demonstrators were killed in Beit Hannoun, and many others were arrested in Hebron and Bethlehem, accused of collecting money for the resistance and distributing anti-Israeli leaflets. In January 1969, large numbers of Palestinian women staged a sit-in strike in front of Israeli prisons and detention centers demanding the release of their imprisoned husbands, brothers, and sons. In response, the Israeli authorities fired on them, killing and wounding many" ("The Struggle of Palestinian Women," 1975: 9).

One of the major protests was a violent reaction to the fire set to al-Aqsa Mosque in 1969 by an Australian tourist, but when al-Haram al-Sharif was under Israeli security control. Two Palestinian female demonstrators, Muntaha Awad from Jenin and Lina Musbah from Nablus, were killed in the protests (Alqam, 2005: 198).

Professor Lisa Taraki, head of Sociology Department at Birzeit University, wrote the following about the period of 1976-1981 of Palestinian women's movement:

> "The period between 1976 and 1981 witnessed a process of democratization of the national struggle, and Palestinian Women's Movement became more complicated and demanding as they focused on mobilizing and organizing a grass-roots women in a comprehensive development approach that abstained the welfare approach of women charitable" (Taraki, 1995).

> "The democratization process that took place in 1970s and 1980s contributed to a change within the resistance movement at the structural and ideological levels," Taraki added, "it created new mass -based organizations with mobilized and organized Palestinians within broad categories and sectors such as youth, workers, women, and students" (Taraki, 1991).

In short,

> "Socio-economic and political factors have been invoked by many scholars to explain the spread of

> politicization and mobilization of women by national secular movements in the seventies and the eighties which led to massive participation of women in the first Palestinian intifada" (Jad, 2010).

In *Daughters of Palestine: Leading Women of the Palestinian National Movement*, Amal Kawar writes:

"Palestinian women's movement is essentially "secular" mirroring the PLO in its orientation, namely being nationalistic, pluralistic, and supportive of democracy. Of the thirty-four Women who established the *Union of Palestinian Women Committees* in Ramallah's Library in 1978, twenty-nine of whom were Muslims and the remainder Christians, almost all were not religious. The few who said they were religious, explained that they practiced some of rituals such as fasting during the month of Ramadan, but that they were not strict in their religious beliefs" (Kawar, 1996).

The members of the Union of Palestinian Women Committees were different from "The General Union of Palestinian Women" in social class and education since that the later had members from refugee camps and cities and middle class, but the members of the new body (the Union of Palestinian Women Committee) were from villages and cities and they were more educated and from upper social class like:

> "Zahira Kamal, born in Jerusalem in 1945, a former activist of the DFLP. She was detained and put under

> house arrest by the Israelis. In 1990, she joined Yasser Abd Rabbo and other comrades to form the Palestinian Democratic Union (FIDA). In 2002 she won the internal election for FIDA becoming the first Palestinian female to assume the post of secretary general of a PLO faction. She was appointed as the first Minister of Women's Affairs in November 2002" (Aldaqqaq, 2014: 39).

Another example is the late Rabiha Diab, who headed the Union of Social Work Committees, which is a women's movement. Rabiha Diab was from a Palestinian village called Dura Al-Qari'a in Ramallah district. Diab graduated from Bethlehem University in Arts. She held the office of the Minister of Women's Affairs. She also held the positions of Member of Parliament in the Palestinian Legislative Council. Other examples include Zahira Kamal, a graduate of Alexandria University in Egypt, Maha Nasser, a graduate of Birzeit University, and Amal Khresha, a graduate of the Jordanian University (Kawar, 1996).

The first women committee established in 1980s represented a nucleus of women of different political factions, mainly of the left, who believed in linking national liberation to social liberation struggle and women's rights to national and political rights (Al-Hassan, 2012). The DFLP allowed women greater roles and recruited more women to its politburo compared to Fatah (Dajani, 1992: 41). This is due to the fact that the DFLP (as well as the PFLP) adopt Marxist-Communist ideology which treats men and women equally (Dajani, 1999: 60).

In the 1970s and 1980s, the leftist-led factions recruited women in the West Bank and Gaza Strip while Fatah mobilized women in the diaspora where it dominated. The Union of Palestinian Women Committees is one of the women's organizations in the West Bank and Gaza Strip. It was established in 1978 by Zahira Kamal, a leading figure of the DFLP (currently the leader of FIDA faction). Maha Nassar, a PFLP female activist, founded the Union of Working Women in 1981. Amal Khrisha founded the Union of Social Work Committees in 1982. The organization was led until recently by the late Rabiha Diab (Kawar, 1996: 102).

Studies on Palestinian women's social and political activities since the late 1970s have focused on "secular" women who established various associations (Abu Amr, 1987); (Hroub, 1994); (Al-Barghouti, 1997); (Abdulhadi, 1998) rather than on pious women, who are the focus of the proposed study.

Gradually, in the 1990s, serious research was done on the activism of pious women in the Arab world. These studies provide valuable background for the current research on Pious Palestinian women activists on al-Haram al-Sharif. For instance, the creation of the General Union of Palestinian Women reflected the concept in the PLO's charter that both men and women must be involved in the liberation of Palestine, which gave a momentum to women. Therefore, Palestinian factions paved the way for women to take active role in their functions. Women were entrusted in mobilizing grassroots and in the early 1980s women involvement in the national movement peaked as factions brought efforts together to launch the first Palestinian uprising or *intifada* in 1987(Aldaqqaq, 2014).

During the First Palestinian Intifada, 1987-1990

> "The Palestinian intifada was considered a defining moment in the history of women's movement in Palestine and gave momentum to their involvement in national activism. For example, women organized demonstrations and protests; several women were martyred and hundreds of women were detained by the Israeli authorities. In addition, women had to assume the role of bread-winners in their families, especially in cases where the man of the household was detained or martyred" (Aldaqqaq, 2014).

I will quote from the Declaration of Independence which addresses many issues and concerns such as the equity and equality between females and males in the future State of Palestine. "Equity and equality between males and females, elimination of all forms of discrimination between the two sexes, constitutional state, rule of law, a place where every Palestinian's dream can come true, among other rights."

> "Palestinian women's activism during the Oslo Accords and post-Oslo Accords phase focused mainly

> on the social issues of women; this was in line with the state-building phase that the PLO and other political parties were undergoing at the time. The focus was on legislation regarding women's issues and women's participation in decision-making positions. In fact, Palestinian women's activism worked/struggled towards the achievement of the social and civil rights of women, all of which were marginalized on the women's movement agenda before Oslo" (Aldaqqaq, 2014:70).

Finally, it is important to note that the Palestinian National Authority (PNA) was not serious in addressing the women's movements' issues (Kuttab, 2004; Jad, 2008). Its leaders considered women's issues to be secondary to national developmental concerns. The PNA's vision for Palestinian women's development was later translated into the foundation of the Ministry of Women's Affairs (MOWA). In all probability, this step was a cosmetic solution to the problems facing women and did not touch on core issues, such as the reform of both personal and criminal law, encouraging women's civic engagement, eliminating all forms of discrimination against women, and equity and equality in opportunities based on equal qualifications among other issues (MOWA.gov.ps, 2013; MOWA.pna.ps, 2013). In sum, Palestinian women's movement activism in general is secular in agenda and goals. This is different from the activism of pious Palestinian Muslim women as we will see in next chapter.

Pious Muslim Women's Activism

From the 1967 War until the First Palestinian Intifada, 1967- 1987

Israel, which took control of the West Bank and Gaza after the 1967 Six-Day War, freed Sheikh Ahmed Yassin from prison -Yassin was detained during Egyptian rule of Gaza (www.historycommons.org). According to David Shipler, a former New York Times reporter, the Israeli government supported the Islamic Movement "to counteract the PLO and the communists (Aly, Feldman and Shikaki, 2013, p. 229, footnote 30). According to Martha Kessler, a senior analyst for the CIA, "we saw Israel cultivate Islam as a counterweight to Palestinian nationalism."

According to the web site History Commons, in the 1970s, Yassin was able to form some Islamic organizations. In the 1980s, he formed Hamas as the military arm of his organizations (http://www.historycommons.org/). This report added:

"In 1973 Israeli military authorities in charge of the West Bank and Gaza allowed Sheikh Ahmed Yassin to establish the Islamic Center, an Islamic fundamentalist organization. With Israel's support, Yassin's organization soon gains control of hundreds of mosques, charities, and schools which serve as recruiting centers for militant Islamic fundamentalism. In 1976 Yassin creates another organization called the Islamic Association that forms hundreds of branches in Gaza. In 1978 the Islamic Association is licensed by the government of Menachem Begin over the objections of moderate Palesinians including the Commissioner of the Muslim Waqf in the Gaza Strip, Rafat Abu Shaban. Yassin also recieves funding from business leaders in Saudi Arabia who are also hostile to the secular PLO for religious reasons" (http://www.historycommons.org/).

Palestinian women who were active in pious organizations were educated and belonged to a new social class. Palestinian women who were active in pious organizations like *al-Jam`iyya al-Islamiyya*, the Islamic Young Women's Association and al-Salah Islamic Association in Gaza at the early 1980s were graduates of the Islamic University (Huroub, 1999). These women appeared inconspicuous. Like most in the urban Arab middle class, their attire was modest and modern worn by older women in the villages and refugee camps. They were, however, partners to some extent in the popular armed struggle (Lahlouh, 2010)."The Islamic Movement in the West Bank and Gaza Strip, on the other hand, was visible in the dramatic growth of the number of mosques built since the 1970s and also in the proliferation of Islamic educational institutes, children's nurseries, youth clubs, health clinics and vocational centers. This social service infrastructure was the core activity of the Muslim Brotherhood's Islamic Center (*al-Mujama al-Islami*) in Gaza; it took on a more overt political face only after the 1987 intifada and is presented since then by Hamas (Kawar, 1996: 114).

The Center was primarily established as a mosque, but attached to it was a medical clinic, a youth sports club, an Islamic festival hall and a center for women's activities and for training young girls (Abu Amr, 1994: 16).

In addition, during this period, a number of Islamic societies affiliated with Hamas were founded. They included al-Salah Islamic Society (established in Gaza in the early 1980s), al-Huda Islamic Society, and the al-Khansa Society in al-Bireh. They greatly increased the political role of Palestinian pious women (Huroub, 1999).

The real beginning of the political, social and religious women's actions dated back to the early 1980s. Palestinian universities and colleges, especially the Islamic University, played a vital role in the spread of trade union and political awareness amongst girls in the Gaza Strip (Bajes, 2012). Soon, many female students got involved in the student councils at Birzeit University, Hebron University and Al-Najah National University. These student councils belonged to various factions including, the Muslim Brotherhood and the Islamic Jihad Movement (the Islamist Bloc of the Muslim Brotherhood, the Islamist Group of the Islamic Jihad (Bajes, 2012); (Salama, 2010). During this period, it was noted that Hamas adopted the approach of the Muslim Brotherhood, and founded many charities for children, prisoners, martyrs and orphans, which made Hamas very popular among the lower classes. Most importantly, Hamas also gained the confidence of the privileged, wealthy people from the cities (Bajes, 2012).

From the First Palestinian Intifada until the Founding of the Murabitat Movement, 1987-2010

Muslim female students took part in the elections of student councils at the universities and colleges of the West Bank and Gaza Strip as early as the 1980s. They were affiliated with the Muslim Brotherhood movement. They operated under the name of the Islamic Bloc. This bloc competed with female activists from Fatah and left wing political parties in recruiting the largest possible number of female supporters. They employed methods of *daʿwa,* (charitable work) such as funding the education of needy female students.

The Muslim Brotherhood movement has played a central role in student movements in the West Bank and the Gaza Strip since 1979 until the present. The Muslim Brotherhood dominated all of the student councils of the Islamic University in Gaza and Hebron University. After Hamas was founded in 1988, the Islamic bloc continued its role of recruiting more supporters until they won the student council elections at Birzeit University in 1997, which was a shock since Birzeit University was historically run by the Nassir Family, which was a Christian family, and this victory occurred after the creation of the PA (Birzeit University's student council's elections 1997); (Bajes, 2012).

The first intifada broke out in late 1987. It gave rise to Palestinian women's participation in politics on both national and Islamic religious platforms. Hamas was founded in 1988. Hamas paid greater attention to the social aspects, particularly the expansion of infrastructure for the social service charities, which cared for the needy families. It exerted remarkable contributions towards the establishment of the Islamic charities, which cared for orphans, the poor and the sick such as Islamic Al-Salah Association in Gaza. During the first intifada of 1987, Palestinian women participated in the Palestinian national struggle, including in various political and religious activities, alongside their fellow men (Jad, 2008); (Al-Ramahi, 2004); (Sabbag, 1998); (Kawar, 1996). Jad writes:

> "Socio-economic and political factors have been invoked by many scholars to explain the spread of politicization and mobilization of women by national secular movements in the seventies and the eighties which led to the massive participation of women in the first Palestinian intifada. . . .Central to the Islamization of Palestinian identity was the Islamization of gender. Hamas, unlike Fatah, spelt out its gender agenda at an early stage. This is a common feature of religious movements which place a great deal of emphasis on the family unit" (Jad, 2010).

Abdulhadi notes:

"The second year of the intifada saw a shift in the local context, which directly altered gender dynamics, thus crushing Palestinian women's hopes for liberation. This change resulted from a combination of the successful attempt by the Islamic Resistance Movement, Hamas, to impose wearing the Hijab, or head cover, on women in Gaza and the harsher measures adopted by the Israeli occupation authorities. . .

In the same year [1993], Palestinian women organized conferences, seminars, and meetings in which violence against women, women's reproductive health and rights, the drop-out rates among school girls, the Islamist imposition of a dress code on women in Gaza, and women's legal status and personal status code were publicly discussed for the first time. A shift was evident in the discourse of Islamist women who deviated from the official line of Islamic Resistance Movement, Hamas, by advocating a new view on women's roles and freedoms" (Abdulhadi, 1998: 650).

Ben Shitrit adds to Hamas, Muslim women make and educate men. However, they need guidance in order to be safeguarded from those who might lead them astray, according to Article 17 of Hamas' Charter. Moreover, the Charter defines home as the place for women where they care for the children and raise them on Islamic values and morals to be ready for Jihad (Ben Shitrit, 2016).

Hamas' Shura (consultative) Council only has one female member (Jamila al-Shanti). Hamas says that the reasons for such a policy are security and safety; to save women from being harassed, like men, by the Israeli authorities. However, women (wives, mothers, sisters) took part in the Hamas election campaign of 2006 (Bajes, 2013: 77). Bajes argues that Hamas excluded women from its top ranks because they chose to (Bajes, 2013). However, according to my analysis of the following Qur'anic verse and *hadith* and the reading of their interpretation, I believe that Hamas's policy is based on religious grounds. The Qur'an says in Chapter 4 (Surat Al-Nisa), verse 34 [4:34] "*Al-rijal qawwamun `ala al-nisa*" (Men are in charge of women by [right of] what Allah has given one over the other and what they spent "for maintenance" from their wealth)." The *Hadith* also states that "a people ruled by a woman will never prosper" (Al-Bukhaari, *hadith* no. 4163).

Female activists in the Islamic Movement

"...have emerged as important players in the Palestinian women's movement after the Oslo Accords were signed between Israel and PLO, particularly in Gaza. The failure of the peace process has provided Islamic Movements with fertile ground to widen their political and social influence and this has resulted in further polarization between the nationalist, secular and Islamic forces" (Richter-Devroe, 2011).

When viewed in a comparative perspective to Hamas's mother-movement in Egypt one should note that in the 2005 elections to the Egyptian parliament, the Muslim Brotherhood nominees included one woman only. The reason for this - as presented by the leaders - was to save women from being harassed, like men, by the Egyptian authorities (Bajes, 2013: 38). Women, regardless of their status (married, single, mother ...etc.) may participate in political and social activities; therefore, women had their share in the election of Muhammad Morsi as president of Egypt (Bajes, 2013). There are also Islamic female leaders who defend women from within the system, like Lama Hourani, who is a Hamas leader in the West Bank. She campaigned on behalf of female workers and protested against a pervasive conservative culture that threatened women's rights. During the 2006 elections of the Palestinian Legislative Council, six women from Hamas list were elected (Al-Hassan, 2012).

In the aftermath of the wining of the elections by Hamas in 2006, an argument broke out among some members of Hamas who were elected to the Palestinian Legislative Council (PLC). Such members include Umm Nidal Farahat from Gaza and Muhammad Abu-Tayr from Jerusalem. They wanted the hijab to be imposed upon Palestinian women, which reminded people of the events during the first intifada in 1987 when women were forced to wear the hijab by Hamas activists. However, the Hamas government of Ismail Haniyeh of 2006-7 reassured people that the hijab will not be imposed on Palestinian women (Lahlouh, 2010: 29).

"With the failure of the Camp David peace talks between Israel and the Palestinian Authority in the fall of 2000, Hamas and other nationalist Palestinian factions including Fatah returned in earnest to armed resistance as a strategy for achieving national liberation. While containing their proselytizing and social efforts, Hamas's agenda of nationalist struggle had remained paramount to the organization during the years of the second intifada (2000-2005)... In the national election of January 2006 Hamas decided to participate in the democratic process by running for seats in the PLC. A Hamas victory in the 2006 election led to a unity government of Fatah and Hamas that soon disintegrated into a factionalist fight between the two organizations. As a result of this conflict, Hamas came to control Gaza Strip from 2007 to the present, while Fatah currently maintains its dominance in the West Bank (Ben Shitrit, 2016: 70).

Islamist women often advocated for, and carried out, various political actions at mosques, charities, homes, during festivals, and at universities in the West Bank, the Gaza Strip and Jerusalem. For example, they played a major part in the media campaign for Hamas, which led to its victory in the 2006 elections (Salah, interview, 2014). They possessed a powerful religious and social discourse inside Palestinian homes, promoting the political Islamic project of Hamas. After the

Hamas movement assumed power in 2006, Palestinian women enjoyed a distinctive status in the Hamas government and the Palestinian Legislative Council through the Ministry of Women's Affairs. In this regard, the mosques everywhere played a major role in the religious mobilization and awareness among women who provided significant support for Hamas. Hamas's Change and Reform movement won the PA legislative elections of 2006 by winning 74 seats out of the 132 seats of the Palestinian Legislative Council. Following the campaign, Hamas acknowledged the role of women in its victory in the elections, for example, Dr. Mariam Saleh, then the Minister of Women's Affairs in the Hamas government, Dr. Salah saidin an interview: "Palestinian Muslim women played prominent role in supporting the Islamic Movement in Palestine (Hamas)" (Salah, interview, 2014).

Conflict Between Secular and Islamic Palestinian Women's Agendas

Islah Jad, professor of women's studies at Birzeit University explained the conflict between the political agendas of secular and Islamist women by writing that Hamas won the legislative elections of 2006 and formed the majority of the Palestinian Legislative Council. Hamas also appointed the first female Minister of Women's Affairs. However, Hamas faced difficulties in running public agencies where most employees were Fatah supporters. Finally, Hamas government failed in the West Bank but took over power in the Gaza Strip.

The Palestinian women's secularist and Islamist agendas clashed in 2006 and 2007. The clash included a fundamentally political conflict. (Jad, 2010) The *murabitat* movement differed from their predecessors as we shall see in the next chapter.

The Murabitat Movement

The *murabitat* movement emerged in 2010 to mobilize women to defend al-Aqsa mosque. The purpose of the movement is to strengthen the hold of Muslims, including women, on al-Aqsa, and to combat the movement of Israeli Jewish women (Sabri, interview, November 2, 2015). Aida Sidawi told me that the Islamic Movement in Israel had established the study circles in 2010 to teach Qur'an, Hadith, and Islamic doctrine. However, the main goal of the study circles was to confront the Jewish religious groups, which contained female members, who come to al-Haram al-Sharif (Sidawi, 2014).

Though the Israeli authorities outlawed the *murabitat* movement in 2016, the *murabitat* are adamant about keeping up what they define as holy work. Sana' al-Rajabi says: "We come to al-Haram al-Sharif to study and pray; we are protecting al-Aqsa so the Jews won't take it" (Sana', interview, November 5, 2015).

Murabitun Study Circles on al-Haram al-Sharif

Pious Muslim Women, Women's Rights, "Agency" and Gender Activism

Pious Muslim women have rejected "feminism" as a western idea, brought to the Middle East by foreign and homegrown secular feminists, who aim to undermine Islam. Professor Islah Jad, one of the founders of the Women's Studies Institute at Birzeit University, wrote: "Women in Islamic movements see this term as alien, politically loaded, Western, irrelevant and integral to colonialist strategies to undermine the indigenous social and religious culture" (Azim, 2013). Jad also writes that many conferences in Gaza were attended by women's groups in order to "present Islamist women themselves as the 'true' and 'authentic' Islamist voice for women's interests. . . These conferences were landmarks in the passage of Hamas gender ideology utter rejection of feminism" (Jad, 2010). Dalal Bajis says that pious Muslim women reject being categorized as feminists by international studies (Bajis, 2013: 14). Feminists, on the other hand, often regard pious women as lacking female consciousness and as being exploited by pious men.

Studies of Muslim pious women in Egypt, the Shi'i section of Beirut, and the Islamic Movement in Israel have reached the conclusion that these women exhibit ideas and actions that may promote women's rights, may be defined as "agency," may have raised gender consciousness and actions, and may be termed "female activism."

In a recent study by Dalal Bajes (2013) on Muslim women's participation in Arab Spring in Egypt and Tunisia and Muslim women in Palestine, Bajes argues that Muslim women's activities are centered on Islamic framework and they seek to achieve political rights to occupy senior posts within Islamic movements. She also argues that Muslim women's role in the early 21st Century is not a spontaneous reaction; it has been the outcome of historic and social developments. The activities of Muslim women are an agency through taking part in political organization that supervise and fund their work to increase supporters in the Arab world. This is consistent with my work on the Murabitat and the activities they conduct, with the political and financial support of the Islamic Movement in Israel and Hamas. This means that the Murabitat are an agency; however, they reject the term feminism and affirm their demand for political rights even if they had feminist nature. The Murabitat are satisfied with the term Islamic Women's Activism, which Badran, Jad, and Bajes confirm.

The Muslim Brotherhood, the movement from which the Islamic movements in Palestine and Israel emerged, had a unique relationship to women from its onset. Imam Hassan al-Bana, the founder of Muslim Brotherhood, said in 1933 when a sisterhood branch was founded that "Women are equal to men in rights and duties. Islam gives women full personal, civil, and political rights. The Qur᾿an and Hadith are full of texts that ensure and safeguard women's rights" (al-Bana, 1986). The

Muslim Brotherhood also believes in social support for women and their participation in the parliamentary elections, which would ensure equality between men and women (Bajis, 2013).

An anonymous article on the Muslim Brotherhood website says:

"The participation of women is crucial to Muslim Brotherhood. The leading role of Muslim Sisterhood within the Islamic Brotherhood movement began with Zaynab Al-Ghazali, who was in charge of the consultation office of the Islamic Brotherhood. In 1937 Zaynab Al-Ghazali established the first Islamic Women's association in Egypt. In the beginning Hassan al-Banna requested the cooperation of Zaynab Al-Ghazali in *da'wa* and political functions. He demanded that the Muslim Women's Society (*Jamiyat al-Sayidat al-Muslimat*) to join the *jama'a* (group); however, al-Ghazali rejected al-Banna's request in order to safeguard the independence of the Society. In 1939 Al Ghazali joined the Muslim Brotherhood for *da'wa* for God and for the religion of Islam" (http://www.ikhwanwiki.com/).

Badran's study (1994) of the activities and views of prominent women in Egypt uses "gender activism" rather than "feminism" which Islamist women reject: "I prefer 'gender activism' to 'feminism' because 'gender activism' covers secular and pious activities. 'Feminism' refers to secularism, which Islamist women reject (Badran, 1994:c203). In this, Badran has given voice to the 'discomfort' which many female activists feel in using the term 'feminism.'

> "I agree that women's activism opens up new spaces for women that might contradict prevailing gender roles. I shall also refrain from using the label feminist to refer to Islamist women, since many of the women whom the term might seek to represent refuse to identify with it. The changes that these women seek to implement are contingent upon various circumstances which might not always challenge gender imbalances. At times, they may even support patriarchal structures. Islamist women regard feminism as superfluous." (Badran, 1994: 203).

Badran also states that there are some women who articulate and practice forms of feminism and yet who refuse to be known as feminists. She has created the term 'gender activism' for these women, leaving the term 'feminist' for those who choose to adopt it" (Badran, 1994: 204).

However, the pious Palestinian women active at al-Haram al-Sharif do not seem to fit this definition; in the interviews I have conducted there was little mention of women's rights in theory or in practice (see: chapter seven) The reason for this seems to be because in Palestine the fight for religious and national rights often overshadows the struggle for women's rights. Other reasons for not mentioning women's rights may include the fact that the lower and middle class women from the Jerusalem area are more religious and have less social consciousness. For instance, Hanadi al-Halawani, who teaches Shariʿa to the *murabitat*, said in an interview, "we believe that Shariʿa protects our rights. And now most of the *murabitat* believe the same" (Hanadi al-Halawani, interview, July 30, 2015).

Professor Islah Jad, follows suit and refuses to use "feminism" to denote all forms of women's activism. Jad supports Badran (1994) in term Gender Activism; she says "I refrain from using the term 'feminist' to denote all forms of women's activism, as does Badran" (Jad, 2010). Jad adds, "I agree that women's activism opens up new spaces for women that might contradict prevailing gender roles. I shall also refrain from using the label 'feminist' to refer to Islamist women, since many of the women whom the term might seek to represent refuse to identify with it. Islamist women regard feminism as superfluous" (Jad, 2010). Khadija Khweis, one of the *murabitat's* leaders said that the term "feminist" means Western women struggling for their rights in Western Culture." Hence, she refuses to identify with the term but asserts that Islamist women have the Qurʾan as a Shariʿa to protect our rights" (Khweis, interview, July 15, 2015).

In Mahmood's study (2005) of the urban women's mosque movement in Cairo, the work of the *daʿiyyat* (female preachers) and the mosque lessons, she challenges gender and feminist theory from a Middle Eastern perspective. Mahmood concludes that the pious women she studied have "agency" through cultivation and performance of gendered Islam. "Agency," she argues, is not a synonym for resistance to gender domination, but a capacity for action to promote Islamic gender norms.

The "capacity for action," such as the cries of *Allahu Akbar*, is used by the *murabitat* to confront Jewish religious groups upon entry to al-Haram al-Sharif and upon exit from the site. The *murabitat* use this "action" also to prevent the Jewish groups from celebrating the visit to the site upon exit. So, the *murabitat's* actions promote a nationalist and religious agenda, not a women's or a gender agenda.

Some of the *murabitat* said that after the al-Quds intifada, they felt that they had power as women and that society encouraged them and honored them for their activities on al-Haram al-Sharif (Zeina Abu Amr, one of the *murabitat's murabitat's* teachers, December 25, 2015). Some rank and file members, such as Amal from al-Isawiya, pointed out that their activities were successful because the number of Jewish women and men entering al-Haram al-Sharif decreased. Also, the Israeli Prime Minister stated that there is no plan to change the status quo on al-Haram al-Sharif (Amal, interview, December 25, 2015). This indicates that like the Egyptian pious women interviewed by Mahmood, the Palestinian pious women active at al-Haram al-Sharif may have developed a sense of "agency" in the political sphere although not necessarily in gender relations.

Mahmood also points out that mosque lessons in Egypt helped recruit women for social and political activities against the secular Egyptian government. In that respect, my findings are similar to Mahmood's, even though the situation in Egypt is quite different from that of Palestine. Study circles for women on al-Haram al-Sharif led to their political activism in the *murabitat* movement against Jewish visitors to the site.

Deeb's valuable ethnography (2006) of publicly pious Shiʿi women in the Dahiya of Beirut, describes social services run by pious individuals and *jamʿiyyat* associations, including those affiliated with Hezbollah. Many of the social services carried out by the women of al-Haram al-Sharif are similar to those described by Deeb and help increase the popularity of political Islamist movements. The *mMurabitat's* social services, however, are informal. But some Palestinians in the Jerusalem area need social services for their families. I met one of the *murabitat* one day at a bank and she asked me about the time of the salary of *ribat* (January 2014). Unlike the pious women of the Dahiyya, however, the women of al-Haram al-Sharif may actually participate in the fight against the Israeli enemy, following their participation in study circles, which Hezbollah does not permit.

The pious women studied by Deeb began to become aware of being excluded based on qualities that were assumed to be masculine, and of the few women in leadership positions in the Dahiyya. Deeb adopts the term "gender jihad" from one of her informants to describe these women's gender consciousness and actions, and how they even subtly challenge the male leadership. Some of the female leaders and the *murabitat's* rank and file said that they can be as good leaders as men, and that the leadership should not be for men only. The female leaders said that in their universities they were leaders of Islamic groups, so why couldn't they be leaders in the future? The public relations efforts carried out by the *murabitat* serve this purpose (along with the primary aim of publicizing the situation at al-Haram al-Sharif – the attempts by Jewish men and women to change the status quo, the efforts by the *murabitat* to fight them, and the harsh treatment they undergo by the Israeli police and the border guard). Some women also said that the experience of the Hamas appointing a woman as the Minister of Women's Affairs in the Palestinian government encouraged them to view women as capable of action (Khweis, interview, November 15, 2015).

Tal's study (2011) of women in the Islamic Movement in Israel showed how the movement developed from providing social and educational services to engaging in political activities, and how women made important contributions. Her detailed descriptions of Islamist women's activities are excellent points of departure for evaluating those of the women of al-Haram al-Sharif. In this study, Tal examines the interaction of the Islamist women from Israel and from the Palestinian territories on al-Haram al-Sharif. Tal used the term "female activism" - rather than "gender activism" - to describe the rise of women's consciousness and actions to promote women. Although the Islamic women's movements in Israel are sister movements to the West Bank pious women, the women leaders and teachers of al-Haram al-Sharif do not use these terms. Nevertheless, at least some of them have a raised consciousness of women's capacity for action, and some are taking actions like publicity to promote the role of women (Sidawi, a *murabitat* leader, interview, November 10, 2014).

Other scholars have different views on the right terminology for the activism of Muslim women. Dalal Bajes, for example says that pious Muslim women in the Islamic World, including Indonesia, the Middle East, Afghanistan, and Malaysia, prefer the term Islamic women's activism to feminism (Bajis, 2013:14). In Ben Shitrit's comparison of the southern branch of the Islamic Movement in Israel and the Shas Torah Guardians' Movement (2013), she critiqued Mahmoud's understanding of the theoretical term "agency" and argued that the movements she studied offer women "powerful libratory narratives." She concluded that these women activists are "highly invested in the idea of the 'autonomous individual'."

The *murabitat* were involved in actions, which Badran, (1994) said "open up new spaces for women that might contradict prevailing gender roles," and which Ben Shitrit labeled "Frames of Exception." One example is that the *murabitat* prayed in the marketplace of the Old City close the Chain Gate in the sight of men, which is not consistent with the Islamic Shariʿa. Members of the *Murabitat* who are on the Israeli security authorities' black list and who are banned from al-Haram al-Sharif committed to such behavior as praying in the street sending out a message, reflecting the harsh treatment of the Israel security authorities and showing the Islamic world that al-Aqsa is in danger. This is the broader goal of the *murabitat*. Nevertheless, these mature, active, pious women prayed behind a young man, showing that they respect this gendered rule of communal prayer (see photo).

Worshippers close to the Chain Gate of the Old City

Also, *murabitat* do not need a male relative (*mahram*) to accompany them when they come out of their homes. Some of them even do not even obtain their husband's permission to go to al-Haram al-Sharif. (Umm Mohammad al-Natsheh, a rank and file member of the *murabitat,* interview, November 29, 2015) perhaps another "opens up new spaces or "frame of exception."

As for expressing ideas that may promote women's rights, Sana al-Rajabi, one of the *murabitat's* leaders and Hiba al-Taweel, a rank and file member of the *murabitat,* said: "We have respect from our husbands, our family and our society, so we have obtained the main right for women, which is 'respect." Husbands go out to work and women stay home to do chores and help children with education. However, that does not stop women from taking *ribat* action (Hiba al-Taweel, and Sana, interview, November 10, 2015). Khadija Khweis said about the political rights for the leaders of pious Islamic women that they should be leaders in the Hamas and in Parliament; that they should be ministers like Mariam Saleh and Jamela al-Shanti in the future (Khweis, interview, July 15, 2015). In conclusion, some *murabitat* leaders, such as Khadija Khweis, Aida Sidawi, and Hanadi Halawani speak of women's rights, including social and political rights, some think that respect is the most important right and some, like the *murabitat's* rank and file, do not mention women's rights at all.

In conclusion, the *murabitat* seem to differ from their pious sisters in Egyptian, Beiruti and other Palestinian Islamic movements regarding women's rights, "agency" and gender activism. The reasons for this will be analyzed in the following chapters. Consequently, I find that the comparison between the Palestinian women's movement in the past and the pious Palestinian women in the fight for women's rights in the present time shows that both groups of women fought for nationalist and not religious goals until the 1980s when the Islamist movements in Israel and in Gaza and the West Bank mobilized women for political goals. The nationalist and religious goals often overshadowed any efforts for women's rights, but the participation of women activists in these movements undoubtedly gave them a sense of empowerment.

The following is taken from an interview with former Mufti Ikrima Sabri (November 2, 2015, interview), which confirms that the reason for creating the Murabitat movement is political:

The idea of creating a Murabitat movement began when the Israeli police banned Palestinian men below the age of fifty from entering al-Haram al-Sharif while allowing women to enter. The ban included male worshippers and teachers.

First circle lessons were established to disguise the Murabitat who would stop attending the lessons the minute Jewish groups arrived to al-Haram al-Sharif.

The Murabitat movement was also created to confront the female members of the visiting Jewish groups in al-Haram al-Sharif. Mufti Ikrima Sabri told me that a number of Islamic leaders including Sheikh Ra'ed Salah, Sheikh Kamal Khatib, Director of al-Aqsa Mosque Sheikh Omer al-Keswani, and the imam of al-

Haram al-Sharif decided to create the Murabitat Movement to confront the female members of the Jewish groups in al-Haram al-Sharif since Muslim men were not allowed to do so.

The interviews with Islamist leaders such as Sheikh Ra'ed Salah, Sheikh Kamal Al-Khatib, and the former Mufti of Al-Aqsa and Palestine Sheikh Ikrima Sabri, the purpose of the Murabiteen and the Murabitat as well as the circle lessons is to gather the biggest number of Muslim women in Al-Aqsa mosque to confront the Jewish groups that visit the area and stop them from entering Al-Aqsa mosque. This step was taken when the Israeli police prevented Palestinian men below the age of fifty from entering Al-Aqsa mosque as well as preventing male teachers from conducting circle lessons. The purpose of the circle lessons is to achieve a political, social, and religious objective of preventing the Jews from taking over Al-Aqsa, destroy it, and build the third temple.

The rest of the chapters discuss the Murabitat's political, social, and religious activities. Part of the Murabitat, especially rank and file Murabitat, joined the circle lessons to get paid by the Islamic Movement in Israel. Another part of the rank and file women joined the Murabitat to escape domestic problems with the in-laws. This reflects the weakness of the secular women's movement in attracting women through women's associations or charitable or cultural projects. The number of Murabitat consequently increased and the Palestinian society and Muslims respected and supported them.

Conclusion

Palestinian women began to play significant social and political roles in the early 20th century. Such roles were similar to those played by women in countries that were colonized such as India, Egypt, and Algeria. The political circumstances of the Palestinians pushed Palestinian women to directly join the national movement in rejecting the British Mandate, the British policies, and the Zionist project. Their activities included joining protests physically and advocating the Palestinian cause.

Education, especially girls' schools in Jerusalem and Ramallah founded in the end of the 19th century, played a crucial role in the empowerment of the Palestinian women's movement and strengthening women's status in the society.

Upper class Palestinian women organized themselves through women's associations and societies in Jerusalem in the early days of the 20th century. However, women became aware that the time and place were not right to demand women's social rights since both Palestinian men and women lacked such rights. The national struggle for liberation took precedence over women's rights. The Palestine Arab Women's Congress, which took place in Jerusalem in 1920, reflected the political role of women that rejected the policies of the British mandate and the activities of the Zionist movement in Palestine. The Palestine Arab Women's Congress, which took place in Jerusalem in 1920, reflected the political role of women who rejected the policies of the British mandate and the activities of the Zionist movement in Palestine. The Congress also concluded with producing a letter containing political demands to Sir John Chancellor, the High Commissioner for Palestine. However, being limited to spouses of bourgeoisie national leaders and due to the internal conflict and weakening of the Palestinian national movement, the women's movement suffered weakness in the aftermath of the 1948 Nakba. This movement was fragmented due to lack of participation of grassroots women. The movement then started to pick up and rise again in refugee camps and rural areas.

Alternatively, women from rural and poor communities contributed to provision of food to the families of the Palestinian fighters during the years of the Palestinian Arab revolt. Other than fulfilling these kinds of traditional roles, some of those women also took part in the actual battles side by side with the male fighters.

Being limited to spouses of bourgeoisie national leaders, the women's movement suffered weakness in the aftermath of the 1948 *Nakba.* This movement was fragmented due to lack of participation of grassroots initiatives by women. The movement then started to pick up and rise again in refugee camps and rural areas. Thc room for participation given to Palestinian women by the PLO was not proportionate compared to what Palestinian women had gained.

However, in the 1960s and 1970s Palestinian women reaffirmed their roles in the national Palestinian movement.

They were able to establish the General Union of Palestinian Women (GUPW) in 1965, which was one of the key achievements after the establishment of the PLO. After 1967, Fatah and the leftist parties allowed women to carry arms and be involved in armed operations. This was evidence of Fatah's and the political left's involvement with grassroots initiatives by women. The women's movement fully supported the PLO. The establishment of the Union of Palestinian Women Committees in Ramallah's Library in 1978, which had secular and pluralistic orientation, was one of the key achievements of the movement in the West Bank and Gaza Strip.

This reflects the conflict and competition between the secular Palestinian women's movement and the pious Muslim Palestinian women's movement in the spread of ideology and for gaining support at home, in educational institutions, and in other places. Pious Muslim women's public participation started in the 1970s, when social and religious organizations, such as *al-Mujama` al-Islami* (the Islamic Center), which were established in Gaza, gave women room to take part in their activities. These activities included advancing social welfare and spreading the religious ideology of the Muslim Brotherhood and of the Hamas at a later stage. In the early 1980s, universities played important role in allowing pious Muslim women sufficient room to maneuver to spread the ideology of the Islamic Movement.

Women's participation in the first intifada in 1987, which involved women from all sectors of Palestinian society, gave women an advanced role in the Palestinian national movement. Consequently, Palestinian parties, whether secular or religious, realized the significance of women's roles in the spread of their ideologies and the recruitment of supporters. Then, there began clear competition between secular and religious Palestinian women's movements.

After the establishment of the Palestinian Authority in the mid-1990s, secular women appealed to the Palestinian Legislative Council for endorsement of new legislations that ensured women's social, cultural, and political rights. On the other hand, pious Muslim women believed that their rights were guaranteed by the Islamic Shariʿa.

The activities of the Muslim women in the Islamic movements and the appearance of the *murabitat* show that pious Muslim women – including the *murabitat* - have delayed demanding women's social rights due to the fact that their main goal was the nationalist goal of liberation. This goal was similar to that of secular Palestinian women's movements in the past. But also, for pious Muslim women, the spread of the Islamic ideology among Muslim women was an exclusive goal. However, the *murabitat's* leaders considered being respected and acknowledged their political role by family and society, as a significant part of their struggle for social and political rights, especially in their effort to freely participate in political and social activities. Some Murabitat leaders speak of women's rights including social and political rights, some think that respect is the most important right and some, like the *murabitat's* rank and file, do not mention women's rights at all.

4. The Setting and Profile of Haram Women Activists

A Day on al-Haram al-Sharif

The day at al-Haram al-Sharif began with the early Morning Prayer at around five o'clock. I witnessed two Israeli police officers patrolling al-Aqsa Mosque after the prayer. The study circles for the *murabitun* start at 07:00. The Israeli police at al-Haram al-Sharif take photos of the *murabitat* arriving at the site. At that time *murabitat* start gathering and have their first study session at 07:30. A group of Jewish people entered al-Haram al-Sharif area from the Dung Gate (*Sha'ar ha-Ashpot* in Hebrew and *Bab al-Magharbe* in Arabic) at 07:30, which is guarded by Israeli police officers. The Israeli police oversee the entry of different Jewish groups. Each group has ten to twenty male and female members guarded by heavily armed police of about fifty officers to protect them.

Jewish worshippers arrive at al-Haram al-Sharif

When the first group enters the Magharbe Gate, cry of *Allahu Akbar* breaks out by a dozen of *murabitat* attending Qur'an study circle, which comes to a stop. The *murabitun* follow with more *Allahu Akbar* cries. The *murabitat* start crying *Allahu Akbar* first because they are the first to witness the Jewish groups enter al-Haram al-Sharif from the Magharbe Gate. The *murabitun* follow when the Israeli security forces become busy with protecting the Jewish visitors rather than keeping an eye on the *murabitun* study circles. The cries go on until the group of Jewish people leaves the area. Some of the *murabitat,* especially leaders like Aida Sidawi and Khadija Khweis, chase the Jewish group all the way to Bab al-Rahmah

(Gate of Mercy, North-East of al-Haram al-Sharif) where Jewish groups face the Dome of the Rock for non-verbal worship. The *murabitat* then raise a huge curtain, which acts as a barrier between the Jewish worshippers and the Dome of the Rock. The Jewish visitors then continue with their journey to Bab al-Silsila (Chain Gate) and leave the holy site. Afterwards, the *murabitat* continue with the study circles. (See photo).

A day at al-Haram al-Sharif:
Murabitat in the morning starting study circle

According to one of the *murabitat* this means that the main purpose of the study circles is to be there when Jewish groups come to the site. It is a political purpose that supersedes the study circles, which stops when the Jewish visitors are at the site of al-Haram al-Sharif. One of the *murabitat* leader and teacher named Hanadi al-Halawani told me that the goal of the *murabitat* is to jeopardize Jewish plans to overtake the site; the study circles are only a justification (Interview, August 20, 2015).

The *murabitat* then take a break to join breakfast (humus, falafel, tea, and juice). According to one of the *murabitat*, the money for the food is donated by charitable people. I had the opportunity to join the *murabitat* in one of their meals (see photo). They have meals inside the mosques or in the open area of al-Haram al-Sharif.

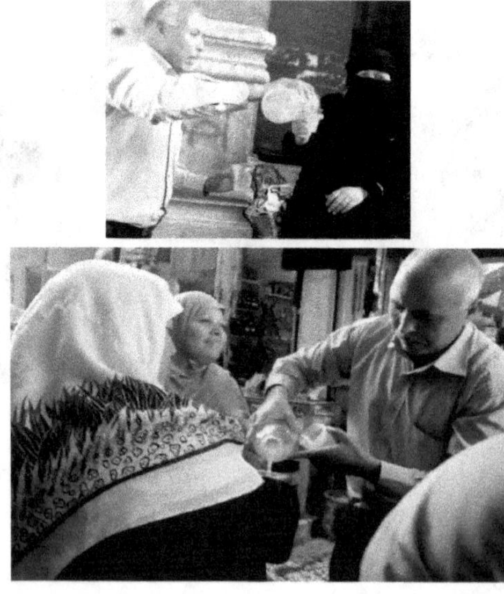

Me serving orange juice to the murabitat after a meal.
This is outside the site. The murabitat considered me as a brother (akh).

My experience with the *murabitat* was that they were very modest and generous. This reflected their hospitality and the brother-sister relationship. They also enjoyed high morals.

After the Muslim's midday prayer (*salat al-thuhr*) at 13:30, another group of Jewish people (men and women) arrived and the cry of *Allahu Akbar* sounded by men and women in al-Haram al-Sharif area. The group of Jewish people stayed on al-Haram al-Sharif until 14:30. The rituals performed by the Jewish group included a 15-minute stop of non-verbal prayer at a short distance from the Dome of the Rock. Then the Jewish groups leave and the *murabitat* go home. The identity cards are handed back on the way out and the Israeli police can arrest wanted ones (leaders and the *murabitat's* rank and file) on their way out.

Other Jewish groups of worshippers arrive at 14:30. The first impression one gets from the arrangement of Jewish groups' visits is that the time of worship on al-Haram al-Sharif is divided between Jews and Muslims as in the case of the Tomb of the Patriarchs in Hebron. It also seems that areas of worship are divided between Muslims and Jews, which Muslims disagree with. However, for Muslims there is a difference between the two mosques. Akram Ziyada, a Salafis leader in Jordan and Palestine, told me that al-Aqsa mosque was mentioned in the Qur᾽an (17-1) and in the Hadith, which urges Muslims to worship at Al-Aqsa Mosque, while the Tomb of the Patriarchs was not (Zeyada, interview, 2013) meaning that the Muslims have to defend al-Aqsa.

Jewish worshippers perform religious rituals at al-Haram al-Sharif facing the Dome of the Rock

The number of female worshippers at the Dome of the Rock on a regular day is 500 excluding *murabitat* who number about 100-150 during the day. The number of Muslim women who come to worship on al-Aqsa increases on special occasions such as on Fridays, in the month of Ramadan, and on Lailat al-Qadr. On regular days, the number of worshippers may reach 10,000. The number may reach 400,000 (maannews.net) including 70,000 women on the last Friday of Ramadan and may exceed half a million on Lailat al-Qadr. On Lailat al-Qadr women actually spend the night in al-Haram al-Sharif accompanied by relatives (see photo).

Women worshippers around the Dome of the Rock at Lailat al-Qadr in Ramadan 2015

On holidays many Palestinian women assemble on al-Haram al-Sharif. At the end of Ramadan feast (*`id al-fitr*) 5,000 women come to celebrate the feast. The same number attends the Morning Prayer on `Id al-Adha or feast of sacrifice. Women prepare special confectionary for the `ids. However, the `id prayers are voluntary prayers rather than compulsory like other prayers. The celebrations of *al-mawlid al-nabawi* (birth of Prophet Muhammad) has similar number of women (5,000) coming to al-Haram al-Sharif for celebrating the birthday. The number of women who stay at Sufis' corners (*al-zawiyya al-afghaniyya*) is 1,000 and the number of women who celebrate the Isra and Mi'raj (Prophet's nocturnal journey and ascension to heaven) is 3,000. The Islamic Movement in Israel joins the *al-mawlid al-nabawi* celebrations with more numbers. The Movement has special celebration called Al-Aqsa Child Day where 1,000 people join, including Arab school children from Jerusalem and Israel proper. The activities conducted at al-Haram al-Sharif show that it is more than just a place of worship. It is a site of celebrating religious occasions, socializing, protesting political and military actions, as well as worshipping God.

Age and Marital Status of the Murabitat

Of the total number of about 1,000 *murabitat*, I interviewed fifty of them. Most of the *murabitat* are in the age group of more than 45 years old, they are mostly married and receive the approval of their spouses in order to take part in the *murabitat* activities. However, a small number of spouses (about five) did not approve of such activities but their wives decided to join anyway. The husbands who reject such activities do so because they fear the reaction of the Israeli authorities.

Examples of *murabitat*, who participate without their husband's consent, include Iman (49) from Kufur Aqab, told me that her husband had refused to allow her to join the *murabitat* but she joined anyway (Iman, interview, March 11, 2015). Sana'a al-Shami (46) from Ras al-Amoud told me that her husband is against her taking part in action of the *murabitat*. However, she joins the *murabitat* despite her husband's objection. (Sana'a al-Shami, interview, November 3, 2015) So she is challenging accepted gender norms in her society to pursue her interest in going to al-Haram al-Sharif. This independent decision may be considered a degree of agency.

Most of the *murabitat* have no dependents, which means that the children are grown up and independent. They can look after themselves. Some of the *murabitat* have grown up daughters who do the chores while their mothers are away. Some middle aged *murabitat* take care of older family members. One of the *murabitat* from Kufur Aqab, aged 50, leaves site after midday prayer to look after her elderly parents.

There are also *murabitat* aged 28 to 40 who have pre-school and primary school children, some of whom are as young as four years old. Young children are sent to kindergartens while *murabitat* are on al-Haram al-Sharif area. Mothers of young children must leave al-Haram al-Sharif at 13:00. For example, Hiba al-Tawil (28) has children in elementary school and in preschool. She told me that she had to leave at 13:00 to prepare lunch for some of her children and pick up her other children from preschool. A small number of the *murabitat* are in the age group of 20-30; they are actually the daughters of some of the *murabitat*. The *murabitat* who teach at schools come on Sundays when schools are closed.

This influences the time each of the *murabitat* can spend on al-Haram al-Sharif. In light of their family responsibilities, younger *murabitat* leave earlier than other *murabitat* who are older and have more free time to be at al-Haram al-Sharif and take part in the *murabitat* activities and socialize with other *murabitat.* Moreover, some of the older *murabitat* are married to *murabitun,* which means they have more time to spend at the site and they go home with their spouses.

Most *murabitat* are supported in their activities by their families. Aya from Kufr Aqab (30) married without children, is encouraged by her husband to be among the *murabitat.* She goes home at 14:00 and prepare for her husband's return from work at 16:00. (Aya, interview, March 15, 2015) Moreover, the *murabitat* are encouraged by other family members (brothers, parents ...etc.) to be member of the *murabitat.* As an example Umm Sa'aid al-Shaludi from Silwan receives the blessing of the entire family for taking part in the actions of the *murabitat* (Umm Sa'aid al-Shaludi, interview, September 20, 2015).

I interviewed one of the *murabitat* who wanted to remain anonymous. She was 35 years old. She told me that she was married to one of the *murabitun* aged 40. They were from al-Isawiya. He was a trader and joined the *murabitun* from Morning Prayer until 09:00 AM when he went to work. This anonymous *murabita* did not need her husband's permission since she came to al-Haram al-Sharif with her husband (interview, July 20, 2015).

In interviews, Hiba (28) and Amal (32) from Wadi al-Joz expressed how they managed to combine family obligations and activism. Hiba said, "My children go to preschool and school. Then I come to al-Haram al-Sharif to join the *murabitat*. Sometimes I bring my youngest son with me." Hiba and her child were arrested once by the Israeli police. The photo of the detained mother and child had 1,000 likes on Facebook. Amal said "I take my children to school and preschool. I return from al-Haram al-Sharif before they finish school to prepare lunch for them." Sana'a, another interviewed *murabitat* member, said, "My children are university students and employed. I go home at 2 o'clock in the afternoon to prepare lunch before the children and their father come home. They encourage me to go al-Haram al-Sharif every day" (Sana'a, interview, September 20, 2015). *Murabitat* with children are also vulnerable to threats from the Israeli police. They accused *murabitat* of being unsuitable mothers to care for children and threatened to take the children away, according to Sana' Rajabi who is one of the *murabitat* (interview, 2015). The age and marital status difference reflect the diversity of the *murabitat* members and a variety of coping mechanisms to find a balance between family and activism and to challenge their husbands' wish to control their activities when necessary.

Geographic and Socio-Economic Background of the Murabitat

Most of the *murabitat* come from the Old City of Jerusalem and the surrounding towns and villages and neighborhoods of Jerusalem such as Ras al-Amoud, Sur Baher and Isawiya. They are holders of Israeli identity cards, which means that they can travel freely without restrictions or require entry permissions into Israel proper. They also have access to al-Haram al-Sharif. This also means that they are not residents of the Palestinian territories. Hence, they can attend study circles and festivities easily. They are also under the Israeli rule. *Murabitat* leaders come from the city, mainly the Old City of Jerusalem, where women are more educated. The *murabitat's* rank and file come from rural areas.

The group of *murabitat* has different economic backgrounds. Some of them are poor, some belong to the middle class (middle class means those who are financially independent but not rich); however, **many** of the *murabitat* are rich but not prestigious. But *murabitat* do not descend from elite families of Jerusalem. The fifty *murabitat* I interviewed and the *murabitat's* leaders are not from well-known families such as the Husaynis, the Nashashibis, the Nuseibas, the Budayris, al-'Alamis or other well-known Muslim families of Jerusalem.

On the other hand, some of the *murabitat* come from poor families, for example, Umm Sa'id al-Shaludi told me that not many of *murabitat* come for the money – the monthly salary of NIS 1,000. Umm Sa'aid added, "But most of the *murabitat* have a religious and holy connection with al-Haram al-Sharif (Umm Sa'aid, interview, September 20, 2015). The poor *murabitat* are also assisted financially by donations from middle class *murabitat* or from other charitable people (Umm Muhammad al-Natsheh, interview, November 29, 2015).

The *murabitat's* leaders are supported by their husbands who are employed by Israeli businesses and earn more than 5,000 shekels a month. So they do not require the stipends provided to teachers and pupils in the study circles. Khadija Khweis, who is married to an Al-Quds University professor, and Zeina Abu-Amr whose husband is a professor of Engineering at Birzeit University - both are *murabitat* leaders-, told me in an interview that they enjoyed a good financial status since their husbands earned good salaries. Most of the *murabitat* are not employed outside the home, although a few had teaching jobs; hence they have free time to join the activities on al-Haram al-Sharif.

Most of the *murabitat* have not enjoyed more than high school education. However, leading *murabitat* and teachers of study circles are often more educated and some even hold master's degrees. The *murabitat* spokeswoman, Latifa Abdulatif, is a graduate in Math from al-Najah National University in Nablus. She speaks English very well (interview, 2014). Khadija Khweis has a Master Degree in Shariʿa from Hebron University. There she led the Islamic female students' movement. As for working outside the home, some of the *murabitat* used to be teachers but lost their jobs with the Israeli Ministry of Education because of their activism (Abdulatif, Khweis).

An interview with Latifa Abdulatif

Religiosity and Political Affiliation of the Murabitat

The *murabitat* interviewed described their degree of religiosity to me. Samiha Shahin told me that her connection with al-Aqsa is *Aqida* (a matter over which Muslims hold conviction, or "creed"). She also stated that she came to al-Haram al-Sharif to pray more than one time a day. She prays alone at many spots so that she may hit the spot where Prophet Muhammad prayed (Samiha Shahin interview, September 20, 2015).

An indication of their religiosity is their dress. Most of the *murabitat* wear Islamist hijabs, such as those worn by Hamas supporters and the supporters of Muslim Brotherhood in Egypt. This means that they do not cover their faces or hands. None of the *murabitat* wears traditional Palestinian dress.

Rather, they wear long coats (*jilbabs*) in dark colors made popular by the Islamist movements. Some of the *murabitat* wear a *niqab*. Few *murabitat* wear *khimars* which cover the whole face (a *khimar* is similar to the *niqab* worn by Salafi women) so that they won't be recognized by the Israeli police cameras (interview with one of the *murabitat*, August 15, 2015) although they are not affiliated with the Salafis (See: photo).

Murabitat's leaders with and without khimar

The Murabitat wearing khimars in order not to be identified by Israeli security surveillance cameras

The leading *murabitat* wear distinctive uniforms including khaki colored jackets such as those worn by press photographers. This makes them stand out as frontline *murabitat*, speakers for Murabitat, and coordinators of activities (see photo).

Leading murabitat wear distinctive uniforms and a banner stating "I am banned from al-Aqsa"

Murabitat women interviewed deny any connections to political groups. However, my observations show that they are affiliated to the Hamas and the Islamic Movement in Israel. Zeina Abu Amr stated that the *murabitat* do not have any affiliation with the Palestinian Authority. I interviewed one of the leaders of the *murabitat* named Zeina Abu Amr; she is on the blacklist of the Israeli police and banned from entering al-Haram al-Sharif. I asked Abu Amr about the political affiliation of the *murabitat* and whether they were members of political organizations. Abu Amr told me that the *murabitat* did not have any political affiliation whatsoever. Abu Amr also denied any affiliation with the Palestinian Authority. However, when I asked Abu Amr about the connection between Hamas and the *murabitat,* she smiled and remained silent (interview, December 25, 2015). In answer to the same question, Khadija Khweis, one of the leaders of the *murabitat,* said that the *murabitat* did not have any connections with any political groups. She added that she had been the leader of the female students at Hebron University, which had been part of Hamas' Islamic block (interview, December 30, 2015).

I also observed that the songs and the slogans of the *murabitat* while at al-Haram al-Sharif reflect hidden support for or affiliation to Hamas. The chants including *khaybar khaybar ya yahud, jaysh Muhammad qad ya'ud* (Oh Jews, remember Khaybar - the army of Muhammad will return) and *yallah yallah ya Qassam, hay al-Aqsa bstanak,* (come on Qassam [the armed wing of Hamas] al-Aqsa awaits you).

The *murabitat's* leaders who led Islamist students' movements at Palestinian universities such as Hebron University and Al-Najah University in Nablus may be affiliated to Hamas. Latifa Abdulatif was one of the leaders of female students at al-Najah University in Nablus and those female students were Hamas supporters.

The fact that the Islamic Movement in Israel paid the *murabitat* salaries was evidence that the *murabitat* were affiliated with the Movement. Also, the Movement bailed out the *murabitat* who were detained by Israeli police. According to Aida Sidawi, the person who paid the bail out money was from the Islamic Movement in Israel (Aida Sidawi, interview, November 10, 2014).

In addition to protecting al-Aqsa from a Jewish control, the political message the *murabitun* and *murabitat* and all Islamic movements in al-Haram al-Sharif send is that they want to establish an Islamic state (not to be confused with ISIS). For example, Hamas and the Islamic Movement in Israel want an Islamic state with Jerusalem or *al-Quds* as the capital (Ra'ed Salah, Al-Quds TV, 2015). On the other hand, Hizb al-Tahrir states in every weekly lesson that they want the caliphate back to lead the Islamic army to liberate al-Aqsa Mosque from the Jews. Samiha Shahin, one of the *murabitat's* leaders, told me that "We support and wait for the establishment of an Islamic state in Palestine, a Hamas Islamic state, in which Jerusalem will be the capital" (Samiha Shahin, interview, September 20, 2015).

At present, the *murabitat* focus their struggle on the assertion that al-Aqsa belongs only to Muslims. They seek to jeopardize Israeli plans to take control of al-Haram al-Sharif. In the interviews I conducted, there was no mention of women's rights in theory or in practice, because in Palestine, the fight for religious and national rights often overshadows the struggle for women's rights. Moreover, other factors that overshadow the women's fight for their rights include socio-economic factors, educational factors, and rural-urban factors. However, women's rights are safeguarded by the Shariʿa. This issue was revealed many times in the *khutbas* (sermons) of Ikrima Sabri in 2014.

Conclusion

The *murabitat* are mostly middle aged (over 45 years) and mostly married. They obtain an approval from the spouses to join the *murabitat* activities. The majority of the *murabitat* come from the Old City of Jerusalem and the neighboring towns and villages. These women have grown up children, so they are relatively free of family obligations and may pursue their interests on al-Haram al-Sharif. They usually have the support of their families, but when they don't, they are even willing to defy their husbands, an independence that indicates how important the work of the *murabitat* is for them and how far they are willing to go to challenge Islamic gender norms.

Some of the *murabitat* are poor; however, the majority of women is from a middle class background and is financially independent. Few of the leaders are well-to-do but not prestigious. The important thing is that none of the women of the elite Jerusalem families are members of the *murabitat.*

The *murabitat* come from inside the city of Jerusalem, but also villages that have become absorbed into the city, as well as villages farther afield such as Kufur Aqab. These *murabitat* belong to the middle class. They are respected and encouraged by their husbands, their family, and their local community for facing Jewish groups visiting al-Haram al-Sharif. Amna (40) a married woman from Kufar Aqab told me that her husband worked in Israel and he respected and encouraged her. She is also supported by her family (Amna, interview, November 16, 2014).

Murabitat wear hijabs, which is a sign of religiosity. There are *murabitat* who wear a *khimar* in order to hide their faces from the Israeli security cameras. Their dress indicates their religiosity, and although they deny political affiliation, it is clear that they are linked to the Hamas as well as the Islamic Movement in Israel, the former by the content of their activities and the latter by financial support.

Women who come to al-Haram al-Sharif may come as individuals to pray and study, as they have done for centuries, as we will see in the next chapter. As Mona, a 46 year old woman from Isawiya, said: "I come here to pray and worship God" (Mona, from Isawiya, December 12, 2014).

5. Women's Prayer and Study on al-Haram al-Sharif

> "When I come to pray on al-Haram al-Sharif, I feel comfortable. I feel that this place is closest to God, so that God is beside me. I believe that one prayer in al-Aqsa Mosque equals five-hundred prayers in other mosques. Maybe I am praying in the place where the Prophet Muhammad prayed with His companions (*sahaba*). My presence protects al-Aqsa from Jewish settler groups and I come to study Shariʿa and Qurʾan at the *Masatib al-'Ilm*," says Samiha Shahin, one of the Murabitat (Shahin, interviews, July 20, 2015 and September 15, 2015).

Women have been coming to pray on al-Haram al-Sharif for centuries. The first part of this chapter is devoted to women's prayer on al-Haram al-Sharif in the past and in the present. I will first survey the information about women's prayer at al-Haram al-Sharif in the past, and then I will describe and analyze the reasons women gave in interviews for coming to al-Haram al-Sharif to pray today. This will be followed by a discussion of gender separation on al-Haram al-Sharif in the past and in the present. The second part of the chapter deals with women's study and the Shariʿa Schools for Girls and Boys on al-Haram al-Sharif.

In the early years of Islam, female ascetics used to reside in al-Aqsa Mosque. (Katz, 2003). Ibn al-Jawzi, who wrote hagiographical accounts, mentions pious female worshippers on al-Haram al-Sharif as early as the 12th century. In one of his accounts, he said that he "saw many women wearing chemises of wool and veils (*khumur*), dwelling in retreat in the mosque (*muta`akifat fi al-masjid*) not speaking during the day." Another anecdote of Ibn al-Jawzi is about ten female devotees who stayed worshipping in al-Aqsa Mosque. Ibn al-Arabi, (d.543/ 1148/) reported "I saw in al-Aqsa Mosque chaste women who did not go out of their place of religious retreat (*muta`akifat fi al-masjid*) until they died as martyrs there" (Katz, 2003:167). "Women in the late 15th century were also reported as attending prayers at al-Haram al-Sharif covering their faces" (Katz, 2003:169).

Taqi al-Din al-Hisni noticed the extensive presence of Muslim women on al-Haram al-Sharif in the 17th century. He disagreed with such presence and argued that it might be a cause of corruption and unnecessary mixing of men and women, which may lead to *fitna* (seduction) or temptation. He argued that women should be forbidden from attending Friday prayers. At the same time, a Franciscan named Eugene Roger who made a pilgrimage to Jerusalem in the 17th century stated that "women never go the mosque at all but on Fridays and every day during the month of Ramadan." Katz says that during the celebrations of the birth of Prophet Muhammad at the end of 17th century, women stayed in one area of the mosque with small boys and girls (Katz, 2003).

At the time of this study, I observed that the women who prayed inside al-Aqsa Mosque were not necessarily *murabitat*.

The number of non-*murabitat* women who come to al-Aqsa Mosque and the Dome of the Rock every day is 300. Prayers at the Dome of the Rock are conducted before prayers at al-Aqsa Mosque. The non-*murabitat* worshippers told me that the purpose of coming to al-Haram al-Sharif was only for worship and that they had no connections to the *murabitat*.

The *murabitat* women interviewed reported many reasons for praying on al-Haram al-Sharif. Some women come to pray in al-Aqsa Mosque "because at home there is too much noise and it is difficult to have a minute of silence to focus on praying," said Rabiha, who comes to pray at al-Haram al-Sharif (Rabiha, one of the *murabitat*, interview, 2015).

Also, Ilham al-Ju`be (43) from the Old City, said "al-Haram al-Sharif provides the opportunity to meet women from all over Jerusalem and make new friends and develop social relationships for future marriages of children" (Ilham al-Ju`be, interview, September 17, 2015). Some widows and divorced women come to pray at al-Haram al-Sharif for psychological reasons; they miss their husbands and come to cry and to pray to God. (Anonymous, interview, November 3, 2015).

Some women come for spiritual reasons; they want to be alone with God and to seek forgiveness from God, because one prayer in al-Haram al-Sharif equals 500 prayers in other mosques according to a Hadith (Samiha, interview, 2015). Also the main reason for women worshippers is a religious connection with al-Aqsa Mosque. While praying, they think of

Fadail Bayt al-Maqdis (the virtues of Jerusalem).." Also praying on al-Haram al-Sharif gives them more and more *hasanat* (credit for good deeds) and preserves the Sunnah of Prophet Muhammad who prayed in this site with all prophets on the night of the *Isra* and *Mi'raj*. Moreover, women feel a connection to Prophet Muhammad and the *sahaba* (Prophet's companions) Samiha also told me that she prayed in a different location of the mosque every day so eventually she would pray in the same place as Prophet Muhammad had prayed and she would feel the connection with Him. (Samiha, one of the *murabitat*, interview, 2015). The *murabitat* believe that praying on al-Haram al-Sharif will be an intercession after their death. This is based on the following Hadith by Prophet Muhammad:

"The deeds of every deceased person are sealed by their death, except for the one who dies as a Murabit (person guarding the Muslim frontiers) in the Cause of Allah; his deeds will continue to be grown (increased) for him until the Day of Resurrection and he will be safe from the *fitnah* (trial) of the grave" (Related by Abu Dawud and Al-Tirmidhy- https://tawheedmovement.com).

Leaders of the *murabitat* emphasized political goals that were intertwined with religious aims. One said that praying at al-Haram al-Sharif increases the *murabitat's* legitimacy and prominence as a good Muslim women and Islamists. The legitimacy of the *murabitat* is to serve the purpose for which the *murabitat* movement was established which is to protect the holy site from Jewish worshippers' presence and to jeopardize Israeli plans to take over the site. This is what Muslim women need to do as a duty (Khweis, interview, September 15, 2015). Another stated:

> "Al-Aqsa is part of the *aqeeda*, it is as important as Islam. If we lose al-Aqsa, we lose our religion. Jewish groups want to destroy al-Haram al-Sharif. Their visits will lead to place and time division of al-Haram al-Sharif. We will be at the site every day; joining the study circles, to stop the Jewish groups from taking control over the site. We meet Jewish groups with *Allahu Akbar* to stop them from praying on al-Haram al-Sharif." (Interview with Aida Sidawi leader at her home, November 10, 2014).

Aida Sidawi described the *murabitat* as *guardians* of the holy site, a new religious and political goal. Katz (2013), however, describes the women who stayed in the mosque to worship as *mu`takifat fi al-masjid* but not as guardians, and none of the women have described themselves as guardians of al-Haram al-Sharif before 2010.

A third *murabitat* leader, Amal (28) from Isawiya village near Jerusalem, spoke in the aftermath of the start of Al-Quds intifada, about how they felt: "The number of *murabitat* has increased, and we have a major role in the intifada. We tell the world that al-Aqsa is in danger, and our actions moved the Palestinians and the Islamic world to support us. We are not related to any political group, and we are not a political movement, but we have political power. The number of Jews on al-Haram al-Sharif has decreased" (Amal, interview, 10 December, 2015). What Amal means by this is that *murabitat* believe that they come to pray, learn, and confront the Jewish visitors. In fact, the *murabitat* have influential supporters for their activities (Ismail Haniya, aljazeeranet, October 11, 2015). Muhamad Halabi declared support for the *murabitat* (https://www.facebook.com/KLMTY/videos) on his Facebook page, before he was killed. Similarly, Ra'ed Jaradat posted a statement of support before he was killed in an attack on Israeli troops (https://www.alaraby.co.uk/society).

Latifa Abdulatif, an active member of the *murabitat*, views their purpose as keeping the Jews away and preventing the Jews from building their Temple on al-Haram al-Sharif. Abdulatif emphasizes women's unique role as replacing men in leading the contest over al-Haram al-Sharif since men are all imprisoned or oppressed by the Israeli police.

Some women prefer to pray alone because joining study circles, they think, is useless; it is too political. Hence, they are against political goals, agendas, and activities. On the other hand, Sana'a al-Rajabi and Aida Sidawi, who support the political goals, told me that "We are guardians for the sake of God. Everybody must protect al-Aqsa so the Jews don't take it; they have their eyes on it" (Sana'a, and Aida, interview, September 20, 2015). So this means that *murabitat* consider protection of al-Haram al-Sharif from the Jews as part of their duties.

In the last few years, the political reasons for Muslims to pray on al-Haram al-Sharif such as protecting al-Aqsa Mosque from Jewish groups, has increased. According to Latifa Abdulatif, women have been coming to al-Aqsa in increasing numbers to pray, to study the Qur'an, and most importantly to protect al-Aqsa from Jewish groups (Abdulatif, interview, September 15, 2015).

The Allocation of Space on al-Haram al-Sharif

In the past, there were varying degrees of separation between women and men praying on al-Haram al-Sharif. Women prayed at enclosures for women (*maqasir*) as early as the tenth century (Katz, 2003). But in the seventeenth century Taqi al-Din al-Hisni complained of the unnecessary mixing of men and women during communal prayers. Traveler Ali Bey observed at the beginning of the nineteenth century that there were separate places within Al-Aqsa Mosque that are reserved for women to hear prayers and sermons. However, al-Nabulsi in the end of the Seventeenth century stated that women might not have been confined to specific areas in al-Aqsa.

In the first half of the fourteenth century women stood in rows behind rows of men, according to the Sunnah, which showed gender separation. There are also women's mosques such as the Dome of the Rock (also named Jami'a al-nisa') on al-Haram al-Sharif (Katz, 2003:168). However, in the late fifteenth century, it was open for men worshippers. Al-Haram al-Sharif preserved space for women to worship, and female worshippers may have their own entrance to a mosque as well as their own courtyard. "Women have a door of their own, through which they enter both the Temple [al-Haram al-Sharif] and the courtyard thereof, and their own aisle in the Temple, wherein they pray apart from the men" (Katz, 2003:168).

At the end of the seventeenth century, Abdul Ghani al-Nabulusi described how people gathered according to their ranks, the elite, and common men and women gathered in one area of the mosque. Here the women are modestly separated from men but apparently remained visible to them (Katz, 2003: 169).

During Ramadan 2015, the Waqf administration put a 10-meter long curtain to separate men from women worshippers inside al-Aqsa Mosque. The Israeli police removed the curtain; therefore, there are no barriers separating male and female worshippers within al-Aqsa Mosque. Consequently, women now occupy a corner of the Mosque where they can pray behind men, according to the precedent of the Prophet. They can, however, be seen by men.

There are no curtains separating male and female worshippers, but during prayer, men line up before women; hence, they cannot see women while praying. This is one of the Shariʿa rules. The preacher asks men and women to follow this rule before praying during times of crowded conditions (Imam Muhammad Hussein, Ramadan 2015). During Friday prayers, for instance, the rows of male and female worshippers intermingle. However, preachers (or imams) call for gender separation. During Ramadan, as well as during other Muslim festivals, it becomes impossible to distance male and female worshippers since they come in such large numbers (female worshippers' number could reach 10,000). So the Dome of the Rock is reserved for women.

In sum, history of women's worshipping on al-Haram al-Sharif shows that gender separation has always been a matter of significance. This separation has religious grounds since Islam is keen on separating women and men during times of worship. This legacy goes back to the early days of Islam. Today, gender separation is still there; however, it is more flexible since men and women can see each other though they worship in separate rows on Fridays and during Islamic holidays and during the special Ramadan prayers such as the *Taraweeh* and *Lailat Al-Qadr* prayers. Also, men can pray in the Dome of the Rock though reserved for women.

Women's full participation in the communal prayer is guaranteed by amplifiers all over al-Haram al-Sharif area including the Dome of the Rock, so women can clearly hear the *khatib* or preacher (unlike some mosques where women are so marginalized that they claim they cannot hear the *khutba* or speech of the preachers).

The *khutbas* are given by men in compliance comply with the Jordanian Waqf rules, and include religious, political, and social messages. A *khatib* may dwell on Palestinian political issues, such as the Gaza war. (I attended a Friday prayer in al-Aqsa mosque in 2014 and the *khutba* was about the Gaza war). The *khatib* asked worshippers to donate money, food, water, and medicine to Gaza. Another *khatib* criticized the way Israeli authorities try to change the Palestinian curriculum taught at Arab schools (*tawjihi*) in Jerusalem to the Israeli curriculum of the *bagrut.* Sometimes *Khatib* Ikrima Sabri talks about women and gender issues, women's rights as prescribed by the Shariʿa, polygamy, and inheritance. He encourages women to demand their rights and not to be afraid of claiming them from male family members. Sabri also talks about justice done to women at Shariʿa courts. Sabri is also a supporter of the *murabitat* (interview, November 2, 2015).

Education on al-Haram al-Sharif

This part of the chapter deals with women's study and the Shariʿa Schools for Girls and Boys on al-Haram al-Sharif. Al-Aqsa Mosque compound and Jerusalem in general have been centers of Islamic learning at least since the Umayyad period and throughout Islamic history (Abdul Mahdi, 1980, p. 11). There were 366 study circles in al-Aqsa Mosque in the 11th century when al-Ghazali visited–and stayed- in the site (http://archive.aawsat.com/); (Mufti Sabri, interview, 2015). And there is evidence that women joined such schools and study circles during the Mamluk period (Abdul Mahdi, 1980: 67). In addition to study circles, women came to al-Haram al-Sharif in the past to listen to popular preachers (*wu'az*) without any barrier between the genders (Katz, 2003: 169).

According to mufti Sabri, fewer women came to al-Aqsa Mosque before 1967 to attend study circles and learn Qurʾan and Hadith. There were no female teachers then. The reason for that was that men were more educated in Shariʿa than women. The number of men with higher education was more than the number of women. Women enjoyed a traditional life in Palestinian society (interview, 2015).

Study Circles

Masatib al-`Ilm are the creation of the Islamic Movement in Israel. They were initiated after founding al-Aqsa Construction Institute in 2008. They included men only and started with few men initially, 30 students attended, but after three years this was expanded to more than one thousand. "These study circles constitute an increased Muslim presence in Al-Aqsa courtyard during all hours of the day, and especially during times when the holy esplanade is open to non-Muslim visitors" (Tzikiyahu, 2015: 6).

In the study circles of the *murabitat*, at different locations of al-Haram al-Sharif, women are taught the Qur᾽an and the Hadith in lessons of one hour each. The teacher either sits or stands among the learners (see: photo).

A study circle

The number of students per study circle ranges between 10 and 30. There are also study circles for non-*murabitat* or *murabitun*). Non-*murabitat* women may attend lessons by Sheikh Abbasi, a Salafi sheikh, who talks about the life of Prophet Muhammad and virtues (Abbasi, interview, 2014).The number of study circles spread out on al-Haram al-Sharif could reach ten.

At first, the teachers at the study circles were people with graduate and postgraduate degrees as well as university professors who specialized in Shariʿa. However, the Israeli authorities decided to stop those teachers from entering al-

Haram al-Sharif and arrested some of them in early 2015 because the Israeli police noticed that the teachers' activities led to more students and they felt threatened by those young teachers. Hence, they were replaced by *murabitat's murabitat's* teachers. (Khweis, interview, September 20, 2015). The *murabitat's murabitat's* teachers; however, do not possess the same knowledge of Shariʿa as the original teachers. Some of them learnt about Islam from their own studies. Aida, for instance, is one of the *murabitat* who became a teacher. When such teachers are denied entry to al-Haram al-Sharif, one of the *murabitat* in the study circles would volunteer to teach despite the insufficient knowledge of Shari'a.

In one of the study circles, the teacher was a 65-year old man named Muhammad al-Sharif holding a diploma in Islamic studies. He taught among the *murabitat*. He was within the age group that did not face Israeli police restrictions on entry to al-Haram al-Sharif (older than 55). Muhammad al-Sharif also taught Qurʾan reciting (interview, 2015).

It can be seen, that male teachers were preferred for the *murabitat* study circles because of their superior education and women were only recruited after the Israeli authorities prevented these young men from entering al-Haram al-Sharif. Similarly, when the female teachers who had some education were barred by the Israelis, the *murabitat's* rank and file took their place. This unique situation provided educated women with an opening, and later some lower class women with an opportunity.

Well-off *murabitat* teach for free at al-Haram al-Sharif. They do it to gain *hasanat* that are rewarded by Heaven to charitable people, according to Islamic tradition. *Murabitat* also urge other women to join them and learn about Islam.

The topics of the study circles are determined by the needs of the *murabitat.* Umm Huthaifa (50) teaches the *murabitat* how to recite the Qur'an. She also teaches Hadith. She is not highly educated. Umm Huthaifa told me that teaching Hadith and reciting the Qur'an do not require postgraduate education (Umm Huthaifa, interview, November 29, 2015).

The Qur'an interpretation (*tafsir*) which the *murabitat* study is *The Interpretation of Ibn Kathir.* In most cases the topics are general but sometimes they are gender-specific. One of the topics that were discussed in the study circles, was polygamy. A *murabitat* member asked the preacher about this issue and he told her to read the part in *Surat Alnisa'a* (Chapter 4 of the Qur'an) and the interpretation of Ibn Kathir about polygamy and its conditions. The study circles are also opportunities for the *murabitat* to socialize.

Learning the Qur'an helps *murabitat* accept their destinies as decided by God who is in control of everything, as they believe. Such belief is actually in the core of Islamic doctrine. They believe that they are better off worshipping on al-Haram al-Sharif than having a career. This negative attitude toward women's work outside the home is very unusual, particularly since the teachers of the *murabitat* had worked outside the home. Moreover, the attitude toward work outside the home is seen as an alternative to boredom; they do not see the purpose of work as the meeting of financial need or as a way to earn money for other things. So the *murabitat* do not worry about their economic situation. Having the honorific treatment by the society and living a simple life are sufficient for them. The money they have is enough. They are supported by working children or spouses or by the Israeli welfare. A *murabitat* leader named Sana'a al-Rajabi- made this comparison: "We as women are better off here in an all-women's group with honor than women who go out to work. All is written in the Qur'an –there is nothing to be afraid of" (interview out door, November 29, 2015).

It is the study circles that teach the *murabitat* about the virtues of al-Aqsa Mosque. The teachers of the study circles even tell *murabitat* which television channels to watch; such as Saudi religious channels. They warn them of the Shia television channels (Aida Sidawi, interview, November 10, 2014).

In any case, the study circles come to a standstill when the groups of Jewish worshippers arrive at al-Haram al-Sharif and the cries of *Allahu Akbar* begin. The *murabitat* then follow the Jewish groups with more *Allahu Akbar* cries and tell them that al-Haram al-Sharif is no place for them (see photo).

Al-Aqsa in Islamic tradition

The study circles were made illegal by the Israeli authorities following the decision to ban the *murabitun*, the *murabitat*, the study circles, as well as al-Aqsa Institute of the Islamic Movement in Israel on September, 9, 2015; consequently, the number of study circles dropped sharply (Rabiha, interview, September 20, 2015.); (See also http: / / www. jpost. com/ Arab-Israeli-Conflict).

Shari'a Schools

Shariʿa schools in al-Haram al-Sharif

There are three schools inside the A-Haram al-Sharif, including the Shariʿa Secondary Girls' School and the Shariʿa Secondary Boys' School, both established in 1978 by the Awqaf Ministry of Jordan to teach Islamic religion at a time when Jerusalem lacked Islamic religious schools and had only Christian schools (Uhud Sabri and Nader al-Afghani, schools' principals, interview, 2015).

The third school is Al-Aqsa School, which was established in 1980. It is actually a group of schools located within al-Haram al-Sharif and the Old City. Al-Aqsa School is a Palestinian public school (run by the Palestinian Authority) (Akram al-Ashhab, school principal, interview, 2015).

The Shariʿa boys' school is located within al-Haram al-Sharif in an historical building that was used by the Jordanian army before the 1967 war. The Shariʿa girls' school is also located within al-Haram al-Sharif on top of the Waqf department building. This building was a Jordanian police headquarters before the 1967 war. The Shariʿa Boys' School has

167 students taught by 12 male teachers who are Jerusalem residents (Al-Afghani, school principal, interview, 2015).

Uhud Sabri, the principal of the Shariʿa Secondary Girls' Schools, is a graduate in Shariʿa from the Jordanian University. She has been the school's principal since 1986. She is Mufti Sabri's sister. A number of the teachers at the school are university graduates and postgraduates. The teachers are residents of Jerusalem. The Shariʿa Girls' School has ninety-five students taught by fifteen male and female teachers. The students get a thirty-minute break during the day to pray and celebrate special Islamic occasions (Uhud, school principal, interview, 2015).

Al-Aqsa schools group has three-hundred and seventy students, including seventy girls. They are first to tenth graders. All students are residents of Jerusalem. The tuition fee at al-Aqsa schools totals 2,400 shekels. Orphaned and impoverished children are exempted from payment of fees (Akram al-Ashhab, interview, 2015).

The Shariʿa schools follow the curriculum taught at public Palestinian schools (the curriculum of the Ministry of Education of the Palestinian Authority) and Jordanian schools. However, there are six additional topics taken from the Jordanian Awqaf Ministry taught at the Shariʿa schools including, Qurʾan, Hadith, Islamic teachings, the Islamic political, social, and economic system, and Islamic rhetoric. Another topic is called the "Islamic world now," which is about the problems of the Islamic world, including its modern political and economic problems. The economic issues include poverty and unemployment. The topic also discusses the political systems of the Islamic world that ensure democracy, such as having parliaments. The schools offer free education. The Hashemite Kingdom of Jordan covers the running costs of the schools (Al-Afghani and Uhud, schools' principals, interview, 2015).

On the other hand, al-Aqsa schools group teaches the Palestinian public schools' curriculum (of the Palestinian Authority) only. There are twenty-three teachers at the schools who work six hours a day. The schools do not teach additional religious education. However, preachers from Israel proper - not members of the Islamic Movement in Israel- preach among students on special occasions providing that they receive the principal's consent. The students of these schools are not taken to pray at al-Aqsa Mosque but they take part in religious ceremonies (Akram al-Ashhab, interview, 2015).

It is worth noting that girls in public school tend to finish high school before they get married, according to a parent of one of the Shariʿa school's girls. However, girls at Shariʿa schools may get married before finishing high school because they are preferred by men and schools encourage them to get married at that age (A parent of one of the Shariʿa school's girls, interview, 2015).

In an interview with a Shariʿa school graduate - currently a student at Bethlehem University- on the topic of marriage, she said, "Marriage is an honor for girls. However, girls may continue university education when they get the chance to do so. They could study humanities or religion at Palestinian or Jordanian university. The girls of the Shariʿa schools are well-received at universities. On the other hand, families support women's work when they graduate from university. Teachers encourage students to gain more education and take part in the development of the society" (Rawan Bseso, a graduate from Al-Shariʿa Girls' School, interview, 2015).

Additionally, Jerusalem has also many private Christian schools, as well as public schools that are run by the Israeli Ministry of Education. Tuition fees at the private schools may reach 2,000 USD. However, parents prefer not to send their children to schools run by the Israeli Ministry of Education. The parents, in most cases, prefer the Shariʿa schools, especially for girls, since such schools are respected by the society and make girls wear *jilbabs* and hijabs and teach them good Islamic manners (A Shariʿa Girls' School's parent, interview, 2015).

POLITICAL ACTIVITIES

The Israeli policy of closing Shariʿa boys and girls schools on al-Haram al-Sharif and forcing students of such schools to stay outside the area encourages the students to join the *murabitun* and the *murabitat.* When the Israel Police prevent students from entering al-Haram al-Sharif area, the students take part in protesting such policies. For instance, on July 15, 2015, the Israeli police closed the doors of al-Haram al-Sharif in the face of the Shariʿa schools' students and other people going into site in order to let Jewish groups worship within the area. They had to wait outside with the *murabitat* who were also prevented from entering al-Haram al-Sharif (Shariʿa school student, interview, 2015). This policy of Israel prompted the principal of the Shariʿa secondary school for girls to declare that the students and staff of the school consider themselves *murabitun* and *murabitat.* The principal also said that "the school teaches following Islam, worshipping God, and obeying the Prophet Muhammad. We are proud to have *murabitat* and *murabitun* among our students and staff. They come every day to the third holiest place of Islam" (Principle of Shariʿa Secondary Girls' School Ohood Sabri, interview, 2015).

Conclusion

The gender-based separation in the Islamic society is based on the religious traditions of Islam where mixing men and women is considered *fitnah* (seduction). Therefore, men and women are separated especially during prayer in order to preserve worshipping from such *fitnah*. However, when the numbers of male and female worshippers becomes extremely large such during Friday prayers and Ramadan, the *Khateeb* (orator) orders men to pray in lines in front of women. The prayer of men who stand behind women's lines is considered invalid.

In addition to prayer, al-Haram al-Sharif is a center for Muslim women to study as they had in previous centuries. The Awqaf department noticed the need for Shariʿa schools on al-Haram al-Sharif. Hence, it established two Shariʿa schools for boys and girls in 1978. The schools are fully funded by the Jordanian government. They teach six Shariʿa topics in addition to the Palestinian school curriculum. There is a third school on al-Haram al-Sharif. This school teaches first to ninth grades only. It is fully funded by the Palestinian Authority.

The schools on al-Haram al-Sharif provide religious education for Jerusalemite children as well as the Palestinian school curriculum. The school children are not involved in political activities (Akram al-Ashhab, interview at his office, 2015). The schools' principals confirmed that their students did not take any part in political activities. However, Israeli security measures such as preventing students from entering al-Haram al-Sharif where their schools are located, forces students to take part in the actions of the *murabitun* and *murabitat* taken outside the site.

Some women are not connected to the *murabitat* and merely pray and hear lectures but do not participate in the study circles. The study circles are important activities for the *murabitat*. They provide the rank and file members with guidance, and they open a path for some *murabitat* to leadership. Moreover, the presence of the *murabitat* in study circles not only increases the numbers of Muslim women at al-Haram al-Sharif but also makes them available for political activities, particularly when Jewish women come to the area to visit and pray by heart. "It is the study circles that teach the Murabitat about the virtues of Al-Aqsa Mosque... Learning the Qurʿan helps Murabitat accept their destinies as decided by God who is in control of everything."

For the *murabitat*, the study circles are opportunities to learn the Qurʾan and Sunnah. Therefore, teachers of the study circles bear the responsibility of delivering lessons. The teachers were first men because they were more educated in Shariʿa. However, when male teachers were detained or banned from al-Haram al-Sharif, *murabitat* educated leaders took over the teaching. Then, these women were also eventually banned from the site, which required that the *murabitat's* rank and file take over the function of teaching the study circles. However, the teaching delivered by the *murabitat's* rank and file was limited to reciting the Qur'an. This shows that the most important goal of the movement is to have *murabitat* always present at the site to confront Jewish visitors.

When the Israeli authorities decided to ban the study circles, the *murabitun* and *murabitat,* as well as Al-Aqsa Association, which paid salaries to the *murabitun* and *murabitat,* the number of study circles dropped significantly. The fear of the Israeli punitive measures also contributed to the drop in the number of the study circles.

6. The *Murabitat's* Activities on al-Haram al-Sharif: *Da'wa* Proselytizing and Social and Political Mobilizing

Blacklisted murabitat praying outside al-Haram al-Sharif

This chapter explains what the goals are of the study circles on al-Haram al-Sharif and how they mobilize women for social and political ends. The study circles discussed above include *da'wa* proselytizing to recruit more women from Jerusalem to the *murabitat*. They also lead to social activities, including support for needy families. The *murabitat* also meet with women from other Islamic movement and join social and political activities such as the "Children in Support of Al-Aqsa Day." Most importantly, from the point of view of the founders and leaders of the *murabitat*, the study circles serve a political purpose and recruit women for political activities. The chapter also explains how *da'wa* is utilized by Hamas and the Islamic Movement in Israel to gain more support and supporters in Jerusalem and the Palestinian territories.

PREACHING *(DA'WA)* AND WOMEN

Da'wa usually denotes preaching of Islam, and the *da' wa* of the Islamic movements targets other Muslims to bring them to the right path as they see it, and to recruit more supporters. Preachers may be a male preacher called a *dā'ī* in Arabic, or a female called a *da'iyyah* (plural *du'at).*

In modern times, *da'wa* has been employed by a number of Islamist and salafi movements to propagate their view of Islam. The Muslim Brotherhood, founded in Egypt in 1928, adopted *da'wa* educational and social activities to expand their movement, and from the outset, they included women in this endeavor (Kassam, 2010: 329). The Hamas, based on the Muslim Brotherhood, considers *da'wa* a main tool for promoting the movement, to which it adds the concept of armed resistance against Israel (embodied in the movement's name - Islamic Resistance Movement (Hamas). When Sheikh Yassin founded his Islamic movement in Gaza in 1970, inspired by the Muslim Brotherhood, he also included women (Kassam: 2010: 329). In 1987, the movement adopted the concept of the armed resistance against Israel. Hamas' policy about women's participation in the da'wa and jihad was expressed in the Hamas Charter of 1988.

THE *DA'WA* OF THE HAMAS AND THE ISLAMIC MOVEMENT IN ISRAEL

The *da'wa* of the *murabitun* and *murabitat* on al-Haram al-Sharif is influenced by the Hamas and by the Islamic Movement in Israel. The role of *da'wa* for the Islamic Movement in Gaza, later the Hamas, launched in mosques in the early 1970s, was to raise awareness among people about understanding their situations. The mosques are direct contact points where people meet preachers and where preachers can send their messages"(Lahlouh, 2010: 14). "*Al-Mujama` al-Islami* (Islamic Center in Gaza) in the early 1970s became the group's main social welfare organization and remains so today. In addition the Islamic Movement carried out *da'wa* activity in mosques as part of their agenda to win more supporters. (Levitt, 2006)

The Islamic Movement in the Gaza Strip realized women's roles in the first stage of the establishment of the Islamic Center Mosque. They recruited women, at mosques and religious classes as well as at universities (Lahlouh, 2010: 14). Miriam Saleh, Hamas' Minister of Women Affairs, spoke about the Hamas women's role in *da'wa.* According to Saleh, "Women can go into any Palestinian house. They can preach, especially women wearing hijabs. Women can also preach at mosques and during religious and social festivities. They can preach at high schools and universities. This is what women have been doing since Hamas' foundation. Women have also contributed to Hamas' winning of the legislative elections in 2006" (interview, 2014).

The policy of Hamas toward Muslim women's role in *da'wa* is expressed in the charter of 1988. Article Twelve of Hamas' Charter stipulates: "From the point of view of the Islamic Resistance Movement, patriotism (*wataniyya*) is part of the religious belief. There is no greater and deeper patriotism than in a situation in which an enemy takes our Muslim land. Then the jihad turns into a religious obligation for every Muslim man or woman. The woman goes out to battle without her husband's permission and the slave without his master's permission."

Article Seventeen of Hamas' Charter stipulates: "In the campaign for liberation, the Muslim woman has a role which no less important than that of the Muslim man because she creates the men. Her role in the guidance and education of the new generation is great. Our enemies also understand this and they believe that if they could educate her and lead her away from Islam, they would win the campaign. Therefore, they invest great efforts in the media, films, and educational materials through their creations - the Zionist organizations, which have different names and forms, such as the Freemasons, the Rotary Clubs, espionage networks and so forth, which are all nests of destruction. These Zionist organizations have huge material resources which enable them to penetrate societies... to fulfill Zionist goals and to spread which serve the enemy. While these organizations are active Islam is missing from the field and foreign to its people. The

Islamic [activists] must fulfill role against the... so that someday Islam will direct the life and liquidates these organizations which are enemies of mankind and Islam."

Article Eighteen stipulates: "Woman in the home of the fighting family, whether she is a mother or a sister, plays the most important role in looking after the family, rearing the children and imbuing them with moral values and thoughts derived from Islam. She has to teach them to perform the religious duties in preparation for the role of fighting awaiting them."

Thus, according to this important document, Muslim women are supposed to participate in the jihad (art. 12) but their role is to be a wife and mother (art. 17, 18). How are these conflicting roles combined by the movement and by the women themselves? Many of the *murabitat*, as we have seen, have already raised their children, while those who still have small children at home, take them to pre-school. The establishment of pre-schools by the Islamist movement undoubtedly enables women to study and work, but here we see that it also enables them to participate in social and political activities. Moreover, as we have seen, the *murabitat* end their day at al-Haram al-Sharif at 14:00 so they can pick up their children and prepare meals before their husbands return from work (Sana, interview, 2015). Moreover, many *murabitat* related that their husbands actually encouraged them to participate in activities on al-Haram al-Sharif. These findings indicate that Palestinian women are able to combine daʿwa and domestic roles.

Ben Shitrit's analysis of Articles 12, 17, and 18 of Hamas' charter argues that the charter gives women a passive role since it treats them as "makers of men," focusing on the biological nature of women as producer of children who would be men and heroes in defense of their homeland and Islam. The idea of women as the biological reproducers of the nation is a recurrent theme in speeches and the movement's publications.

"This role is a personified most ubiquitously in the movement's discourse in the image of Umm Nidal Farhat. Crowned as the Khansa of Palestine, she is the ultimate symbol of maternal contribution and sacrifice, as three of her children died in martyrdom operations while her only remaining living son is imprisoned. Her tragic fame came from a videotape in which she encourages and bids farewell to one of her sons before he embarked on a martyrdom attack on an Israeli settlement in 2002. She has been widely celebrated by Hamas as a role model for the 'pious women of the nation'" (Ben Shitrit, 2016: 75).

Moreover, Ben Shitrit claims that:

> "Women in the house and the family of jihad fighters, whether they are mothers or sisters, carry out the most important duty of caring for the home and raising the children upon the moral concepts and values which derive from Islam and educating their sons to observe the religious injections to preparation for the duty of jihad that is awaiting them" (Ben Shitrit, 2016: 73).

However, Hamas' women play an important role in *da'wa* at universities, mosques, and homes. This was noticeable in Hamas winning of the students' council elections at Birzeit University in 2016 (Hamas Election Campaign, 2016). On the other hand, Hamas' institutions and organizations such as the Shura Council and Hamas' politburo do not give women significant roles, though their female supporters were active in campaigning for Hamas (Bajis, 2013).

The Islamic Movement in Israel also followed the approach of the Muslim Brotherhood toward women - that they can perform *da'wa* to recruit more supporters. In the early years of the Islamic Movement's organizing, women who were mostly wives and family members of the movement's founders played a supportive, but limited role. Their contribution at the time was to encourage their husbands, who spent long days and nights away from home, traveling across the country for their *da'wa* work and spending money out of their own pockets for the sake of the Islamic project. (Ben Shitrit, 2016: 91).

In this respect, Sheikh Sarsour and other founding leaders mention the women in those early days emulated the model of Prophet Muhammad's first wife, Khadija, who supported him when he was struggling to spread his message. Sheikh Ibrahim Sarsour added "after that we noticed that the vast majority of women in those times didn't attend prayers in our mosques, so we began with that. We began to call upon women to come to the mosque, to attend sermons, to attend the Friday sermon for instance, to attend lectures in mosques and in cultural centers, and when we, men, didn't succeed to address women, we came to the conclusion that women can address women better" (Ben Shitrit, 2016: 91).

The Islamic Movement in Israel became aware of the role of women in *daʿwa* at homes, mosques and universities. It starts at home through educating children about the Islamic religion, the proper way to worship, and the right morals. The next step is to target mosques, schools, universities, businesses, factories, and farms. The Islamic Movement in Israel also employs social activities through charitable societies in order to gain more supporters. Social activities include supporting poor and needy families, sick people, and needy students. Because of their social activities, the Hamas and the Islamic Movement in Israel earned people's trust (Al-Hroob, 1999).

Ben Shitrit writes that one of the activities of the Islamic Movement in Israel and creates extensive daʿwa programs such as preaching in homes and mosques for female students and mothers. This was to teach those specific Qurʾanic verses and their interpretation, the stories of the life of the Prophet Muhammad as well as the women who helped him in this period, for example Khadija and Asma'a bint Abi Bakr (Ben Shitrit, 2016).

The leadership of the Islamic Movement in Israel relied on women with strong social relations and those involved in social welfare and who have leadership characteristics. Among the leading women in the *da'wa* activities of the Islamic Movement was the wife of the leader of the movement (Sheikh Ra'ed Salah), Umm Omar (Tal, 2011). The activists in this field preached religious upbringing of children and focused on families' ways of convincing young girls of the significance of wearing hijabs (Tal, 2011). The Movement helped these women to establish specialized societies that looked after women and children such as *Sanad* Mother and Child Association and Muslim Women (*Muslimat*) for Al-Aqsa Association. The later was active in religious and political *da'wa* and had many members (Tal, 2011).

Da'wa on al-Haram al-Sharif

The *murabitun* and *murabitat* conduct *da'wa* at the study circles (*Masatib al-`Ilm*). The *murabitat* started *da'wa* at homes to encourage women to join the *Masatib al-`Ilm* and increase the number of *murabitat* in al-Aqsa Mosque. Safiyah from Silwan (30) told me in an interview that *murabitat* went to houses in neighborhoods to encourage women to take part in *ribat*, explain the importance of *ribat* in Islam, and the importance of al-Aqsa Mosque, and role of *ribat* in stopping Jewish groups from taking over al-Aqsa Mosque. Teachers in the study circles encourage *murabitat* to invite women and girls within their families, including their extended families (*hamula*) to join the *murabitat* at al-Aqsa Mosque (Safiya, interview, September 25, 2015).

Other goals of *da'wa* on al-Haram al-Sharif include reaching out to women and preaching among them the ways of safeguarding themselves by wearing hijabs and *jilbab*s as well as studying the Qur'an, hadith, and raising their children in the teachings of Islam (Sidawi, interview, November 10, 2014). According to *murabitat* leader Khadija Khweis, the hijab for Muslim women is a symbol of Islam, Islamic teachings, piety, and moral liberation. Through the hijab, Muslim women can demonstrate to the world the reality and dynamics of the gender equality within Islam. This in turn, reflects the beauty of Islam at all levels of society: individual, family, and the community (Khweis, interview, July 15, 2015). Another goal is political advocating standing in the face of Jewish groups entering al-Haram al-Sharif (Sidawi, interview, November 10, 2014).

Informal Social Mobilization

In addition to *da'wa*, the Muslim Brotherhood worked through the zakat committees, which gave in-kind and cash aid to the poor and needy families (Lahlouh 2010). They also opened medical centers that provided free medical treatment to poor families. The Muslim Brotherhood also managed to collect donations from internal and external sources to build mosques and Qur'an centers, organize religious book exhibitions and cultural festivals (Lahlouh, 2010: 14). This type of charitable activities and social services has been documented among pious women in Egypt and Lebanon as well (Badran); (Mahmood); (Deeb).

Many West Bank towns, especially Ramallah and al-Bireh, witnessed the foundation of several charitable societies sponsored by Hamas such as al-Huda, al-Khansa, and Islamic society schools that have more classes of religious education than other schools. These societies also give aid to poor and needy people (Jad, 2008: 113).

Social support was among the activities of the women of the Islamic Movement. Such services involved raising money for poor families, visiting sick and disabled people, teaching women, and teaching religious lessons. These women's activities also involved paying visits to towns and organizing meeting with young women as well organizing educational trips.

(Ben Shitrit, 2016: 92).

The *murabitat* on al-Haram al-Sharif also have social goals include caring for the poor, the orphans, collecting donations for needy families whether in the West Bank or Gaza, including Gaza patients who are treated at the Makassed Hospital in Jerusalem. One of the *murabitat's* rank and file named Huda Abu Sninah (50) from Isawiya, told me: "We collect food donated for Gazan patients at the Makassed Hospital. We also provide first aid" (Huda Abu Sninah, interview, July 15, 2015).

Murabitat collect charitable donations (*zakat*) at the end of Ramadan. Muslims believe those who give zakat can expect reward from God in the afterlife, neglecting to give zakat can result in damnation. But where does the money of zakat go? The zakat money goes to needy students, impoverished people, and charitable organization such as the zakat Committee of al-Aqsa. Some of the money also goes to the Islamic Movement in Israel, which is more trusted by worshippers, as I noticed during Ramadan 2015.

Also there are many *murabitat* efforts to help the women during festivals, especially Ramadan, when large number of people numbers prayed on al-Haram al-Sharif. For example, they provided first aid for the older women.

Providing first aid is among the murabitat activities at al-Haram al-Sharif

The social charitable activities of the *murabitat* are informal, which means that they do not have organizations set up for this purpose, like, for instance, the women in Beirut's *Dahiya.* Informal contacts between the women are organized to collect money for a certain family, Gaza families coming to al-Makassed Hospital, poor students, the poor, orphans, etc. One or two of the women take the money collected and bring it to the needy. Two or three women go alone without men accompanying them. Informal charity projects are all women-based.

MOBILIZING WOMEN FOR POLITICAL ACTIVISM

"We are a group of *murabitat* Muslim women who attend masateb al-i'lm to learn. We also stand in the face of the Jews' attempts to take control over al-Aqsa Mosque" (Samiha, interview, July 15, 2015).

Warning message to the women of al-Aqsa:
Women for theTemple organizes a Torah program at al-Aqsa

The mere act of praying or studying at al-Haram al-Sharif is regarded by some leaders and rank and file members of the *murabitat* as political since it strengthens the Muslim presence there. The presence of the *murabitat* on al-Haram al-Sharif also makes them available for political activism against organized groups of Jewish men and women who come to pray there. The founders of the *murabitat* - Ra'ed Salah and Sheikh Kamal al-Khatib - regarded this as the primary purpose of the modern study circles- ." . . to protect al-Aqsa Mosque from Jewish settler groups" (in an interview with Al-Jazeera satellite channel on September 15, 2015). And the *murabitat's* leaders also advocate standing in the face of Jewish groups entering al-Haram al-Sharif as a primary goal (Sidawi, interview, 2015).

Women usually face less restrictions of movement by the Israeli authorities then men do on entering al-Haram al-Sharif. So when the Israeli authorities limit the entrance of men, the women can take over their political activities. The women are not treated better by the Israeli police, which do not differentiate between men and women according to my personal observation. Moreover, a number of *murabitat* leaders and teachers are subject to Israeli police entry restrictions to al-Haram al-Sharif. In many cases, the Israel Police issued orders to stop Aida Sidawi, who is one of the *murabitat's* leaders, from entering al-Haram al-Sharif for three months. The police order also banned Aida Sidawi from being anywhere within 200 meters from al-Haram al-Sharif. The irony of the police order is failing to realize that Sidawi only lived

20 meters away from the site she is banned from (Sidawi, interview - conducted at Sidawi's home, November 10, 2014). Hanadi al-Halwani is a *murabitat* teacher who was also banned from al-Haram al-Sharif for three months (from Ramadan 15 or July 1 to October 2015). Al-Halwani was consequently deprived of the special Ramadan prayer of Taraweeh on al-Haram al-Sharif, Friday prayers, the Id al-Fitr prayer, and Id al-Adha prayer (Al-Halwani, interview, July 20, 2015).

One of the *murabitat's* rank and file whose name is Sahar al-Natsha was also banned from entry to al-Haram al-Sharif for a month (July 15 to August 15, 2015). Khadija Khweis, a *murabitat* leader, received a ban from entering al-Haram al-Sharif by the Israeli police. She was banned from the site from May 20 to October 20, 2015. (Khadija Khweis, interview, conducted outside the walls of al-Haram al-Sharif, August 23, 2015) (See photo).

Khadija Khweis banned from entry to al-Haram al-Sharif

Agroup of women banned from intering in al-Haram al-Sharif

This did not deter them and the blacklisted *murabitat* are distributed at the gates of Al-Aqsa Mosque to yell *Allahu Akbar* in the face of Jewish groups as they leave the area. They also organized prayer for women outside of the gate, in the sight of passers by. *Murabitat* women were also arrested. Charitable people who support the Islamic Movement in Israel provide financial support to *murabitat* detained by the Israeli authorities.

Israeli Border Police arrest one of the murabitat

The political aspect of visiting al-Haram al-Sharif is evident to women as soon as they arrive in the morning when the Israeli police take the identity cards of the *murabitat* upon entry into al-Haram al-Sharif area, patrol the area, and take pictures of the *murabitat.* This is emphasized when the Jewish groups arrive with heavy police guards. At this point, other Muslim women's activities stop, and the activists follow the Jews around yelling *Allahu Akbar* and *Khaybar Khaybar ya Yahud...*" The Khaybar chant refers to a famous battle of Muhammad and his followers against the Jews who cultivated the oasis.

The zealousness of the *murabitat* is shown when they erect a temporary barrier between the Jewish prayer groups and the Dome of the Rock, where the Holy Temple was believed to have stood. They raise a five-meter long cover between the Jewish groups and the Dome of the Rock when the groups start praying in the vicinity of the mosque. The cover acts as a barrier between the Jewish worshippers and the mosque. The significance of the place where Jewish worshippers perform religious rituals is that they believe that it was the place where the Temple once stood. This act sends a message to the Jewish worshippers: You may not pray here and you will not take over al-Haram al-Sharif (A *murabitat* member, interview, August 2015). The *murabitat* also participate in political demonstrations and carry out public relations through the media aimed at the Arab and Muslim world, according to one of their leaders, to send a message to Arabs and Muslims that Israel *bullies* Palestinian women and has no respect for them.

There are two ways of mobilizing women for demonstrations on al-Haram al-Sharif. The first involves women who know about developments in events on the news and decide to go to prove that this site is for Muslims only. The second involves women who are called upon by leaders of Islamic movements to take part in activism in the holy site.

For public relations, activists used social media such as Facebook, as well as news channels, and material such as photos of funerals of people killed in the intifada, to urge women to go to al-Haram al-Sharif and to publicize activities. This gave the activism wider Palestinian context since it involved non-*murabitat* women to take action in Jerusalem and reflect the Palestinian identity of the city. The *murabitat* are photographed while confronting the Jewish groups on al-Haram al-Sharif and while being attacked by Israeli police. I held a number of interviews with a number of *murabitat* over the telephone. *Murabitat* carry cell-phones and take pictures or make videos of activities on al-Haram al-Sharif. They have a Facebook profile, which is updated regularly by a number of the *murabitat* and journalists who operate on al-Haram al-Sharif. Liwa Abu Rumeilla is a journalist from Jerusalem. She works for Palestine TV and has a Facebook profile, which she updates with videos from al-Haram al-Sharif. Her videos often go viral. The *murabitat* send messages to Palestinian society as well as the Arab and Islamic Worlds about the threats surrounding al-Aqsa Mosque, including the destruction and Judaization of the compound, as well as the way Muslim women are mistreated by Israeli police. These messages have a direct impact on the social and religious traditions of the society. Consequently, the messages contributed to the breaking out of the al-Quds intifada in 2015. Moreover, a number of Palestinian youths carried out attacks on Israeli targets to revenge the *murabitat* and their ill-treatment by Israeli troops.

Women who come to al-Haram al-Sharif are exposed to many conflicting political and religious groups. They witness the entry of Jewish groups to the area and the actions taken by the Israeli police. They become aware of conflicts and political activities. Hence, they may become supporters of Hamas and/or the Islamic Movement in Israel. Female worshippers may be able to see the contributions the Islamic Movement in Israel has made by setting up the study circles.

On September 9, 2015, Israel National News website posted that the Israeli Defense Minister Moshe Ya'alon, signed an order "declaring the groups of Islamists (the *murabitun* and the *murabitat*) who regularly harass Jews on the Temple Mount... as illegal." Ya'alon also stated that "the activists regularly riot on the Mount, curse, shout, and throw various objects at the Jews who ascend the Mount, and sometimes attack police as well" (http://www.israelnationalnews.com/News/News.aspx. 9/9/2015).

One day after the signing of the order by the Israeli Defense Minister, which rendered the *murabitat* as illegal, I interviewed a number of *murabitat* on al-Haram al-Sharif and asked them about it. The reaction of the *murabitat* was that "we are here to stay. We shall defend al-Aqsa Mosque. We shall prevent Jewish settlers from taking over al-Haram al-Sharif. We do not recognize the order of Ya'alon. We shall continue to worship on al-Haram al-Sharif" (Khweis, interview, September 10, 2015). In addition the Israel authorities' oppressive measures treated men and women similarly by placing women under custody. The Israeli authorities fired Khadija Khweis and Latifa Abdulatif from the education system for their relations with the murabitat. A number of murabitat were also denied state benefits for taking part in the murabitat movement (Murabitat, interviews, 2015).

I asked in my interviews with the *murabitat* about their political orientation. They first denied affiliation to any political movements. However, they admitted having connections with the Islamic Movement in Israel and with sheikh Ra'ed Salah. They are also connected to Al-Aqsa Association, which was created by the Islamic Movement in Israel for the purpose of protecting al-Aqsa Mosque from Israeli plans. However, *murabitat* admitted no connection with the Salafis, Sufis, or Hizb al-Tahrir. Zeina, who is one of the *murabitat*, denied any connections between the Palestinian Authority and the *murabitat* movement. She said to me: "We [the *murabitat*] are not connected with the P.A. We refuse the grants they give to people to do pilgrimage to Mecca and Medina." Zeina failed to answer my question about *murabitat's* connection with Hamas. (Zeina, interview, 2015).

The Israeli police continue to take punitive measures against the *murabitat* including detention and imposing fines, according to Aida Sidawi, one of the *murabitat* who is banned from al-Haram al-Sharif (Sidawi, interview, November 10, 2014). A number of the *murabitat* were detained at the Ramla prison. Sidawi was detained once and was taken to court. She told the judge that she had been detained because she had shouted *Allahu Akbar* in al-Haram al-Sharif area. The judge freed her since the law did not criminalize such an act. Khadija Khweiswas fined by the court 1,500 NIS for the same activity. However, she was bailed out by an unknown person, which means there is a movement behind the *murabitat.* The *murabitat* are taken immediately to court when they get arrested. Sidawi said in an interview at her home, which is located in the Old City of Jerusalem ten meters away from al-Aqsa:

"We are the *murabitat.* We started in 2010 with Muslim women from Israel proper. We were more than 1,000 women. We participated in the study circles where we studied Qur᾿an and Hadith. Now the Israeli authorities consider us illegal; consequently, the number of the *murabitat* had dropped to 300. There are 55 *murabitat* on Israel's police blacklist. However, for us the blacklist is a gold list. *Murabitat* used to get paid a thousand shekels a month. A preacher earned 1,500 shekels a month. We don't get paid these days. We do not need to get paid. We come to al-Aqsa to pray. Al-Aqsa is in my heart. Every Muslim is obliged to protect al-Aqsa. It is the least I can do. The Jews want to take over al-Aqsa Mosque/al-Haram al-Sharif. We stand as the guardians of al-Aqsa to protect it from the Jews. We are guardians for the sake of God. This is a gift from God" (Sidawi, interview, November 10, 2014).

The *murabitat* chant Hamas songs, and praise the activities of Hamas against the occupation. This is all taking place under the nose of Israeli police. That means that the Islamic Movement and Hamas are working on al-Haram al-Sharif together through women (and men). For instance, on Child's Day, which the Islamic Movement in Israel organized in 2014 (the Islamic Movement organizes this festival annually), female protesters on al-Haram al-Sharif chanted Hamas' songs during the protest and raised Hamas flags.

Researcher with Mariam Saleh, a senior Hamas official

The *murabitat* also meet female political leaders from the Islamic Movement in Israel. Some Jerusalem women suffered arrests by Israeli police on December 8, 2015, for being part of the Islamic Movement.

Sometimes *murabitat* are subpoenaed at al-*Qishla* police station at the Jaffa Gate to collect their identity cards (see subpoena). Blacklisted *murabitat* are not allowed entry into al-Haram al-Sharif. For instance, 64-year-old East Jerusalem resident Zeinat Aweda al-Jilad, an activist in the all-female *murabitat* group, from the Jerusalem neighborhood of Al-

Isawiya, was arrested by Israeli police for suspected ties with the northern branch of the Islamic Movement on December 8, 2015. She spent three days in Ramla prison and five days house arrest. She was banned from al-Haram al-Sharif for 15 days. (Zeinat, interview, December 19, 2015) The Israeli Prime Minister's Office describes [the *murabitat*] as "a salaried group of activists aimed at initiating provocations on the Temple Mount. This action significantly raised tensions on the Temple Mount. A large portion of the recent attacks were carried out against the backdrop of this incitement and propaganda" (*Haaretz*, English edition, November 17, 2015).

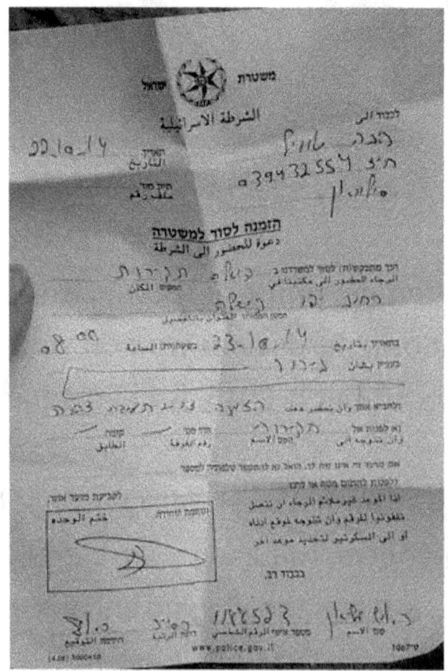
משטרת ישראל
الشرطة الإسرائيلية
הזמנה לסור למשטרה
دعوة للحضور الى الشرطة
www.police.gov.il

Israeli police: Subpoena a murabitat member (Hiba Al Tawil)

One of the murabitat *praying at an Israeli detention center*

The *murabitat* gained more support from Palestinian society after the breakout of the al-Quds intifada in October, 2015. Since then, they are treated with much respect and even honored for their activities.

The attitude of other Islamist political movements to al-Haram al-Sharif and *murabitat* differ. Abu-Sarah, one of the leaders of Hizb al-Tahrir in Jerusalem told me that the Hizb al-Tahrir movement did not encourage its female supporters to take part in the *murabitat* activities. However, Hizb al-Tahrir is not against such activities. They consider the *murabitat* activities insufficient. Abu Sarah said, "We need more activities. We shall wait for the caliphate's army, not the Islamic State, to stop the Jews from taking over al-Haram al-Sharif."

Female supporters of the Salafis come only for daʿwa. A Salafis leader from Anata, near Jerusalem, said Salafis did not support the *murabitat* activities, nor do they recognize them. Salafis believe that *murabitat* activities may actually cause more harm than good to al-Haram al-Sharif such as causing access restrictions to the area. *Murabitat* women are exposed to Salafi ideas in the study circles such as extremely conservative interpretations of the Qurʾan on gender issues. I witnessed only one *murabitat* teacher who wore a *niqab*. Her name was Umm Huzayfa. She taught *murabitat* how to recite and interpret the Qurʾan. Additionally, a few *murabitat* wear a *niqab*.

Observing political power of Hamas on al-Haram al-Sharif, I found that Hamas is more in control of the compound than before and has more supporters. This is obvious when looking at the Hamas banners and slogans on al-Haram al-Sharif. Hizb al-Tahrir has significant presence on al-Haram al-Sharif, which can be seen from its flags and banners. The Jordanian authority controls the *Awqaf* services (security guards and schools) on al-Haram al-Sharif. The Palestinian Authority (PA) wants to take over *murabitat* activities through providing subsidized *hajj* and *umrah* (pilgrimage) services. However, a number of the *murabitat*, who are probably Hamas supporters, refuse to be under the PA. In any case, the PA does not have any political power on al-Haram al-Sharif.

When a major event or development occurs, such as the kidnapping and murder of Muhammad Abu Khdeir by Jewish extremists on Ramadan 14, 2014 or July 11, 2014 regular women and *murabitat* came to al-Haram al-Sharif to protest and show solidarity with the families of the victim. For example, non-*murabitat* women took part in a massive protest in front of the Dome of the Rock, which I witnessed, to condemn the killing of Abu Khdeir and the Israeli occupation (see photo).

Non murabitat-Fatah banner with picture of Muhammad Abu Khdeir during protest on al-Haram al-Sharif

I participated in this demonstration with non-*murabitat* women. The *murabitun* also send messages similar to those sent by *murabitat*. (See photo).

Political activities of murabitat include sending a message to the Islamic world

Conclusion

The Islamic Movement in Israel became aware of the importance of the role of women in *daʿwa* to spread the ideology of the Movement and increase its supporters. These women were mainly those who were involved in social welfare and enjoy leadership characteristics. They were contacted by the Movement. The *daʿiyat* of the Islamic Movement in Israel were educated and charismatic women. Among the leading female figures of the Islamic Movement is Sheikh Ra'ed Salah's wife.

Daʿwa in general is not restricted to men. Women can take part in such activity. This has been seen throughout history where women (in the Muslim Brotherhood in Egypt, for instance) have played important roles in *daʿwa*. This has been realized by the leadership of the Islamic Movement in Israel, which involved women in *daʿwa* at schools, colleges, mosques, homes, and associations. *Daʿwa* focused on social aspects of women's Islamic life including wearing the hijab as an attire that safeguards the women's respect and makes her more marriageable.

Daʿwa does not stop at the Shariʿa lessons, it also used for political purposes to recruit more supporters for the Islamic Movement using different means, most importantly lessons in homes, mosques, market places, and even on buses as well as during social events. Muslim women and rank and file members of the *murabitat* who may come to al-Haram al-Sharif to pray and study experience the political dimension of their activities on a daily basis. In the study circles, they are recruited to daʿwa proselytizing, social activities and political action.

The *daʿwa* in the study circles aims to bring more women to al-Haram al-Sharif and to strengthen the *murabitat*. The *murabitat* do not, however, have formal daʿwa institutions, nor do they travel long distances to expand the movement like the women of Hamas, the Islamic Movement in Israel, or their counterparts in other parts of the Arab world. The *murabitat* do learn about the role of women in Islam and in the religious national struggle which they may pass along to other women.

However, *daʿwa* is not restricted to the study circles. *Murabitat* took *daʿwa* to neighborhoods and extended families to invite women to join *ribat* and explain its importance in the protection of al-Aqsa Mosque. These actions were instructed by teachers at the study circles in order to recruit more and more *murabitat*. The objective of *daʿwa* on al-Haram al-Sharif is the spread of Islamic teachings concerning women including the Islamic dress and education and raising of children.

The charitable and social service activities of the *murabitat* are informal, not organized as that of movements of pious women in Egypt, Lebanon, Israel and Palestine. Women praying or studying on al-Haram al-Sharif are mobilized for political action when they interrupt their religious activities to combat the Jewish groups that come to pray at the Temple Mount. These actions are documented and disseminated by public relations activities that enhance the image of the *murabitat.* The *murabitat* took over the roles of Muslim men and the *murabitun* when these were blocked by the Israeli authorities. Eventually, *murabitat* leaders were arrested and *murabitat* were banned from entering al-Haram al-Sharif. The Israeli authorities state that this was necessary because the *murabitat* continued their struggle from prison and from outside al-Haram al-Sharif, gaining even more recognition. In these political actions, they were supported financially and morally by the Islamic Movement in Israel and the Hamas.

7. Voices of the Murabitat and Perceptions of the Movement

The voices of women members of political movements like the *murabitat* are rarely heard, so it is extremely valuable to hear what their views are. Why did they join the *murabitat* and what did they learn? What did they learn about Jews? How did this experience affect them? How do they view their role as Muslim women in Palestinian society? Moreover, in this study, the views of these not very educated homemakers who are rank and file members of the *murabitat* are compared to the more educated and more sophisticated *murabitat's murabitat's* teachers and leaders. Finally the views of all of these women are compared to the opinions of male leaders.

THE *MURABITAT* SPEAK

The *murabitat's* rank and file related that they came to al-Haram al-Sharif for a variety of religious, psychological, social, economic and political reasons. Rabiha, one of the *murabitat's* rank and file (interviewed on September 20, 2015), said that she came to the site of al-Haram al-Sharif "to be in a place not far from God; to feel close to Prophet Muhammad who did the Mi'raj from here.' Al-Mi'raj is, according to the Qur'anic verse (17:1), the miraculous ascension from al-Aqsa Mosque to the heavens. The verse also describes the "Prophet Muhammad's

Night Journey (the Isra) on the winged steed Buraq from the Sacred Mosque [in Mecca] to the Farthest (Al Aqsa) Mosque (Reiter, 2008: 27).

Furthermore, al-Haram al-Sharif is a place far from the everyday social problems of the *murabitat's* rank and file such as bickering among the daughters-in-law and neighbors gossiping. (Rabiha, interview, September 20, 2015)

There are psychological reasons for being on al-Haram al-Sharif as well. In one incident, I asked one of the murabitat about her feelings when inside the holy site. The first reaction of the lady was that she started crying. She said that "I have problems with my two daughters-in-law. They do not respect me. I am all alone at home but when I come to al-Aqsa Mosque, I feel relaxed. It is all peaceful and quiet here. There are no problems here. The murabitat respect me more than my children and daughters-in-law. I study the Qur᾿an and the Hadith for more information about my religion. I have murabitat friends. We discuss my problems at home. This makes me feel more at ease and gives me comfort. I forget all problems at home with my daughters-in-law. I would rather stay here than stay at home." Because of these reasons the murabitat spend time on al-Haram al-Sharif learning about Islam, socializing, and protesting Jewish groups' presence there. For them, it is a place to go out to rather than to stay at home all the time.

The Murabitat feel that they are in touch with God while being inside the site. Psychologically, they feel satisfied and at peace and they believe that God is more likely to answer their prayers. Some women say that after they go to al-Haram al-Sharif, they are socially honored by families and neighbors, including men. Religious education also widens women's knowledge of Islam.

The *murabitat's* rank and file feel that they are in a holy place so they obtain the *fada'il* (virtues) of al-Haram al-Sharif (Leila, one of the *murabitat's* rank and file, interview, July 27, 2015). The tradition goes that one prayer on al-Haram Al-Sharif is equivalent to 500 prayers in another place" (Reiter, 2008: 32).

One woman, Rabiha (48) from Silwan, who is a rank and file member of the *murabitat*, narrates:

> "My neighbor told me about the study circles at al-Aqsa Mosque and she invited me to attend a number of lessons. The idea was to my liking. I felt comfortable inside while attending the study circles on Islam, Qur'an, and Sunnah. There are many problems at home with my daughters-in-law. Attending the study circles keeps me away from all problems. It improves my knowledge and understanding of Islamic religion and Qur'an" (Interview, October 2, 2015)

Some *murabitat* women also said that:

"Inside the site, all the time, we feel that we commune with God by more *tasbih* [recurring expression of short sentences glorifying God using fingers or beads]. Psychologically, we feel good because we have no problems while there. It gives us hope that God will give us what we ask for. We are here to learn about our religion and to establish social connections to help find future spouses for the children. We feel that it is better to come here than to stay at home." (Elham al-Jubeh, interview, September 20, 2015).

Elham Al-Jubeh meant by "it is better to come here than to stay home" that al-Haram Al-Sharif was a place to learn the Qur᾿an and Hadith, to worship God, and to socialize. These are advantage that cannot be found at home.

One of the *murabitat* from Beit Hanina, who preferred to remain anonymous, told me that:

"my sister is one of the *murabitat.* She told me to go to the study circles, which I did. My relationship with al-Aqsa was purely religious; for *ribat* and *hasanat* [points earned for good deeds]. *Ribat* stays with me until Judgment day. I am here to learn Qur᾿an and Sunnah. I don't take part in actions with political nature. I leave after study circles end" (Interview with one of the *murabitat,* November 29, 2015).

Some of the *murabitat* talked about the benefits of *ribat* in Islam according to Qur᾿an and Hadith:

"Our actions and *ribat* will give us *hasanat,* for example: Suad (50) from the Old City of Jerusalem, told me that, "*ribat* in al-Aqsa Mosque brings me closer to Allah. It gives me *hasanat* (good points) and wipes away the *sayi'at* (bad points). It makes me go to paradise. Al-Aqsa Mosque is the place of ascension of Prophet Muhammad to heaven" (Suad, interview, September 27, 2015).

Aya (30) from Kafr `Aqab, emphasized:

"I wanted to learn new ideas about Qur'an and Sunnah. My husband advised me to join the *murabitat* and to attend the study circles. My husband is one of the *murabitun* in al-Aqsa Mosque. He is 30 years old. I attended the study circles to learn more about the Qur'an and the Sunnah" (Interview, June 28, 2015).

Some of *murabitat* admitted that they came to earn money, according to Umm Sa'id Shaludi from Silwan (55). She told me that "some *murabitat* stopped being *murabitat* and stopped attending the study circles when their salaries stopped" (Interview, September 20, 2015).

They also come to al-Haram al-Sharif to defend it. They consider such defense as a religious obligation (or *fard*, like praying).When asked about her motivation to attend al-Haram al-Sharif, Umm Muhammad al-Natshe (45) from Beit Hanina, one of the *murabitat* activists said:

> "I came to the *murabitat* because women from my family or neighbors recruited me. My sister is one of the *murabitat's* leaders. She asked me to join the *murabitat*. She talked about the importance of *ribat*, the *hasanat* earned in *ribat* and preventing the Jews from taking

> over Al-Aqsa Mosque. These, according to my sister, were actions to be taken in life to win Paradise. My sister's argument was powerful. I attended the study circles and I resisted Jewish presence in al-Aqsa Mosque. Now I am on the blacklist" (Muhammad, Interview, November 29, 2015).

In sum, many of the *murabitat's* rank and file do not initially come to al-Haram al-Sharif for political reasons, yet some are motivated by ideological conviction.

The *murabitat* reported that they learned the basics of Islam for everyday life. They felt that they gained new information about Islam which made them more modest and better Muslim women at home in treating their husbands and their children. They learnt how to solve problems and how to help their children be good to their parents as indicated in verse 23 of Surat Alisra'a (Chapter 17 of the Qur'an), which reads "Thy Lord hath decreed, that ye worship none save Him, and (that ye show) kindness to parents. If one of them or both of them to attain old age with thee, say not 'Fie'unto them nor repulse them, but speak unto them a gracious word." (The *murabitat* also learnt that taking interest on money lent or borrowed is forbidden in Islam. Hence, they encourage their spouses to stay away from paying or taking interests on their money. They consider wearing hijabs and jilbabs as good conduct and in line with the teachings of the Qur'an.

Elham al-Jubeh (43) from Beit Hanina, told me that:

"We talk about social issues. We talk about our problems. We exchange views about solutions to problems. We talk about the fact that fewer girls get married and high dowries as a reason that deters men from marriage. A suggestion to reduce this issue was to reduce dowries and ask the Mufti to discuss the issue of marriage and reduction of dowry in the Friday prayer's speech so that many people would know about it. Inheritance is another issue we discuss" (Elham Al-Jubeh, interview, September 17, 2015).

Amna (40) from Kufur Aqab, said:

> "I especially liked the stories about *Sahaba* and *Sahabiyat* which showed what women did in Muhammad's time... I have joined the *murabitat* to study the Qur'an and learn about the life of the Prophet. I admire the roles of the *Sahabiyat* in Islam such as *al-Sayida* Khadija, the wife of Prophet Muhammad and Asma'a bint Abi Bakr. *Sahabiyat* are my role models and leaders in the defense of al-Aqsa." (Amna, interview, September 6, 2015).

Omm Rami Al-Kilani (50) from the Old City of Jerusalem, said:

> "I joined the study circles when they started in 2010 to teach Islamic religion and education, ethics, Prophet's life, caliphs and their just policies. I want to teach my children about Islam and ethics so that they can be respected in the Palestinian community and to have a good chance finding spouses...I learned to respect my husband and to obey him according to Islam. The Prophet SAS said, "I looked into jahanam (hell), and saw most in there were women who had disobeyed their husbands" (Omm Rami Al-Kilani, interview, July 5, 2015).

Nuha (50) from the Old City of Jerusalem, said

> "I joined the study circles to study the Qur'an and the Sunnah, especially the sayings of the Prophet. I learned to obey my husband, look after him, and not to upset him. The Prophet says: 'If it had not been for polytheism, I would have asked a woman to worship her husband'. This means that a husband must be obeyed in sickness and in health" (Nuha, interview, September 24, 2015).

Thus, one of the important things that the *murabitat* felt they learned in the study circles were religious texts and models supporting patriarchy. They did not mention some of the knowledgeable and politically active women from the time of the Prophet, such as 'Aisha bint Abi Bakr, or sayings of the Prophet supporting women's learning or attendance at communal prayers.

Most of the *murabitat's* rank and file were housewives, so their contact with Jews was limited. At al-Haram al-Sharif, they learned about the Jewish holidays based on the behavior of the Jews who visited there.

> "We learn that women and men must defend al-Haram al-Sharif from the Jews. It is an honor to defend the site now and in the afterlife. We feel like guardians of al-Aqsa and Islam. It is a Jihad. While Israeli security

> forces keep arresting men, we have to take the role of defending al-Aqsa. *Sahabiyat* like Umm Amarah, Asmaa bint Abu Bakr, and Sumayyah Umm Ammar would have done the same thing." (*Murabitat*, interviews, 2014-2015).

Huda (50) from Isawiya, said:

"I know that Jews pay more visits to al-Aqsa Mosque on Mondays. They pay more visits on Thursdays, before the weekend. They come in smaller number on Sundays, the beginning of the week. They do not come during their weekend (Saturdays). Jewish women come in larger number during Jewish holidays such as Rosh Hashanah and Sukkot. We are distanced from al-Aqsa Mosque during Jewish holidays" (Huda, interview, July 15, 2016).

They also learned new things about Jewish religion such as keeping away from the holiest places. (Hiba Al-Taweel, interview, September 15, 2015). "We are afraid that their activities [of the Jews] would lead to changing the status quo and the destruction of al-Aqsa Mosque and the Dom of Rock." (*Murabitat*, interviews, 2015). On the other hand, one of the *murabitat* told me that she had seen a Jewish woman praying; her reaction was: "Look she believes in God" (Interview, August 25, 2015).

In short, the *Murabitat's* rank and file on al-Haram al-Sharif learn some very negative and even inaccurate things about Jews and their experience teaches them that Jews are protected by the Israeli authorities. At least one woman, however, was surprised to learn that the Jewish women were as devoted to God as they were.

The *murabitat's* rank and file spoke about how the experience affected them and how they felt. Some said that it gave them social prestige in family and in neighborhood for themselves and for their children. Sana' Al-Rajabi told me that "Our presence and our *ribat* at al-Aqsa Mosque and attending the study circles gave us [*murabitat*] great status among family, neighbors, and the Jerusalem community. Everyone respects us. My husband, children, and neighbors respect me." In a comparison between *murabitat* with working women, al-Rajabi said, "Everyone respects us as *murabitat.* Women who work at schools or hospitals do not have the same respect. They are only respected for their salaries. We, the *murabitat,* are more respected and are a source of pride for the Palestinian community (Sana, interview, November 3, 2015).

Ribat makes *murabitat* feel strong. When they confront Jewish visitors, they have to physically stand up and face them. This gives *murabitat* the strength and will to play the role of a guard protecting al-Haram al-Sharif. Part of this strength is fed by the respect *murabitat* gain from the society for being *murabitat.* Moreover, going to al-Haram al-Sharif sometimes requires a degree of social independence. When I interviewed Zeina Abu Amr about the *murabitat,* she said, "We are a group that studies Shariʿa. We are a small community of teachers, students, leaders and guardians that protect al-Aqsa. Hence, we have a degree of social independence in many activities such as having breakfast together, collecting money for poor families in Jerusalem, and visiting sick Gazans at hospital" (Zeina Abu Amr, interview, November 29, 2015).

Murabitat are aware of the important role they play in society. Sana al-Rajbi was very clear about the role of the murabitat and the role of Muslim women when she made a comparison between murabitat and secular women in the Palestinian society. She said "Women can do important things rather than just stay at home. I have an honor that working secular women such as nurses or teachers do not have." (Sana, interview, 2015).

The *murabitat's* rank and file seem to accept the role of Muslim women in Palestinian society, and think they are treated fairly compared to men. In their actions, these women may, however, disobey the roles of women according to the Shariʿa. "As Muslim women, we follow the Shariʿa. Inheritance law allows a woman to receive half of what a man receives. Women accept this as fair. However, they relinquish their inheritance to their brothers either out of fear or kindness" (Ilham al-Ju`be, interview, September 17, 2015).

Umm Huthaifa (50) from the Old City of Jerusalem, told me:

> "My husband is concerned that the Jews might beat me up and detain me. He is concerned about losing his

> job in Israel as punishment for being married to a *murabita* who had been banned from al-Aqsa Mosque four times. Hence, he disagrees with my presence at al-Aqsa Mosque. However, I still join the *murabitat* and attend study circles" (Umm Huthaifa, interview, November 2015).

This is ironic considering that they are taught in the study circles the importance of obedience to the husband. However, Islamic tradition argues that obedience needs to be within the boundaries allowed in Shariʿa. For instance, verse 36 of Chapter 33 of the Qur'an states "A believing man or a believing woman, shall not, when God and His Messenger decide a matter, have their own decision in the matter."

Hence Islam made the husband the protector and maintainer of the wife and gave him the responsibility of heading the household. This means that it is obligatory for her to obey him. Allah says (interpretation of the meaning):

> "Men are the protectors and maintainers of women, because Allah has made one of them to excel the other, and because they spend (to support them) from their means" (al-Nisaa' 4:34)

The interviews I held with the *murabitat* throughout 2015 show that the *murabitat* felt content about the topics they studied at al-Haram al-Sharif. They said they wanted to gain new information about Islam. The *murabitat* said they wanted to do more for the benefit of Islam and that they felt the holy site enhanced their spiritual feelings. All in all, the *murabitat* felt that the study circles made them better Muslim women at home since they learnt how to treat their husband and the children and how to be modest. They learnt how to solve problems and how to help their children be good to their parents as indicated in verse 23 of *Surat Alisra'a* (Chapter 17 of the Qur᾿an), which reads:

> "Thy Lord hath decreed, that ye worship none save Him, and (that ye show) kindness to parents. If one of them or both of them to attain old age with thee, say not 'Fie' unto them nor repulse them, but speak unto them a gracious word."

The *murabitat* also learnt that taking interest on money lent or borrowed is forbidden in Islam. Hence, they encourage their spouses to stay away from taking interest on a loan or borrowing money. They consider wearing hijabs and *jilbab*s as good conduct and in line with the teachings of the Qur᾿an.

As for the role of women in the *murabitat* movement, the *murabitat's* rank and file women say: "We need leaders to organize us in many groups or study circles in many places on al-Haram al-Sharif. The leaders can help us choose the lessons or issues to be taught to the *murabitat.* Female leaders can be like male leaders by coordinating activities and connections with the Islamic Movement in Israel, which helps us in all of our activities" (Umm Rabia'a, interview, August 2, 2015).

Asked for information about the movement or permission to join them, rank and file members referred me to their leaders. Similarly, the *murabitat's* rank and file did not talk to the press but refer queries to Zeina Abu Amr –a *murabitat* leader- for any statements about the *murabitat* (July 15, 2015). Nevertheless, the *murabitat* are convinced that *w*omen should only lead other women.

The *murabitat's* rank and file fear the reaction of the Israeli authorities. They are less educated than their leaders; hence, they do not discuss political or religion issues related to women and women's rights that the Shariʿa grants. Zeina Abu Amr, one of the *murabitat's* rank and file, said to me in an interview, "Strong women can face the Israel Police and talk to the media. I fear that the police may find out about this interview" (Zeina Abu Amr, interview, September 20, 2015).

THE MURABITAT'S MURABITAT'S TEACHERS AND LEADERS SPEAK

There is a degree of overlap between teachers and leaders because all of the leaders also teach and no less important: some of the teachers go on to become leaders. For the teachers, teaching is an important step to becoming a leader. Umm Muhammad said, "I am a counselor at a school. I want to be a leader in the future" (Interview with Umm Muhammad, September, 20, 2015).

For the teachers, teaching is an important step to becoming a leader. Omm Muhammad said, "I am a counselor at a school. I want to be a leader in the future." (Interview with Omm Muhammad and researcher's notes, September, 20, 2015)

Nevertheless, the teachers and leaders think the most important goal of teaching is to lead the Murabitat to face Jewish groups on al-Haram al-Sharif, to increase the number of *murabitat* to support Hamas and the Islamic Movement in Israel and to impart knowledge of "true Islam" among women, according to their ideology in the *tafseer* (interpretation) of the Qur'an. (Khadija Khweis, interview, July 15, 2015).

Murabitat leaders related that after Hamas won the elections 2006, they saw an opportunity for leadership in the Hamas government of 2006. Hanadi al-Halawani told me that she could, as a Muslim woman, take part in the protests against Jewish groups' visits to al-Haram al-Sharif and be a leader in the Palestinian society like Mariam Saleh, the minister of women's affairs in Hamas government (Hanadi, interview, September 20, 2015).

The *murabitat* come to al-Haram al-Sharif every day according to schedule. The schedule sets the time and place of the *murabitat* presence on al-Haram al-Sharif. The blacklisted *murabitat* (those on the blacklist of Israeli police) stay outside al-Haram al-Sharif since they are not allowed in. They stay at different locations near the gates of al-Haram al-Sharif. However, most of the *murabitat* are found inside the holy site at different locations in order to be ready to face the Jewish groups who enter the site. They stay in touch via mobile phones to coordinate activities.

Some *murabitat* had been student leaders at universities before graduation, and had also practiced *da'wa.* Khadija Khweis told me in November 2014 – during one of my earliest interviews with *murabitat*- that the reason she had become a *murabitat* leader and on what authority: "I have the expertise needed for leading. I was a student leader at Hebron University. I organize *murabitat's* activities in confronting Jewish groups' visits. I also have good connections" (Khadija Khweis, interview, November 5, 2014). Clearly she has a sense of her own skills and ability to lead compared to the rank and file members.

Similarly, Latifa Abdulatif showed the same self-confidence when she said: "I led female students at Al-Najah University. I knew Hamas' leaders from the study circles on al-Haram al-Sharif. I worked as math teacher with the Israeli Education Ministry but I lost that job after becoming a *murabitat* leader" (Latifa Abdulatif, interview, December 20, 2014). Being a *murabitat* leader is a social advantage; it brings honor and respect to the leaders and their families, according to *murabitat* leaders such as Aida Sidawi, interview at Aida Sidawi's home, November 10, 2014).

According to Latifa Abdulatif, *murabitat* leaders had contacts with male leaders during their college years (Latifa Abdulatif, interview, November 20, 2014). Some leading *murabitat* are married to *murabitun* leaders such as Zeina Abu Amr whose husband, Jamal Abu Amr, is himself a leading member of the *murabitun* (Zeina Abu Amr, interview, September 20, 2015).

The teachers and leaders think the most important goal of teaching is imparting knowledge of "true Islam" to women. For leaders, teaching also helps to organize *murabitat* for political actions. If Jewish groups enter al-Haram al-Sharif during the study circles, lessons are stopped and students are told to chase the Jewish groups with *Allahu Akbar* cries. (Latifa Abdulatif, Hanadi al-Halwani, and Khadija Khweis). Latifa Abdulatif told me: "We teach the *murabitat* in the study circles to protect al-Haram al-Sharif and to defend it against the Jews who wish to destroy it" (Abdulatif, interview, December 20, 2014).

Other *murabitat* leaders' political goals, which are behind the teaching, include increasing and supporting the Islamic movement against the secular parties such as the PA. Hanadi al-Halawani said that *murabitat's murabitat's* teachers participated in study circles for political purposes such as increasing the supporters for the Islamic Movement in Israel against the PA and the secular parties. (Hanadi al-Halawani, interview, July 30, 2015).

Murabitat leaders aim for political goals in their teaching including *da'wa* about the importance of *ribat* and the connection between al-Aqsa and Islam and to increase the number of *murabitat* in al-Aqsa Mosque (Hanadi, interview, July 30, 2015). Other political goals include the support for the Islamic Movement in Israel and its activities on al-Haram al-Sharif. (Khadija Khweis, interview, July15, 2015).

The teachers and leaders are much more political than the participants. The *murabitat's murabitat's* teachers and leaders deny the rights of Jews on site. Khadija Khweis and Hanadi al-Halawani say that there are no religious rights for Jews in the holy site; it is only for Muslims. (Khweis and al-Halawani, interview, July 30, 2015). The teachers said that Jews have no connection to al-Haram al-Sharif and the proof is that they do not know where the *Bet haMikdash* is.

Murabitat leaders also hold traditional Islamic views about Jews. Khadija Khweis said "Jews are not to be trusted. Jewish tribes of Medina violated the treaty with Prophet Muhammad and became allies with the infidels against him though he had neighborly relationships with them. The Jews did not obey the Prophets so they did many evil things. They were evil toward the Prophet Muhammad; they threw garbage at his house; they broke their treaty, they were liars, they wanted to kill him." Samiha Shaheen told me that "many Jews try to pray on al-Haram al-Sharif in groups. They sometimes come as tourists. I saw the Waqf security guards trying to stop them from praying" (Samiha Shaheen, interview, September 20, 2015).

Murabitat's Murabitat's teachers feel that they have important religious and political duties. They were proud of what they did and that their actions earned them the respect of the community and the families. Zeina said: My husband, family, and the *murabitat* respect me for what I do" (Zeina, interview, September 20, 2015).

Teaching gave some *murabitat* women an opportunity of acquiring a leading position in the future. Also, it helps in establishing social relationships and connections with the Islamic Movement in Israel. They learn from Islamic Movement in Israel how to face Jewish groups and conduct media campaigns. They learn to encourage women and girls to come to al-Haram al-Sharif on the same days that the Jewish groups come to the site and during holidays, so that there will be more participants in the festivals held at the site (Khadija Khweis, interview, September 15, 2015).

The *murabitat's* leaders feel that women are capable of doing important things and being recognized by society; not just stay at home. Hanadi al-Halawani, Khadija Khweis, Zena Abu Amr, Latifa Abdulatif, Aida Sidawi, and Sana al-Rajabi believe that *ribat* and earning the society's honor and respect are more important than having a job in itself (Interviews with *murabitat* leaders, November 2014-December 2015). Sana Al-Rajabi said, "I have more honor as one of the *murabitat* than women who work at schools or hospitals."

Asked if she felt equal to men in Palestinian society, Khadija Khweis said: "In my job I feel equal to men." She rejected the term "feminist" asserting: "I am not a feminist. I am a Muslim woman. Feminism is a European concept that applies to European women and culture. We are Muslim *murabitat* women. We are respected in our society. We wear hijabs and *jilbabs*. I am a teacher and leader of the *murabitat*. I know my rights, which Shariʿa grants me."

Zeina Abu Amr said on the same issue, "What we do on al-Haram al-Sharif has nothing to do with feminism. We are a group of Muslim Women. We pray, study, and do *ribat*. We are not a women's movement but we do believe in women's rights. (Zeina Abu Amr, interview, September 20, 2015).

Asked if she wanted to be a leader in the Palestinian society like the men, Khadija Khweis smiled and answered, "Yes. Hamas allocated good political positions to women in its politburo and government in 2007. So I would like to be a leader in the Palestinian society (Khadija, interview, July 15, 2015).

"The question of women's roles receives significant attention because of its foundational significance for society." An almost universally repeated phrase among *murabitat's murabitat's* teachers that speaks to this centrality goes "woman is half of society" but in fact she is the entire society, because she is responsible for rearing the next generation of Muslims; girls will become mothers and influence their children, we help them build their character and through this work reform society. When women come closer to religion, society becomes better." (Ben Shitrit, 2016: 51).

Asked if they think that Muslim women in Palestinian society are treated fairly or unfairly compared to men, *murabitat's murabitat's* teachers and leaders respond that Islam gives women more rights than western culture. Women can work, go shopping, go out by themselves, and visit locations in West Jerusalem such as Mamilla Park and Jaffa Street. Women are also entitled to inheritance even in the case of divorcee. Women do not need a *mahram* to come to al-Haram al-Sharif; they come alone (Khadija Khweis, interview, July 15, 2015).

Murabitat's Murabitat's teachers and leaders believe that they are treated fairly and with and respect. They are even encouraged by the Palestinian society and the Jerusalem community to do what they do. Hanadi al-Halawani, a *murabitat* teacher, told me that "the Israeli police arrested and released me. Many people in the Old City of Jerusalem respect me for that. They came to visit me after my release. They sent me messages of Facebook. Many people in the Jerusalem community and all the *murabitat* respect me. They encourage us to continue our activities in al-Aqsa to prevent Jewish groups from taking over al-Haram al-Sharif (Hanadi, interview, July 30, 2015).

Although the *murabitat's murabitat's* teachers and leaders reject the term feminist - as do most Islamists - they have adopted the term "women's rights." On the other hand, they repeatedly refer to respect rather than independence or agency. Nevertheless, they are much more aware of the opportunities for women in Palestinian society than the *murabitat's* rank and file. Moreover, the curriculum that they select to teach the women emphasizes obedience rather than independent action.

The *Murabitun* Leaders and the Male *Murabitat* Leaders Speak

Male leaders on al-Haram al-Sharif and male leaders of *murabitun* respect and honor the *murabitat*. Talal al-Rajabi and Muhammad Abu Farha said, "We respect the *murabitat's* leaders" (Talal al-Rajabi, Muhammad Abu Farha, interview, November 29, 2015). All of the *murabitun*, the *murabitat's* rank and file, teachers and leaders respect the *murabitat* and say they are the guardians of al-Aqsa and that they face the Jewish groups **when men are away** (my emphasis). We respect and appreciate the role of Muslim women in the Palestinian society and the Muslim women in Islamic Movement in Israel (*Murabitun*, interviews, 2015).

The relationship between female leaders and male leaders, however, is not so good because the women are more educated. The female teachers sometimes know more about Islam than the leaders of the *murabitun* because the latter are interested mainly in politics. Some of the *murabitat's* leaders are less educated compared to other *murabitat* leaders.

Noticeably, the Murabiteen leaders are more focused on politics which can be noticed in their circle lessons that are more about politics than religious kissues and coordination with the Islamic Movement and its activities. Abu Farha (60) from the Old City and Talal al-Rajabi (63) from Silwan *murabitun* leaders, complain that "we ask female leaders not to conduct many activities against Jewish groups, but they do not listen to us and do as they like" (Abu Farha, and Talal al-Rajabi, interview, September 15, 2015).

Moreover, female teachers and leaders are more interested in educating women in Islam than male leaders to achieve the main goal of preventing Jewish groups from coming to al-Haram al-Sharif. Male leaders are more interested in numbers.

I observed that on al-Haram al-Sharif, *murabitun* and *murabitat* leaders teach the study circles for one hour only. Then they collect cash and in kind donations from charitable people who have close relations with the Islamic Movement in Israel. The *murabitun* cry *Allahu Akbar* in the face of Jewish visitors for a very short time; then *murabitat* continue the process.

However, male leaders control the money, because the relationship between male leaders and the Islamic Movement, which gives the money to them, is easier than the relationship with the women. Also, the female leaders of *murabitat* have an *indirect* good relationship with the male leaders of the Islamic Movements in Israel. They stand by the *murabitat* in all of their activities and bail them out when they get arrested (Khadija Khweis, interview, July, September, December 2015) Khweis also said that "there are two kinds of male leaders - the ones on the table and the ones under the table - the latter kind controls the money but stays in the shadows."

Male teachers teach *murabitat* for political goals.–Male leaders place more emphasis on preventing Jewish groups from taking over or destroying al-Haram al-Sharif compared to the female leaders (Abu Farah al-Sahoory, Talal al-Rajbi, Khadija Khweis and Hanadi al-Halawani). Mohammed al-Sharif, a study circles teacher, told me that he had taught *murabitat* in order to increase their number on al-Haram al-Sharif. This he does by explaining the relationship between Islam and al-Haram al-Sharif. Other purposes for teaching the study circles include strengthen the Islamic Movement in Israel, defending al-Haram al-Sharif from Jewish presence, and protecting al-Aqsa Mosque." (Al-Sharif, interview, November 29, 2015).

There are other social activities for the Murabitat leaders. The leaders of the *murabitat* engage in various activities. Khadija

Khweis, a *murabitat* leader, takes on the large burden of coordinating between leaders of the *murabitat* and the *murabitat's* rank and file in lobbying as many women as possible to join the *murabitat*. The *murabitat* communicate information to the media about developments on al-Haram al-Sharif, which mainly consists of the visits of Jewish groups. Khweis is also in charge of social activities; she collects donations for impoverished families and for the treatment of sick Gazans who are treated at Jerusalem hospitals. Moreover, Aida Sidawi, another leader, divides blacklisted *murabitat* into groups. Each group goes to one of the gates of al-Haram al-Sharif such as *Huta and al-Majlis*. Each group cries *Allahu Akbar* to draw the attention of the crowd and the media. The cries are in the face of Jewish groups on their way out of al-Haram al-Sharif.

On the *murabitat* and the role of women in Palestinian society, Mufti Ikrima Sabri said:

> "*Murabitat* and other Muslim women have played an important role in the Palestinian society in confronting the Israeli occupation especially in Jerusalem. They challenge and seek to stop Jewish groups from entering al-Haram al-Sharif. Muslim women work side by side with men, such as the *sahabiyat*, who stood by Prophet Muhammad in early days of the *da'wa* such as Khadija, the Prophet's wife, and Asma bint Abi Bakr and Ruqaia."

Sheikh Ra'ed Salah repeated the often mentioned respect for the *murabitat*, who stand alongside men in the defense of al-Aqsa. "We at the Islamic Movement are proud of establishing the study circles, the *murabitat*, and the *murabitun*. The *murabitat* are the Islamic army" (An interview with Al-Quds satellite channel, September 15, 2015).

Influence of I slamic Movement in Israel and how impact and how the circle lessons effects on Jews groups and jews plans "The amplified presence of Muslim citizens of Israel at al-Aqsa also represents a response to the steady increase in the number of Jewish visitors to the Temple Mount. In an interview to the London al-Quds al-Arabi newspaper in November 2013, project director Hikmat Na'amna described the study circles as 'a way to undermine the plans to Judaize al-Aqsa'. Na'amna explained the project's strategy: continuous Muslim presence on the mountain in the form of Qur'an study circles of men, women, and school children, dispersed over the length and width of the compound, at increased concentrations along the routes of the Jewish visitors – who, due to restrictions of Jewish law, follow a relatively fixed route along the perimeter of the Dome of the Rock. In this manner, from their positions in the study circles, the Muslims can track the Jews' movements and respond in real time to any act that they consider a provocation. The Association's website expressly describes the study circles as "the first line of defense of al-Aqsa Mosque" (Tzikiyahu, 2015: 6).

The mufti says our goal today is to increase the number of Muslims on al-Haram al-Sharif to strengthen the Sunnah. Ribat is a type of jihad. Whoever comes to pray in al-Aqsa and to defend it is a murabit. It's a kind of worship. The Mufti supported his argument by quoting Abu Hamid al-Ghazali who visited al-Aqsa at the end of eleventh century. Al-Ghazali cried when he learnt that there were only 366 study circles in al-Aqsa. He considered such numbers as too insufficient to teach Islam properly" (Mufti Sabri, interview, 2015).

In short we can conclude all the activities of Murabitat, Murabteen and the Islamic Movement in Israel not to allow to divided al-Haram place and time and afraid to destrioy the Haram from Jews and The purpose of women's involvement in political activism is to prevent Jewish groups from entering al-Haram al-Sharif, defend al-Aqsa, jeopardize any plans to rebuild the Third Temple . According to interviews with Murabitat About the activities of Jewish women, the murabitat said, "We refuse all types of visits by Jews to al-Haram al-Sharif. We will not allow the Jews to pray in the site because we are afraid that their activities would lead to changing the status quo and the destruction of al-Aqsa Mosque and the Dome of Rock." (Murabitat, interviews, 2015).

In short, the Muabitat and the Murabiteen and the Islamic Movement in Israel were afraid of the activities of the Jewish groups since they aim to divide Al-Haram al-Sharif between Jews and Muslims and to destroy Al-aqsa, the *murabitat* said,

"We refuse all types of visits by Jews to al-Haram al-Sharif. We will not allow the Jews to pray in the site because we are afraid that their activities would lead to changing the status quo and the destruction of al-Aqsa Mosque and the Dome of Rock." (*Murabitat*, interviews, 2015)

Moreover, the purpose of Murabitat's involvement in political activism is to prevent Jewish groups from entering al-Haram al-Sharif, defend al-Aqsa, jeopardize any plans to rebuild the Third Temple. (see photo)

Indivisible

Azam al-Khatib, head of the Waqf department in al-Aqsa, said, "We respect the *murabitat* and defend them against the acts of aggression of the Israeli police and army. We respect their role in the defense of al-Aqsa" (Azam al-Khatib, interview, November, 23, 2015). Aside from the traditional concept of respect for women, Khatib expresses that the women need the defense of men, despite women's impressive activities at al-Haram al-Sharif and the attacks they have suffered.

Dr. Ahmad Yusuf, advisor to Ismail Haniyeh, said:

> "We respect the role of the *murabitat* and appreciate their efforts. They are fighters who honor the Palestinian people. Their role in al-Aqsa Mosque is similar to the role of the *sahabiyat* who contributed to Islamic *da'wa* in the early days of Islam such as *al-Sayida* Khadija, the wife of Prophet Muhammad and Asma'a bint Abu Bakr" (interview, June 3, 2015).

In conclusion, the *murabitat's* rank and file related that they came to al-Haram al-Sharif for a variety of religious, psychological, social, economic and political reasons, while female and male teachers and leaders emphasized religious learning, and men focused on political aims even more than the women.

Regular *murabitat* who come to pray and study and are mobilized for political activities said they were there to protect al-Aqsa Mosque from the Jews and prevent them from taking over al-Haram al-Sharif (*Murabitat,* interviews, 2015). They added that they wanted to tell the Jews and the Israeli government that "al-Aqsa is Islamic property and only for Muslims. It is not just for Palestinians." Few *murabitat* said "Al-Aqsa is for Muslims and Palestinians. We are here to fill al-Aqsa all the time and to increase our strength and numbers." Some of the *murabitat* said they supported the Islamic Movement in Israel.

The *murabitat* participate in many political activities and social and religion activities. They meet Jewish visitors of al-Haram al-Sharif with *Allahu Akbar.* They chase Jewish groups and tell them that Israel lies to them and that al-Haram al-Sharif is no place for them. "Don't listen to your leaders," they say (See photo).

Murabitat chase Jewish visitors on al-Haram al-Sharif

The *murabitat* reported that they learned the basics of Islam for everyday life supporting patriarchy. They also learned basic negative views of Jews but seeing Jews for themselves sometimes gave them a positive view.

My observations of the study circles led to the conclusion that such classes also cover issues like Jewish attempts to take control of al-Aqsa Mosque, Jewish groups visiting the site, and the support of the rabbis and the Israeli government to the Jewish groups that come to al-Haram al-Sharif. They also teach the *murabitat* that Israel seeks to divide al-Aqsa between Jews and Muslims.

The *murabitat* also report that they learned about their role in the political efforts to protect al-Haram al-Sharif. This political element of the lessons was important to female teachers and leaders, and practically the only important thing for male teachers and leaders.

Male leaders support murabitat. They respect them and encourage them. In fact, some murabitat are from the families of the male leaders. They also support and give great respect to women at the study circles. They believe that women who study on al-Haram al-Sharif make better mothers since they can assist in their children's education. I met with two men who were married to murabitat. They expressed their feeling of honor for being married to murabitat who defend al-Haram al-Sharif against Jewish presence.

Male leaders are in contact with the murabitat and with other male Islamic leaders. Male leaders respect murabitat and they have good knowledge of the political situation on al-Haram al-Sharif. Male leaders will often contact female teachers to plan future activities and they use teachers to mobilize women because students listen to teachers and not to male leaders. Murabitun leaders have contacts with other male leaders from the Islamic Movement, Mufti, Waqf guards, and other Islamic movements. They have no contacts with secular movements. Some of the murabitun leaders have small connection with Fatah and the Palestinian Authority. Leaders in Jerusalem and this connection is limited to arrangement of Hajj and Umra (Murabteen, Interview, 2015).

Most of the *murabitat* and *murabitun* – leaders as well as rank and file members - expressed extremely conservative views about the roles of women in Palestinian society and the accomplishments of the *murabitat*. If the rank and file members did not come with these views, they were inculcated with them in the study circles where the curriculum was set by the female teachers and leaders. Female teachers and leaders were aware of feminism and rejected it, but adopted the term "women's rights." Some female leaders did, however, envision greater roles for pious women in Palestinian politics based on the precedent of the Hamas government in the West Bank. Nevertheless, the view that *murabitat* women earned "respect" was common to all – women and men, rank and file members and leaders. This is because the society in general views the *murabitat* as guardians of al-Aqsa Mosque. They are distinguished by being persistent despite the punitive measures taken by the Israeli authority against them. While men are being prevented from entering the site, the women are left in the front line.

The *murabitat* are spread all over al-Haram al-Sharif. When I asked the *murabitat* what they learnt at al-Haram al-Sharif and how they felt about it, they said: "We learn that women and men must defend al-Haram al-Sharif from the Jews. It is an honor to defend the site now and in the afterlife. We feel like guardians of al-Aqsa and Islam. It is a Jihad. While Israeli security forces keep arresting men, we have to take the role of defending al-Aqsa. *Sahabiyat* like Umm Amarah, Asmaa bint Abu Bakr, and Sumayyah Umm Ammar would have done the same thing." (*Murabitat*, interviews, 2014-2015).

Murabitat are often middle-aged mothers and homemakers from lower and lower middle class families. Generally speaking they are not very educated, except for the leaders who teach at the study circles. The latter are educated people; they have postgraduate degrees in subjects other than Shariʿa. Regular Murabitat come to pray, to study and to study the Qurʾan and the Hadith on al-Haram al-Sharif.

In conclusion, the Murabitat told me that it was their activities on al-Haram al-Sharif that led to the al-Quds intifada of October 2015. During this intifada, Prime Minister Netanyahu took the decision to ban Israeli ministers and MKs from entering al-Haram al-Sharif/ Temple Mount. Hiba, one of the Murabitat, told me that "We have obtained the greatest victory. Now we have political power and greater numbers. Our political goals are materializing. We will continue our activities." (Hiba, interview, November, 2015).

Summary and Final Conclusions

The passages concerning the Holy City of Jerusalem in the Qurʿan as well as in the Torah, in addition to the Jewish and Islamic traditions, have contributed to fueling the Israeli-Palestinian conflict. Since Jerusalem is a focal point from a historical, religious, symbolic, and political viewpoint, Muslims and Jews have been competing to conduct their own activities in the city. Muslim and Jewish women have been given opportunities to contribute to the activities in the city; most importantly, in the holiest of locations for Muslims and Jews, al-Haram al-Sharif/ the Temple Mount. The Islamic Movement in Israel has since 1996 led the activities in the city. The Movement established the *murabitun* and *murabitat* on al-Haram al-Sharif, as one of its key groups to carry out its activities, in order to confront the visiting Jewish groups and to ensure the Islamic identity of the site. Among the activities of the Islamic Movement in Israel on al-Haram al-Sharif are the study circles. The purpose of the study circles is to recruit more and more *murabitat* who will stop any Israeli attempts to take over al-Haram al-Sharif. However, one of the important subjects dealt with in the study circles is guidance to become "good Muslims" which in the case of women means upholding Islamic patriarchal values.

The escalating religious and political historical conflict between Palestinian Muslims and Israeli Jews over the Haram al-Sharif/Temple Mount have since the 1920s, and increasingly since 1967, invariably led to the establishment of the *murabitun* movement to combat the Jewish Temple Mount activists and to prevent them from taking over the site.

The decision to establish the *murabitat* movement was not a "coincidence" or "spontaneous," it was planned carefully by Islamic leaders on al-Haram al-Sharif, especially by those who were members of the Islamic Movement in Israel. It was also built against the background of the Islamic Movement women's interest in and activities for al-Aqsa (Tal). The objective was to oppose Israeli encroachments and in particular the Jewish women of the Temple Mount organizations. The *murabitat's* leaders have connections with the leaders of the Islamic Movement in Israel.

It is worth noting that the basic motives that bring Jewish and Muslim women to the holy site are the same. Both groups believe that the site is closest to God and on it prayers are more likely to be answered. However, the *murabitat* also say that they fear Jewish activities that aim to destroy al-Aqsa Mosque. Noticeably, both groups have political aims in their activities in Al-Haram al-Sharif.

The role of the Palestinian women's movements of the past must not be forgotten for their contribution to the building of the *murabitat* movement. Their activities included establishing associations, centers, and unions. Their focus was on national rights; usually with a secular orientation but occasionally with a religious underpinning.-The leadership of the ~~past~~ Palestinian women's movement 1920's-1948 was from Palestinian families from the social elite with some middle class participation. Lower class rural women did however participate in the Qassam movement and in the 1936-1939 uprising. As the movement evolved, its membership shifted from the hands of the upper and upper middle class to lower class women, and from urban to rural women. The first intifada in 1988 was a major turning point because of the extensive participation of women of all backgrounds and the involvement of the Palestinian Islamist movement in the armed resistance.

The rank and file of the *murabitat* interviewed in this study are unique in that they belong to the middle class, they are not highly educated and most are over 40 years of age. They originate from the Old City and other neighborhoods of Jerusalem (which were villages in the not too distant past). They carry Israeli identity cards. The *murabitat's* members do not seem to fit the common profile of Palestinian female activists. The female *murabitat's murabitat's* teachers, however, are highly-educated, upper middle class women who have worked outside the home, are related to prominent men, and come from villages and cities outside of Jerusalem – such as Hebron and Abu Dis. They fit the common profile of Palestinian activist women.

In view of their socio-economic profile, it is not surprising that the rank and file of the *murabitat* initially come to al-

Haram al-Sharif for spiritual and religious purposes - to pray and to study. Some came to al-Haram al-Sharif for psychological, social and even economic reasons. Aside from prayer, these women participate in the study circles to learn more about Islam. The political content of the study circles was satisfying to the founders of the *murabitat* as well as the male and female leaders. Learning about women's modesty in Islam and obedience to their husbands was a prominent aim of the female leaders and teachers and the information was successfully absorbed by the women in the study circles.

The Secondary Girls School (*al-Shar'aiyya lill-banat*) does not, as a rule of thumb, take part in the activities of the *murabitat*. However, when the Israeli police prevent students from going to their school, a number of the girls join the *murabitat* outside al-Haram al-Sharif and shout *Allahu Akbar* with them in the faces of the Jewish visitors.

In the study circles, the rank and file women become exposed to *da'wa* (proselytizing) and engage in some informal charitable and social activities. But these differ from similar endeavors of their sisters in Islamic movements who have highly organized *da'wa* and charity associations.

Through their presence at al-Haram al-Sharif and through the study circles organized and financed by the Islamic Movement in Israel, the *murabitat's* rank and file members are mobilized for political activities–protecting al-Haram al-Sharif from Jewish Temple Mount activists. By being at al-Haram al-

Sharif, the Murabitat are subjected to the religious and political dimensions of the site as they are checked by Israeli security forces and watch Jewish groups coming to Al-Haram, al-Sharif. They confront the Jewish prayer groups, shouting pro-Muslim and anti-Jewish slogans, and forming a barrier between the Jews and the presumed site of the Holy Temple. The *murabitat* also pop balloons and spray water from balloons at the Jewish visitors; however, the women do not throw rocks at the Jewish visitors. Women who come to al-Haram al-Sharif are also politicized by being exposed to many conflicting political and religious groups and by meeting female political leaders from various movements.

The *murabitat's* teachers and leaders have political experience and their activities on al- Haram al-Sharif are politically oriented. When Ra'ed Salah began political activities on al-Haram al-Sharif, these politically active women joined their leaders whom they knew from university, to save al-Haram al-Sharif from encroachment by Jews. Nevertheless, they also viewed the study circles as a vehicle to teach women about their roles as modest Muslims and obedient wives as well as political activists.

The *murabitat's* leaders' public relations initiatives publicize the actions of the *murabitat* to protect al-Haram al-Sharif from the Jews. They also publicize that the *Murabitat* are being harassed and arrested by the Israeli security forces, even though they are women. The bravery of the *murabitat* is exhibited in many ways, whether it is shown in front of the Israel security forces, in prison, or outside al-Haram al-Sharif after they have been excluded. All of these images were broadcast in Palestinian media, Arab media, and international media; this contributed to mobilizing Arab and international support for the campaign in defense of al-Haram al-Sharif and in protest against the Jews

Despite the capability exhibited by the *murabitat*, the idea that the actions of Muslim female activists merely earn them "respect" from their families and from society is prevalent among men and women, leaders and rank and file members. Thus, this rather conservative notion seems to have been successfully inculcated from the leaders to the rank and file members. Few women expressed the idea that women's activism demonstrated their competence or their independent thought and action. Some leaders and teachers *Murabitat* were inculcated with extremely negative views of Jews in the study circles, and these ideas reinforced their experiences on al-Haram al-Sharif where they came into contact with the Israeli security forces, Jewish activist groups protected by the police and with the limitations on Muslim activities there. Nevertheless, a handful of the *murabitat's* rank and file learned from their contact with Jews about Jewish holidays and about Jewish devotion to God.

Pious Palestinian women active in the early 1990s in non-governmental Palestinian women's associations expressed their sense of "agency," – the capacity to act independently and to make their own free choices - and criticized the political and religious leadership using Islamic tools (Rabab Abdulhadi, 1998). The Murabitat interviewed did not express these views. By contrast, the experiences of Islamist women in the political ranks of Hamas during the years 1997-2003 indicate that Palestinian Islamist women created a space for the activities of women's groups, who were thus bestowed with an air of moral legitimacy in public life. The concept of "moral legitimacy" is similar to the notion of "respect" achieved by the *murabitat* since 2010.

Muslim religious movements active 2008-2012 in Israel and the West Bank offer women "powerful liberatory narratives," and their female activists are "highly invested in the idea of the "autonomous individual." *Murabitat* members interviewed for this study rarely, however, expressed the idea of being an autonomous individual. There were only a few exceptions to this rule. One woman came to al-Haram al-Sharif despite her husband's objection, one teacher took this role upon her despite her lack of learning, and one or two women leaders thought in terms of a future political career for themselves. The majority of the *Murabitat* have adopted the concept of "women's rights" from feminism, applying it to the Sharia, and the notion of "respect" for women in place of "agency."

Similarly, pious women in Egypt and the Shi'I section of Beirut exhibit ideas and actions that may promote women's rights. Most of the *murabitat* do not seem to have gender consciousness. One reason for this is that the Egyptian situation is very different from the Palestinian case, because in Palestine the fight for religious and national rights often overshadows the struggle for women's rights. Therefore Badran's term "gender activism" is not applicable to the *murabitat.* Similarly, Mahmoud's use of the theoretical term "agency" - derived from western liberalism and employed by some social scientists - does not seem relevant to Palestinian pious women. The gender consciousness and actions of the women in the Dahiya was dubbed "gender jihad" by one of the informants in Deeb's study. This phrase was not, however, mentioned by the *murabitat* interviewed. It would seem that the socio-economic and geographic background of the rank and file *murabitat* women as well as the content in the study circles impelled them to accept a rather patriarchal view of Islam and Palestinian society.

In sum, the Murabitat were established by the Islamic Movement for political reasons, and women who come to al-Haram al-Sharif for other religious and social aims experience the political aspect of the site and are mobilized for political action. Their actions undoubtedly are a major contribution to the Palestinian struggle to maintain control of al-Haram al-Sharif. Nevertheless, they view their achievements in the context of a rather conservative opinion of women and do not differ much from the outlook of men in this regard.

Name – Date of Interview	Age, Function	Marital Status and Dependents	Education	Place of Residence	Date of *Ribat*	Religion Interest	Political Interest	Method of *Ribat*	Punishment from Israel
Aida Sidawi 10-11-2014 20-9-2015	55, (Leader)	Married, no children father served 20 years in Israeli prison	Secondary-school	Old City	2010 in Masatib al-`Ilm	Al-Aqsa *Aqidah* (doc-trine) and written in Qur'an and Sunnah	Al-Aqsa is a symbol for Palestinian and Islamic Identity	Studying, and teaching in Masatib al-`Ilm	Banished from al-Aqsa 5 times for 1 year, number one on the black list
Khadija Khweis 5-11-2014 20-4-2015 15-7-2015 23-8-2015 20-9-2015 29-11-2015 29-12-2015	40, (Leader and teacher)	Married to a Shari'a Prof. at Al-Quds Univ.	M.A. in Islamic Shari'a from Hebron Univ.	Al-Toor	2010 in Masatib al-`Ilm	Al-Aqsa in her mind and thought for Muslim	No political interest	Teacher in Masatib al-`Ilm	Banished from al-Aqsa 5 times for 2 year, number 2 in the black list
Zeina Abu-Amr 15-7-2015 20-9-2015 10-11-2015 20-12-2015 10-7-2016	45, (Leader)	Married to a Prof. of engineering at Birzeit Univ.	M.A. in Islamic History from Al-Quds Univ. Teacher in Masatib al-`Ilm	Old City	2011 teacher in Masatib al-`Ilm	Al-Aqsa religious place only for Muslim	Symbol for Palestinian Identity	Teacher in Masatib al-`Ilm	In Black list
Latifa Abdullatif 20-12-2014 15-7-2015 15-9-2015	30, (leader, speaks English) speaks to foreign media	Married , taught math in Israeli Education Ministry before *ribat*	B.A. in math from Al-Najah National Univ. in Nabulus	Old City	2010 all her life in al-Aqsa for praying	Al-Aqsa in her Heart written in Qur'an and Sunnah	Symbol for Palestinian Identity , her massage be aware from Religious War in the Haram	In Masatib al-`Ilm	Sacked from Israeli Education Ministry for her *ribat* in the Haram
Hanadi al-Halwani 20-7-2015 30-7-2015 15-9-2015	32, (leader and teacher)	Married	B.A in Islamic Shari'a from al-Quds Univ.	Wadi al-Jooz	2010 teacher in Masatib al-`Ilm	Al-Aqsa in Qur'an and Sunnah	Protect al-Aqsa from Jewish settlers	Teacher in Masatib al-`Ilm	Banished from al-Aqsa 4 times for 1 year, number 3 in the black list.
Sana'a al-Rajabi 20-7-2015 15-9-2015 20-9-2015 3-11-2015 29-11-2015	45, (potential leader)	Married, children are employed	Secondary school	Old City	2012 learning Qur'an in Masatib al-`Ilm	Al-Aqsa Aqidah in Qur'an and Sunnah	National Symbol for Palestinian *murabitat* now Political Power	Study Qur'an	Banished from al-Aqsa 9 times, held in al-Ramla prison number 4 in the black list
Hiba- al-Taweel 15-9-2015 3-11-2015 29-11-2015 20-12-2015	28 (potential leader)	Married encouraged strongly by husband	Secondary school	Wadi al-Jooz	2011, Learns Qur'an in Masatib al-`Ilm with her 3-year-old child	Al-Aqsa Aqida in Qur'an and Sunnah	No political interest-al-Aqsa for Muslim *murabitat* now Political Power	By her Mother, one of the *murabitat*	Banished from the Haram, ar-rested twice. Photo with child in detention went viral
Sana'a al-Shami 3-11-2015	46	Married,	Secondary school	Ras al-Amod	2011 in Masatib al-`Ilm	Al-Aqsa all my life Aqida in Qur'an and Sunnah	We are now political power before and after Al-Quds intifada	My sister was a *murabita* member from 2010 encouraged me to study Qur'an	On police black list. At-tacked by 4 Israel troops who ripped off her Hijab
Anonymous 3-11-2015	54	Divorced, children married	Elementary school	Kufr Aqab	20 in Masatib al-`Ilm	Al-Aqsa is my home, where I pray and forget life's stress	*murabitat* have political power, they protect al-Aqsa from the Jews	2011, learning Qur'an in Masatib al-`Ilm to solve social problems	On black list, banished twice

Name – Date of Interview	Age, Function	Marital Status and Dependents	Education	Place of Residence	Date of *Ribat*	Religion Interest	Political Interest	Method of *Ribat*	Punishment from Israel
Um Rabia'a 2-8-2015	55, unemployed	Married, encouraged by husband	Secondary school	Al-Aysawieh	2010 learning Qur'an in Masatib al-`Ilm	Religious relation with al-Aqsa , written in Qur'an	No Jews to visit al-Aqsa, and protect al-Aqsa from Jews	By lessons in Qur'an and Shari'a in Masatib al-`Ilm	Harassed by the Israeli police
Anonymous 16-11-2014	23, teacher in elementary girls school	Single, encouraged by father	B.A -in Education from Hind al-Hussini College	Aysawieh	From 2010 only in my holiday and summer holiday	Al-Aqsa Aqida in Qur'an and Sunnah	National identity for Palestinian	My father, a murabitun member, encouraged me to be a *murabitat* member	The Israeli police seize my ID card upon entry and hand it back upon exit of al-Haram al-Sharif
Anonymous 16-11-2014	60	Married	Non-educated, attends religious lessons	Old City	2010 in Masatib al-`Ilm	Al-Aqsa in Qur'an	Protect al-Aqsa from the Jews	Attends lessons in Qur'an in Masatib al-`Ilm	The Israeli police seize my ID card upon entry and hand it back upon exit of al-Haram al-Sharif
Safiyah 25-9-2015	30	Married	Diploma in Business	Silwan	From 2010, in Masatib al-`Ilm	Al-Aqsa in Qur'an and Sunnah	To stop the Jews from taking over the Haram	To learn Qur'an and Hadith	The Israeli police seize my ID card upon entry and hand it back upon exit of al-Haram al-Sharif
Amna 16-11-2014	40	Married	Secondary school	Kufr Aqab	2012 in Masatib al-`Ilm , my husband encouraged me	Al-Aqsa in Qur'an – I feel very well in the Haram –no sadness in the Haram	No Jews in al-Aqsa, al-is Aqsa for Muslims. I refuse Jewish visits	Family encouraged me to be Murabitat member to study Qur'an	The Israeli police seize my ID card upon entry and hand it back upon exit of al-Haram al-Sharif
Omm Rami Kelani 5-12-2014	50	Married	Secondary school	Old City	2010- started with *halqat al- al-I'lm* and Masatib al-`Ilm	I have a religious relation with al-Aqsa and al-*ribat* is *fard*	We have political power. We lead in the society.	With my friend Hanan, we went to al-Aqsa to study in Masatib al-`Ilm	The Israeli police seize my ID card upon entry and hand it back upon exit of al-Haram al-Sharif
Aya 15-3-2015	30	Married Encouraged by husband, no children	Elementary education	Kufr Aqab	2013	Al-Aqsa is in the Qur'an. I pray to be pregnant with a child	Protect the Haram from the Jews	Encouraged by husband	The Israeli police seize my ID card upon entry and hand it back upon exit of al-Haram al-Sharif
Anonymous 26-7-2015 29-11-2015	51	Married	Secondary school	Old City	2010- began *ribat* with Masatib al-`Ilm	Al-Aqsa written in Qur'an and Hadith	Protect al-Aqsa from the Jews	Pray and attend halqat al-I'lm	The Israeli police seize my ID card upon entry and hand it back upon exit of al-Haram al-Sharif
Anonymous 26-7-2015	14		11th grade Student at Shari'a girls' school inside the Haram	Wadi al-Jooz	From 2013, during holiday and when school is out	I love al-Aqsa because prophet Muhammad prayed there	Protect al-Aqsa from Jewish settlers	My father and my friends at school encouraged me to be in the Murabitat	Sometimes the Israeli police stop us from going to school

Name – Date of Interview	Age, Function	Marital Status and Dependents	Education	Place of Residence	Date of *Ribat*	Religion Interest	Political Interest	Method of *Ribat*	Punishment from Israel
Anonymous 20-9-2015	57 Unemployed	Married Son, 20, in Israeli custody	Elementary school	Isawiya	2010- joined *halaqat al-I'lm*and Masatib al-`Ilm	Strong religious feeling about al-Aqsa as mentioned in the Qur'an and Hadith	Stop the Jews from entering Al-Haram al-Sharif	Encourage by husband (one of the *murabitun*)	The Israeli police seize my ID card upon entry and hand it back upon exit of al-Haram al-Sharif
Aya Abu Nab 20-9-2015	17 (Khweis' trainee to become a leader)	Single	12th grade	Isawiya	2013 Joined through a friend	Through friends; mostly *murabitat*	Learn Qur'an at *halaqat al-I'lm*	Khadija, my friend, a Murabitat leader	Banished twice for 15 days due to shouting at Jewish settlers
Samiha Shahin 15-7-2015 15-9-2015 20-9-2015	52 (leader)	Married Youngest son is 18	Secondary school	Old City	2013 joined the *Masatebal-I'lm*	I developed a strong religious relation with al-Aqsa, the Prophet, and the *sahaba* while praying on al-Haram al-Sharif	Protect al-Aqsa from Jewish control	Protest massacre of Muslim Brotherhood members in Egypt	Banished for 15 days
Huda Abu Sninah 15-7-2015	50	Married	Secondary school	Isawiya	2010 I study Qur'an in *Masatebal-I'lm*	I have a strong religious connection with al-Aqsa because the Prophet was here	Protect al-Aqsa from the Jews. I volunteer to teach about historical sites in the Haram	My Husband encourage me to join *Masatebal-I'lm*	The Israeli police seize my ID card upon entry and hand it back upon exit of al-Haram al-Sharif
Elham Al-Jubaeh 17-9-2015 20-9-2015 30-9-2015	43 (media activist, has relations with secular women's organizations)	Married	Diploma in Media	Old City	2013 Learnt Qur'an and Hadith at *Masateb al-I'lm*	I have strong religious connection with al-Aqsa because the Prophet was here	Prevent Jewish settlers from controlling the Haram	My friend encouraged me to join Masatib al-`Ilm to study Qur'an	Banished for 30 days; detained for 3 days; ID card seized upon arrival and handed back upon leaving al-Haram al-Sharif
Eman 11-3-2015	43, (comes to the Haram only during Holiday)	Married,	B.A in Arabic Literature	Kufr Aqab	2013	Strong religious connection with al-Aqsa since it is mentioned in the Qur'an	Protect al-Aqsa from the Jews	My friend told me about the Qur'an lessons in Masatib al-`Ilm	The Israeli police seize my ID card upon entry and hand it back upon exit of al-Haram al-Sharif
Anonymous 11-3-2015	40	Married	Diploma in Business	Ras al-Amod	2012	I have special relation with al-Aqsa mosque since the Prophet was there	Protect the Haram from Jewish settlers	I come to pray and I join to Masatib al-`Ilm to learn Qur'an	The Israeli police seize my ID card upon entry and hand it back upon exit of al-Haram al-Sharif
Omm Said al-Shaludi 20-9-2015	55	Married, Married children	Elementary school	Silwan	2013	I am here for God. I have strong religious relation with al-Aqsa	Protect al-Aqsa from the Jews	My husband encouraged me to join the *ribat* with him	The Israeli police seize my ID card upon entry and hand it back upon exit of al-Haram al-Sharif

Name – Date of Interview	Age, Function	Marital Status and Dependents	Education	Place of Residence	Date of *Ribat*	Religion Interest	Political Interest	Method of *Ribat*	Punishment from Israel
Anonymous 20-9-2015	49	Married	Secondary school	Shau'fat	2010	Al-Aqsa is part of Islamic religion	To feel more Muslim in al-Haram al-Sharif	Protect the Haram	The Israeli police seize my ID card upon entry and hand it back upon exit of al-Haram al-Sharif
Majeda Hawash 20-9-2015	62	Married, Married children	Elementary education	Old City	2010	Strong religious connection with al-Aqsa since it is mentioned in the Qur'an	Defend Al-Aqsa against the Jews	I started *ribat* with Masatib al-`Ilm	Arrested 3 times Banished for 15 days
Anonymous 20-9-2015	15 years	Single	Student at the Shari'a Girls School	Old City	I joined the Murabitat when Police stop us from going to school	I love al-Aqsa, it is written in the Qur'an and Hadith	Protect al-Aqsa from Jewish settlers	Joined the Murabitat and developed social relationships with them	Banished for crying *Allahu Akbar*
Wafa'a 24-9-2015	38	Single	Diploma in Education unemployed	Old City	Joined the Murabitat in 2013	Strong religious relationship with al-Aqsa	Protect al-Aqsa from Jewish settlers	Learn at the Masatib al-`Ilm	The Israeli police seize my ID card upon entry and hand it back upon exit of al-Haram al-Sharif
Zenat Aweda 19-12-2015	62	Married	Elementary school	Old City	2013	Strong religious relationship with al-Aqsa since the Prophet prayed there	Protect the Haram from the Jews	My husband encouraged me to study in Masatib al-`Ilm	The Israeli police seize my ID card upon entry and hand it back upon exit of al-Haram al-Sharif.I am on the blacklist of the Israeli police.
Anonymous 24-9-2015	40	Married	Secondary school	Kufr Aqab	2012	Religious relation with al-Aqsa	Protect the Haram from the Jews	My in-laws encouraged me to study in Masatib al-`Ilm	The Israeli police seize my ID card upon entry and hand it back upon exit of al-Haram al-Sharif
Anonymous 18-4-2015	50	Married	Secondary school	Isawiya	2010	Al-Aqsa is in the Aqida	Protect al-Aqsa from the Jews	Masatib al-`Ilm	The Israeli police seize my ID card upon entry and hand it back upon exit of al-Haram al-Sharif
Sana'a 18-4-2015	40	Married, Child in preschool	Junior high school	Old City	2014	Al-Aqsa is mentioned in the Qur'an and Sunnah	Protect al-Aqsa from the Jews	Masatib al-`Ilm to learn Qur'an	The Israeli police seize my ID card upon entry and hand it back upon exit of al-Haram al-Sharif

Name – Date of Interview	Age, Function	Marital Status and Dependents	Education	Place of Residence	Date of *Ribat*	Religion Interest	Political Interest	Method of *Ribat*	Punishment from Israel
Sameera 18-4-2015	46	Married	Secondary school	Old City	2014	Al-Aqsa is in the Aqida	Protect al-Aqsa from the Jews	Her family encouraged her to learn Qur'an	The Israeli police seize my ID card upon entry and hand it back upon exit of al-Haram al-Sharif
Nadia 20-4-2015	60	Married	Elementary school	Silwan	2010	Al-Aqsa is in the Qur'an	Protect al-Aqsa from the Jews	Husband is among the *murabitun*	The Israeli police seize my ID card upon entry and hand it back upon exit of al-Haram al-Sharif
Anonymous 20-4-2015	55	Married, Married children	Secondary school	Kufr Aqab	2010	Al-Aqsa is in my heart since the Prophet prayed there	Protect al-Aqsa from the Jews	Masatib al-`Ilm	The Israeli police seize my ID card upon entry and hand it back upon exit of al-Haram al-Sharif
Nida 20-4-2015	37	Single	Secondary education	Old City	2014	Al-Aqsa is in the Qur'an	Protect al-Aqsa from the Jews and support the Murabitat	Learn Qur'an	The Israeli police seize my ID card upon entry and hand it back upon exit of al-Haram al-Sharif
Anonymous 20-4-2015	30	Married	Secondary school	Isawiya	2013	Al-Aqsa is in the Aqida	Protect al-Aqsa from the Jews	Learn Qur'an a friend encouraged me	The Israeli police seize my ID card upon entry and hand it back upon exit of al-Haram al-Sharif
Amany 20-4-2015	42	Married	Secondary school	Isawiya	2012	Al-Aqsa is in the Qur'an and Sunnah	Protect al-Aqsa from the Jews	Masatib al-`Ilm	The Israeli police seize my ID card upon entry and hand it back upon exit of al-Haram al-Sharif
Omm Muhammad 20-4-2015	41 (tourist guide historical locations in al-Haram al-Sharif, speaks Hebrew)	Married	Secondary school	Old City	2010	Al-Aqsa is in the Aqida	Protect al-Aqsa from the Jews	Masatib al-`Ilm	The Israeli police seize my ID card upon entry and hand it back upon exit of al-Haram al-SharifIsraeli police stops me from speaking Hebrew with Jewish groups about Islamic tradition on al-Haram al-Sharif.
Mona 20-4-2015	46	Married	Elementary school	Isawiya	2012	Al-Aqsa mean Islamic religion	Protect al-Aqsa from the Jews	Masatib al-`Ilm	The Israeli police seize my ID card upon entry and hand it back upon exit of al-Haram al-Sharif

Name – Date of Interview	Age, Function	Marital Status and Dependents	Education	Place of Residence	Date of *Ribat*	Religion Interest	Political Interest	Method of *Ribat*	Punishment from Israel
Amal, July 9, 2015	39	Married	Secondary school	From Isawiya,	2012	Al-Aqsa is in the Aqida	Protect al-Aqsa from the Jews	Learn Qur'an and Shari'a	The Israeli police seize my ID card upon entry and hand it back upon exit of al-Haram al-Sharif
Anonymous 28-6-2015	60	Married	Illiterate	Old City	2013	Praying in al-Aqsa and learn Qur'an	Protect al-Aqsa from the Jews	Learn writing and reading	The Israeli police seize my ID card upon entry and hand it back upon exit of al-Haram al-Sharif
Aya 28-6-2015	45	Married	Secondary school	Kufr Aqab	2010	Al-Aqsa is in the Aqida	Protect al-Aqsa from the Jews	Masatib al-`Ilm	The Israeli police seize my ID card upon entry and hand it back upon exit of al-Haram al-Sharif
Manal 28-6-2015	40	Married	Diploma in Education unemployed	Old City	2012	Al-Aqsa is in the Aqida	Protect al-Aqsa from the Jews	Masatib al-`Ilm to learn Qur'an	The Israeli police seize my ID card upon entry and hand it back upon exit of al-Haram al-Sharif
Anonymous 28-6-2015	57	Married	Secondary school	Al-Toor	2010	Al-Aqsa is in the Qur'an	Protect al-Aqsa from the Jews	Masatib al-`Ilm	The Israeli police seize my ID card upon entry and hand it back upon exit of al-Haram al-Sharif
Anonymous -27-7-2015	36	Married	Secondary school	Al-Toor	2013	Al-Aqsa ismy religious and social life	Protect al-Aqsa from the Jews	My friend encourage me to join the Murabitat	Banished for 1 month
Miriam 27-7-2015	22	Single	Secondary school	Old City	2012	Al-Aqsa is in my religion	Protect al-Aqsa from the Jews	Learn Qur'an and Hadith	Banished and blacklisted
Sua'ad 27-7-2015	50	Married	Secondary school	Old City	2010	Al-Aqsa is Aqida	Protect al-Aqsa from the Jews	Masatib al-`Ilm	Banished for 15 days
Anonymous 27-7-2017 Wears khimar	40	Married	Secondary school	Old City	2010	Al-Aqsa is in the Qur'an	Shouts *Allahu Akbar* when Jewish settlers enter the Haram	Masatib al-`Ilm	Banished for 1 month
Liyla 27-7-2015	42	Married	Secondary school	Silwan	2010	Al-Aqsa is Aqida	Protect al-Aqsa from the Jews	Masatib al-`Ilm	Banished and blacklisted
Anonymous 29-11-2015	61	Married	Elementary school	Kufr Aqab	2010	Al-Aqsa is Aqida and in my religion	Protect al-Aqsa from the Jews	My Husband, one of the *murabitun*, encourage me	Banished and blacklisted
Omm Muhammad al-Natsheh 29-11-2015	45	Married	Secondary school	Beit Hanina	2010	Al-Aqsa is Aqida	Protect al-Aqsa from the Jews	Masatib al-`Ilm	Banished and blacklisted
Omm Hudaifa 29-11-2015	50	Married	B.A. Shari'a from Hebron University	Old City	2010	Teacher in Masatib al-`Ilm in Qur'an reciting and interpretation	Protect al-Aqsa from the Jews	Masatib al-`Ilm , I work as a teacher in Qur'an and Hadith	Banished and blacklisted

Name – Date of Interview	Age, Function	Marital Status and Dependents	Education	Place of Residence	Date of *Ribat*	Religion Interest	Political Interest	Method of *Ribat*	Punishment from Israel
Anonymous 29-11-2015	54	Married	Secondary school	Beit Hanina	2010	Al-Aqsa is in my religion and in the Qur'an	Protect al-Aqsa from the Jews	My sister encouraged me	Banished
Anonymous 29-11-2015	41	Married	Secondary school	Kufr Aqab	2010	Al-Aqsa is in my religion and in the Qur'an	Protect al-Aqsa from the Jews	Masatib al-`Ilm	The Israeli police seize my ID card upon entry and hand it back upon exit of al-Haram al-Sharif
Rabiha (20-9-2015) (29-11-2015 29-11-2015	48	Married	Illiterate	Silwan	2014	I feel happy and content in Al-Aqsa	Protect al-Aqsa from the Jews	My in-laws encouraged me to learn to read and write at the Haram	The Israeli police seize my ID card upon entry and hand it back upon exit of al-Haram al-Sharif
Anonymous 29-11-2015	34	Married	Secondary school	Silwan	2012	Al-Aqsa is in the Aqida	Protect al-Aqsa from the Jews	Masatib al-`Ilm	The Israeli police seize my ID card upon entry and hand it back upon exit of al-Haram al-Sharif
Asma'a 29-11-2015	16 (comes with her mother when school is out)	Single	11th grade	Old City	2014	Al-Aqsa is in my Aqida and I learn Qur'an	Protect al-Aqsa from the Jews	My mother encouraged me to learn Qur'an	Israeli police check my ID card
Abdurrahman Abu Ras (male) 29-11-2015	65	Married	Secondary school	Qalansaweh	2010 March of the Banners	Al-Aqsa is in the Aqida and Qur'an	Protect al-Aqsa from the Jews	Masatib al-`Ilm	Banished four times
Talal al-Rajabi (male leader) 29-11-2015	63	Married	Secondary school	Silwan	2010	Al-Aqsa is in the Aqida	Protect al-Aqsa from the Jews by shouting *Allahu Akbar*	Masatib al-`Ilm	Banished for three months
Muhammad al-Sharif 29-2015	69	Married	Diploma in Islamic Studies	Silwan	2010	Al-Aqsa means Islamic religion	Protect al-Aqsa from the Jews, teach *murabitat* religion, al-Aqsa is a symbol for Palestine	I work as a teacher in Masatib al-`Ilm	Banished and harassed by Israeli troops
Ahmad al-Tawiel-29-11-2015	65	Married	Secondary school	Old City	Security guard in the Haram for 40 years	Al-Aqsa is in my heart and in the Qur'an and Hadith	Protect al-Aqsa from the Jewish settlers	Security guard	Banished and harassed by Israeli troops
Muhammad Yaqoub Abu Faraeh 29-11-2015	66	Married	Secondary school	Old city	2010	Al-Aqsa is Aqida in the Qur'an and Sunnah	Protect al-Aqsa from Jewish control	I pray in Al-Aqsa. I live nearby. I come to Masatib al-`Ilm	Banished for one month
Gila Fein, interview, January 24, 2016	35								
Arnon Sigal, interview, December 20, 2015	40 (leader and reporter)								

Appendix A: List of Interviews*Names and Dates
Interviews with the murabitat and murabitun on al-Haram al-Sharif

Palestinian Women from Occupied East Jerusalem
Calling for Protection

Appendix B: Jerusalemite Women'S Coalition/ October 30, 2015

We women of occupied East Jerusalem call for immediate protection as we witness and suffer the widespread and serious violations of Palestinian human rights, including physical attacks and injuries, severe psychological threats, and persecution by the Israeli settler-colonial state and settler entities.

We urge the international community to act and defend the rights of Palestinian children, women, and men, including the right to a safe life amidst the constant attacks, excessive and indiscriminate use of force used by the Israeli oppressive apparatus, acts of violence and daily terror committed by Israeli Jewish civilians, including settlers. This brutality is intimidating our lives, provoking our youth, willfully causing death and bodily and psychological harm, and disabling and injuring of our community members.

We, a group of Palestinian women, mothers, sisters, daughters and youth–and in the name of the "Jerusalemite Women's Coalition"–call upon the international community to protect our families, community, and children. We are calling for the protection of our bodily safety and security when in our homes, walking in our neighborhood, reaching schools, and clinics, work places, and worships venues.

We are calling for protection, for we feel displaced even at home, as the Israeli soldiers, armed settlers, border patrol, and police invade our homes, attack our families, strip-search our bodies, and terrorize us all.

We women of occupied East Jerusalem feel as if we are orphans, without any protection from the Palestinian Authority or the international community, as the Israeli state terrorizes our homes, educational institutions, and public spaces. The state's imposition of collective punishment and sanctions invade not only our physical spaces and bodies, but also our psyches. We live in a state of fear and horror, not knowing how to face the omnipotent power of the highly technologized settler colonial entity, and militarized Israeli state that regularly executes Palestinians in the streets. Palestinians in occupied East Jerusalem have been abandoned, subject to the discriminatory policies of a violent state and its security and police apparatus.

The current political violence and the lack of any protection, as the Israeli security apparatus is protecting Jews only, jeopardizes women's safety and her economic, social, psychological, and bodily rights, as well as children's and men's safety and security. We call for protection, and the implementation of Security Council Resolution 1325 on women, peace, and security, and urge human rights defenders to protect our community from the Israeli machinery of oppression. Our children must be allowed to reach their schools in peace, and our parents and elderly must be able to reach their work places, health institutions and welfare services with safety. We request that we are able to walk in the streets without fearing the attacks of the Israeli security apparatus and its armed settlers.

We are calling for the protection of women and girls, who are particularly vulnerable to various forms of state violence and mass atrocities. The economic strangulation of Palestinians by the Israeli settler-colonial powers, that have thus far resulted in the total dependency on the Israeli entity, further traps the lives of Palestinians. The feminization of poverty and the economic strangulation of Palestinians in occupied East Jerusalem enslave Palestinians. The feminization of slavery in the colony is apparent when watching Palestinian women turn into domestic workers humiliated, controlled, and oppressed in Israeli public and private entities.

We are aware that humanitarian law attempts to challenge the inherent inhumanity of wars and colonial criminality by requiring international actors to protect civilians. International humanitarian law suggests moral boundaries of the exercise of power in situations of mass violence. International humanitarian law's main object is primarily to protect and aid victims of violence.

We, the women of occupied East Jerusalem, are politically orphaned. We are victims without protection, as the Palestinian Authority has no right to protect us in our city, and the Israeli state treats us as terrorists that should be humiliated, attacked, violated, and controlled. The guerrilla state style tactics used in occupied East Jerusalem, be it the attacks on Palestinians in the streets, the beating of the young and old, the attacks on children going to and from school, the invasion of violent settlers to our neighborhoods and homes, the control of our life, water, cell phones, internet, mobility, health, economy, and accessibility to other resources, have situated us in human cages–segregated, restrained by Israeli laws and security theology, unable to know what to anticipate and what will come next.

Having to endure all the above difficulties, which have been escalated by Israeli cabinet resolutions and otherwise ignored due to global amnesia, we are calling for protection and urgent actions to prevent further agonies, uprooting, demonization, and suffering.

Jerusalemite Women's Coalition /Al-Tajamo' al-Nasawiy al-Maqdasy.

The Coalition includes a group of Women NGOs and Jerusalemite feminists from all segments of society.

Appendix C: List of photographs

A study circle with the murabitun

An activity organized by the Islamic Movement in Israel.
Sheikh Ra'ed Salah stands in front row

A murabitat leader holding the Qur'an l
ed by Hanadi al-Halwani

The sign says it all: I am banished from Al-Aqsa Mosque

Heavily armed against the heavily dressed:
Murabitat on al-Haram al-Sharif

Murabitat wearing khimar during protest on al-Haram al-Sharif

An all-men demonstration on al-Haram al-Sharif

Awaiting the new Islamic Caliphate on al-Haram al-Sharif

Khadija Khweis leads Murabitat in a protest

Summer camp for children from Tamra on al-Haram al-Sharif

Celebrating al-Aqsa Child Day-organized by the Islamic Movement in Israel

Hamas' political activity on al-Haram al-Sharif

Iftar meal funded by the United Arab Emirates

Murabitun and murabitat and Hamas
protest the coup d'état in Egypt and show support for Morsi

Jewish settlers march outside the walls of the Old City

The sign in Hebrew says entry to the Temple Mount is Forbiodden for Jews (Ir Amim)

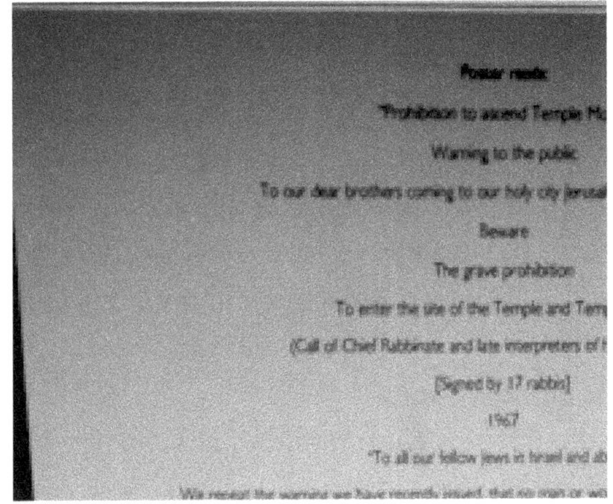

Poster reads:

"Prohibition to ascend Temple

Warning to the public

To our dear brothers coming to our holy city

Beware

The grave prohibition

To enter the site of the Temple and

(Call of Chief Rabbinate and late interpreters of

[Signed by 17 rabbis]

1967

"To all our fellow Jews in Israel and

Reference: Ir Amim

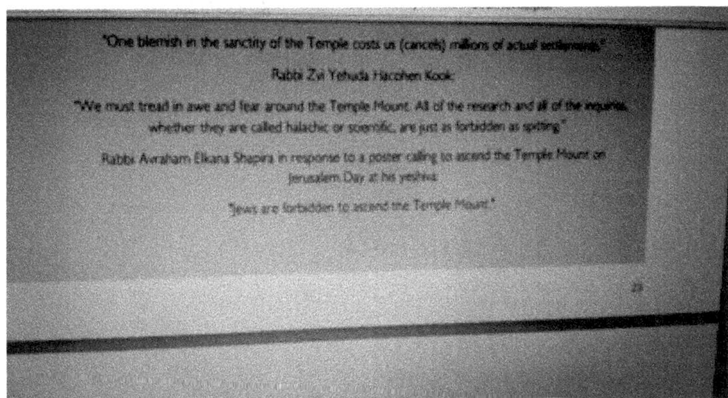

"One blemish in the sanctity of the Temple costs us (cancels) millions of actual settlements"

Rabbi Zvi Yehuda Hacohen Kook

"We must tread in awe and fear around the Temple Mount. All of the research and all of the inquiries, whether they are called halachic or scientific, are just as forbidden as spitting"

Rabbi Avraham Elkana Shapira in response to a poster calling to ascend the Temple Mount on Jerusalem Day at his yeshiva

"Jews are forbidden to ascend the Temple Mount."

The sign warns Jewish people against entry to the Temple Mount (Ir Amim)

BIBLIOGRAPHY

Abdul Hadi, Faiha. *Al-Musahama al-Siyasiya llilmar'a al- al-Filastiniyya 1965-1982* (Political Contribution of Palestinian Women 1965-1982). Ramallah: Markaz al-Mar'a al-Filastiniyya, 2015 [Arabic].

Abdul Hadi, Faiha. *Tareekh al-Haraka al-Wataniya al-Filastiniyya wadawr al-Mar'a feeha* (History of the Palestinian National Movement and Women's Role in It). Albireh: Markaz al-Mar'a al-Filastiniyya lil-Abhath wal-Tawtheeq, 2006 [Arabic]

Abdulhadi, Rabab. *The Palestinian Women's Autonomous Movement Emergence, Dynamics, and Challenges*. Gender and Society, vol.12, no. 16 (1998), pp. 649-673.

Abdul Mahdi, Abdul Jaleel, *Alharaka Alfikriya fi Thil Almasjid Alaqsa fi Al'asrayn Alayubi walMamluki* (Ideological Movement in The Ayubi and Mamluk Eras). Amman, Ministry of Culture Publication, 1980 [Arabic].

Abu Amr, Ziad. *Islamic Fundamentalism in the West Bank and Gaza.* U S A: Indiana University press,1994.

Abu Awdeh, N. & Kuttab, E. *Palestinian Women's Movement: Paradoxes and Argumentative Debates. Review of Women's Studies, 2, 21 – 36.* Ramallah: 2004.

Abu - Amr, Ziad. "The Significance of Jerusalem: A Muslim Perspective," *in Palestine- Israel Journal II*: 2 (1995), PP.23-31.

Abu Amr, Z. *Islamic Fundamentalism in the West Bank and Gaza: Muslim Brotherhood and Islamic Jihad.* Bloomington: Indiana University Press, 1994[Arabic].

Abu 'Aliya, 'Abd al-Fatah Hasan. *Al-Quds: Dirasa Ta'rikhiyya Hawla al-Masjid al-Aqsa wal-Quds al-Sharif* (Jerusalem: A Historical Study on Al-Aqsa Mosque and Jerusalem). Riyadh: Dar al-Murih, 2000 [Arabic].

Abu Awdeh, N. & Kuttab, E. *Palestinian Women's Movement: Paradoxes and*

Argumentative Debate. Review of Women's Studies, 2, (2004) 21 – 36.

Abu- Lughod, L. *Remaking Women- Feminism and Modernity in the Middle East.* Princeton: Princeton University Press, 1998.

Abu Raiya, Isam. *Developmental leadership: The Case of the Islamic Movement in Umm al-Fahm in Israel.* MA thesis, University of Worcester, 1991.12-45.

Abu Raiya, Isam. "The 1996 Split of the Islamic Movement in Israel: Between the Holy Text and Israeli-Palestinian Context." *in International Journal of Politics, Culture, and Society, I.*: 17 (2004), PP. 439-455.

Ahmed, Leila. *Women and Gender in Islam: Historical Roots of a Modern Debate.* New Haven: Yale University Press, 1992.

Ahmad, Rif'at Sayyid. "*Al- Quds 'unwan al—Intifada wa-Rumuz al-Muqawama.*" (Jerusalem - The goal of the Uprising and the Symbols of the Resistance), Al- 'Arab (London), November11, 2002. Published also at www.elquds.net [Arabic].

Ahmad, Yousef. Adviser to Isma'il Hanieh.(interview in his office in Gaza, June 3,2015) p.174

Al-Albani, Muhammad Naser al-Din. *Sahih al- Jami' al- Saghir.* Beirut: Al- Maktab al- Islami, 1986. [Arabic].

Aldaqqaq, Ihab. *A History of Partnership and A Future of Challenging Cooperation.* Columbia University, 2014.

Alqam, Nabeel. *Tareekh al-Haraka al-Wataniya al-Filastiniyya wadawr al-Mar'a feeha* (History of the Palestinian National Movement and Women's Role in It). Albireh: Jam'iyat In'ash al-Usra, 2005[Arabic]

Amara, Muhammad. "*Al-Tabi` al-Islami lil-Sira` fi al-Quds* (The Islamic Nature of the Struggle over Jerusalem)" in Mahmud, Shafiq Jasir Ahmad (ed.). Al-Quds fi al-Khitab al-Mu`asir (Jerusalem in Contemporary Discourse). Zarqa: Jami`at al-Zarqaa' al-Ahliyya (1999), pp. 35-64.[Arabic].

Amirav, Moshe. "Sanctity and Politics on the Temple Mount," in *Islam, Society and the Space in Jerusalem, Past and Present,* edited by Nimrod Luz, *Hamizhah Hehadash 44 (2004)* [Hebrew].

Al-'Arif, 'Arif. *Al- Mufassal fi Ta'rikh al-Quds* (Jerusalem History in Outline) Jerusalem. al-Andalus, 1986.

Al-Hamad, Jawad, *Studies on the Thoughts of the Islamist Resistance Movement of Hamas 1987-1996.* Amman: Middle East Studies Centre, 1997.

Al-'Asali, Kamil Jamil. *Bayt al- Maqdis fi Kutub al-Rahalat 'ind al- Arab wal Muslimin* (Jerusalem in Arab and Muslim Travel Narratives). Amman: The Author, 1992[Arabic].

Assaf, Omar. *Harakat al-Mu`almun fi Flastin1967-2000.*(Teachers Movement in Palestine 1967-2000.) Ramallah: n. p. 2003 [Arabic].

Associations of Women's Committees for Social Work, *Our Mission, Vision, and Core Values.* www.AWCSW.org. Retrieved October, 8th 2013.

Al-Aqsa Mosque Compound Targeted- Lurking Dangers between Politics and Prophecies. Jerusalem: PASSIA, 2015.

Arenfeldt, Pernille. And Nawar Al-Hassan Golley. *Mapping Arab Women's Movements: A Century of Transformations from Within.* Cairo: The American University in Cairo Press, 2012.

Aweidah, Samyia. *Women, Armed Conflict and Loss - The Experience of Bereaved Women in Mutual Psychological Support.* Jerusalem: Women Studies Center, 2007.

Badran, Margot. *Feminists, Islam and Nation: Gender and the Making of Modern Egypt.* Princeton: Princeton University Press, 1995.

Badran, Margret. *Gender Activism: Feminists and Islamists in Egypt.* Boulder: Westview Press, 1994.

Bajes, Dalal, *Al- Haraka al-Tulabiyya fi Flastin* (The Islamic Student Movement in Palestine). Ramallah: 2012 [Arabic].

Bajes, Dalal. *Al-Nisa'a al-Islamiyat fi al-Alam al-Arabi min Radat Fi'el ila Waqi'a* (Islamist Women in the Arab World from Reaction to Reality). Al-Qahira, Dar al-Salam liltiba'a wal-Nashr, 2003 [Arabic]

Barghouthi, Eyad. *Al- Aslamah wa al-Sayyasah fi al-Aradi al-Muhtalah.* (Islamization and Politics in the Occupied Palestinian Territories). Ramallah: n.p.2003 [Arabic].

Barghouthi, Eyad. *Al-Aslam al-Sayyasi fi Flasten.* (Political Islam in Palestine: Behind the Policy). Jerusalem: Media and Communications Centre, 2000[Arabic].

Barzaq, Mukhlis Yihya. *Al- Quds min al-Masjid al- Haram illa al-Masjid al-Aqsa* (Jerusalem from the Sacred Mosque [in Mecca] to Al-Aqsa Mosque), Beirut: Jerusalem Institute, May 2003. Available at www.al-quds –online.org [Arabic].

Baydun, 'Isa Mahmud. *Dalil al- Masjid al- Aqsa al- Mubark* (Guide to al-Aqsa Mosque). Kafar Kanna: Markaz al-Takhtit wal- Dirasat, 1993[Arabic]

Ben Solomon, Ariel. "Israel's Islamic Movement: Overcoming Obstacles," *The Jerusalem Post,* 15 May 2016. Accessed 5 June 2016.

Ben Shitrit, Lihi. "Women, Freedom and Agency in Religious-Political Movements: Reflections from Women Activists in Shas and the Islamic Movement in Israel." *Journal of Middle East Women's Studies,* vol.9, no. 3 (2013).

Ben Shitrit, Lihi. *Righteous Transgressions - Women's Activism on the Israeli and Palestinian Religious Right.*United Kingdom: Princeton University Press, 2016.

Ben Shitrit, Lihi. *Domesticating the Holy: Women for the Temple and the (In) Divisibility of Contested Sacred Places.* University of Georgia: 2014.

Benvenisti, Meron. *Jerusalem, the Torn City [Mul ha- Hamash ha – Segurah].* Jerusalem Wiedenfeld and Nicholson, 1973 [Hebrew].

Ben- Ze'ev, Efrat, and Issam Aburaiya. *"Middle- Ground' Politics and the Re-Palestinization of Place in Israel, "International Journal of Middle Eastern Studies* 36 (2004), PP. 639- 655.

____, City of Stone, *The Hidden History of Jerusalem. Berkeley,* CA: University of California Press, 1996.

Breger, Yitzhak Reiter, and Leonard Hammer, *Holy Places in the Israeli-Palestinian Conflict* (New York: Routledge, 2010).

Chabbi, J. and Nasser Rabat. "Ribat," Encyclopedia of Islam 2nd ed., VIII (1997).

Cohen, Hillel. *The Rise and Fall of Arab Jerusalem – Palestinian Politics and the City since1967.* London and New York: Routledge, 2011.

Cohen, Hillel. *Year Zero of the Arab -Israeli Conflict 1929.* Brandeis University Press, 2015.

Dajani, Abla. *Al-Mar'a al- al-Filastiniyya fi Muwajahat al-Ghazw al-Suhyuni* (Palestinian Women in the Face of Zionist Invasion). Al-Qahira: Dar al-Mustaqbal al-Arabi, 1992[Arabic]

Dakwar, Jamil. "The Islamic movement inside Israel: An Interview with Shaykh Ra'id Salah" *Journal of Palestinian Studies,* Vol. 36, 2 (Winter, 2007).

Dapnna, Sharfman. *Palestine in the Second World War. Strategic Plans and Political Dilemmas: The Emergence of a New Middle East.* U S A: Sussex, 2014.

Daraghmah, Izzat. *Al-Haraka al-Nisa'iya fi Falasteen, 1903-1990* (Women's Movement in Palestine 1903-1990). al-Quds: Maktab Dia'a Lildirasat, 1991 [Arabic]

Dawlat, Filastin. *Majzarat Al-Aqsa, Shahadat wa –Watha'iq* (Al-Aqsa Massacre, Testimonies, and Documents). Itihad Lijan al- Mar'a lil – 'Amal al-Ijtima'I [PLO: The Women's Union for Social Action], 1992 [Arabic].

Dayan, Moshe. *Milestones: an Autobiography.* Jerusalem and Tel Aviv: Idanim and Dvir, 1976 [Hebrew].

Deeb, Lara. *An Enchanted Modern: Gender and Public Piety in Shi'i Lebanon.* Princeton: Princeton University Press, 2006.

Dumper, Mick. *Islam and Israel: Mulsim Religious Endowments and the Jewish State,* Washington D.C: Institute for Palestine Studies, 1997.

Dumper, Mick, andnd Craig Larkin. "Political Islam in Contested Jerusalem: The Emerging Role of Islamists from within Israel Divided Cities/Contested States." Paper No. 12, 2009. Available at: http://www.upwc.org.ps

Dumper, Mick, and Craig Larkin. *The Struggle for Jerusalem's Holy Places.* London: Routledge, 2013.

Dumper, Michael. *The Politics of Jerusalem Since 1967.* New York: Columbia University Press, 1997.

Finkelstein, Israel, and Neal Asher Silberman. *The Bible Unearthed: Archaeology's New Vision of Ancient Isreal and the Origin of Its Sacred Texts.* New York: Simon and Schuster, 2002[Hebrew translation: Reshit Yisrael: Arkheologia, Mikra ve- Zikaron: Tel Aviv University, 2003.

Fleischmann, Ellen. *The Emergence of the Palestinian Women's Movement, 1929-39.* Institute Journal Palestinian studies" Vol. 29. 1999- 2000.

Fleischmann, Ellen. "Jerusalem Women's Organizations During the British Mandate 1920-1930." Jerusalem: Passia, 1995.

Fleischmann, Ellen. *The Nation and it's "New" Women: the Palestinian Women's Movement, 1920- 1948. Berkeley:* University of California Press, 2003.

Fleischmann, Ellen. *"The Other 'Awakening': The Emergence of Women's Movement in the Modern Middle East, 1900-1940"* in Margaret l. Meriwether and Judith E Tucker, eds. *A Social History of Women and Gender in Modern Middle East.* Boulder Westview Press, 1999, pp. 89-134.

Ghada, Talahami. *Historical Dictionary ofWomen in the Middle East and North Africa.* Ghada Talahami .U K :The Scarecrow Press,2013, p.141)

Greenberg, Ela. *Preparing the Mothers of Tomorrow: Education and Islam in Mandate Palestine.* Austin: University of Texas Press, 2009.

Halem, Sara. “The young Woman at the Forefront of Jerusalem’s New Holy War.” In Newsweek. 2012. PP. 12-4.

“Israel Defiled Al-Aqsa,” Ynet News, August 22, 2008, http://www.

ynetnews.com/articles/0,7340,L-3586354,00.html.

Hamdan, Nadia. *Waqi’a al-Musharaka al-Siyasiya llilmar’a al-al-Filastiniyya* (Reality of Political Participation of Palestinian Women). Ramallah: Matba’at Abu Ghosh, 2001 [Arabic]

Hammami, Reem. “From Immodesty to Collaboration: Hamas, the Women’s Movement and National Identity in the Intifada.” In Joel Benin and Joe Stork (eds.), Political Islam: Essays from Middle East Report. New York: I .B. Tauris,1997.

Hammami, Rema and Jamil Hilal and Salim Tamari. *Civil Society in Palestine: “Case Studies.”* San Domenico: European University Institute, 2001.

Al-Hassan, Anwar. *Mapping Arab Women’s Movement* .Cairo: American University press, 2012.

Al- Hut, Bayan Nuwayhid. *Al- Qiyadat wa al- Mu’assasat al-Siyasiyya fi Filastin,* 1917-1948 [The Political Leadership and Institutions in Palestine, 1917- 1948]. 3rd ed. Beirut: Institute for Palestine Studies, 1986. [Arabic]

Hroub, Khalid. *Hamas: al-Tafkeir al-Sayyasi wa al-Mumarassah.(Hamas- Political Thought and Practice.)* Washington DC: Institute for Palestine Studies, 1998 [Arabic].

Hroub, Khalid. *Hamas: Al-Fikr wal-Mumarasa al-Siyasiyya* (Hamas: Ideology and Political Practice). Beirut: Institute for Palestine Studies, 1999 [Arabic].

Hroub, Khalid. *Al-Islamiyun fi Filastin: Qira'at ,Mawaqif wa-QadayaUkhra*_(The Islamists of Palestine: Reading, Positions and Other Matters). Amman: Al-Bashir,1994[Arabic].

Al-Husayni, Yusuf Kamil Hasuna. *Filastin wal-I`tida`at al-Isra'iliyya `ala al-Muqaddasat Al-Islamiyya* (Palestine and Israeli Desecrations of the Islamic Holy Places). Hebron: 2000 [Arabic].

"Ihtifalat al-watan bi-dhikra al-isra' wal-mi'raj," Al-Quds, November 28, 1997[Arabic]

Inbari, Moti. *Jewish Fundamentalism and the Temple Mount.* New York: New York University Press,2009.

Inbari, Moti. "*The Oslo Accords and the Temple Mount, a Case Study: The Movement for the Establishment of the Temple,"* HUCA 74 (2003), PP. 1- 45.

Inbari, Motti. *Messionic religious Zionism confronts Israeli Territorial Compromises*: Cambridge University Press, 2012.

Itzar Be'er. *Dangerous Liaison the Dynamics of the Rise of the Temple Movements And Their Implications.* Jerusalem: Ir Amim, May 2013 [Hebrew].

Eran Tzikiyahu, *Bayan: The Arabs in Israel,* The Konrad Adenauer Program for Jewish-Arab Cooperation, Issue no. 6, December 2015.

J.Breger, Marshal. And Yitzhak Reiter. *Holy Places in the Israeli –Palestinian Conflict.* New York: Routledge, 2010.

JABR, Ahmad Fahim. *Wujuduna al- Hadari fi Bayt al- Maqdis* (The Presence of our Civilization in Jerusalem). Jerusalem: *Markaz al-Quds lil- Abhath wal- Tawthiq,* 1999 [Arabic].

Jad, Islah. *Local Feminism: Between Islamism and Liberal Universalism.* Institute of

Development Studies Bulletin, 39, (2008) 34-41.

Jad, Islah. "Islamist Women of Hamas: Between Feminism and Nationalism."Revue Des Mondes Musulmans et de la Mediterranee, no. 128(2010) also available on website: http:/ www./remmm.revues.org/6971.

Jad, Islah. *Feminism between Secularism and Islamism: The Case of Palestine (West Bank and Gaza).* Beirut and London: Conflicts Forum, (2010), also available on website: http://remmm.revues.org/6971.

Jad, Islah. *Women at the Crossroads: The Palestinian Women Movements Between the Secular, National and Islamic Identities.* Ramallah: Muwatin, 2008.

Jbara, Taiser. *Ta'rikh Filastin al- Hadith* (The Modern History of Palestine). Amman: Dar Al -Shuruq, 1998 [Arabic].

Jose, Raphael. "The Significance of Jerusalem: A Jewish Perspective." Palestine- Israel Journal 11:2 (1995), pp.32-40.

Ju'ba, Nazmi. *Al-Quds:Awraq al-Mu'tamar al-Dawli `an al-Quds.* (Jerusalem: Papers of International Conference about Jerusalem). Amman: Ministry of Culture, 2009 [Arabic].

Karam, Azza. *Women, Islamism and the State: Contemporary Feminisms in Egypt.* London: Macmillan Press and New York: St. Martin's Press,1998[Arabic].

Katz, Kimberly. Jordanian Jerusalem: *Holy Places and National Spaces.* Gainesville: University Press of Florida, 2005.

Katz, Marion. *Women in the Mosque- A history of Legal Thought and Social Practice.* New York: Columbia University Press, 2014.

Kawar, Amal. *Daughters of Palestine – Leading Women of the Palestinian National Movement.* Jerusalem and New York: Women's Committees in the Occupied Territories and SUNY,1996.

Kazi, Hamida. *Palestinian women and the national liberation movement: a social perspective.* Khamsin: Journal of revolutionary socialists of the Middle-East (November13,2013).

Alkhalili, Ghazi. *Al-Mar'a al- al-Filastiniyya wal-Thawra,* (Palestinian Women and the Revolution). Beirut: Markaz al-Abhath, 1977[Arabic]

Klein, Menachem. *Jerusalem, the Contested City.* London: Hurst& Company in association with the Jerusalem Institute for Israel Studies, 2001.

Klein, Menachem. *The Jerusalem Problem: The Struggle for Permanent Status.* Gainesville: University Press of Florida, 2003.

Kuttab, Eileen. "The Palestinian Women's Movement: From Resistance and Liberation to Accommodation and Globalization." Genève: Graduate Institute Publications, 2009.

Kuttab, E. *Palestinian Intifada in the Shadow of Globalization. Review of Women's Studies,*. Ramallah: 2003.

Lahlouh, Alla. *Al-Aganda al-Ijtima`iyya li-Hamas.* (The Social Agenda of Hamas) Ramallah: 2010 [Arabic].

Livneh- Kafri, Ofer. *Jerusalem in Early Islam. A Compilation of Articles [Iyunim be – Ma'amadah shel yerushalayim ba Islam ha-Kudum:* Kovets Ma'amarim]. Jerusalem: Yad Yitzhak Ben- Zvi, 2000 [Hebrew]

Luz, Nimrod. *Al- Haram Al- Sharif in the Palestine Arab Public Discourse in Israel.* Jerusalem: Floersheimer Institute for Policy Studies, 2004 [Hebrew].

Mahmoud, Saba. *Politics of Piety: The Islamic Revival and the Feminist Subject.* Princeton: Princeton University Press, 2005.

Matthew, Levitt. *Hamas Politics, Charity, and Terrorism in the service of Jihad.* U S A: The Washington Institute for Near East Policy, 2006.

Maqadima, Ibrahim. *Ma'alim fil- Tariq ila Filastin* (Guideposts on the Road to Liberating Palestine). Occupied Palestinian Territories: Alim Institute, 1994[Arabic].

Mernissi, Fatma. *Doing Daily Battle: Interviews with Moroccan Women.* Translated by Mary Jo Lakeland. New Brunswick, N.J,1988.

Mernissi, Fatma. *The Forgotten Queens of Islam.* Minneapolis: University of Minnesota Press and Women's Press, 1993.

Middle East Studies Center. *Israel seizes Jerusalem in accordance with the strategic plans.* Amman: -dar –al-Bashir in 1996 [Arabic]

Moghadam, Valentine. M. *Identity Politics and Women: Cultural Reassertions and Feminisms in International Perspective.* Boulder: Westview Press,1994.

Mujir al- Din al- Hanbali. *Al- Uns Al- Jalil bi- Ta'rikh al- Quds wal- Khalil* (The Sublime Friendship in the History of Jerusalem and Hebron), Beirut: Dar al- Jalil, 1973 [Arabic].

Musallam, Sami F. *The Struggle for Jerusalem.* Jerusalem: PASSIA, 1996.

Al- Nahawi, Adnan Ali Rida. *Ala Abwab al-Quds.* (at the Gates of Jerusalem). Riyadh: Dar al –Nahawi, 1993 [Arabic].

Al- Nashashibi, Nasser al- Din. *Who Killed King Abdullah?* Dar al- Uruba, n.d. [Arabic].

Nashwan , Jamil. *Al –Ta`lim fi Filastin min al-Dawla al-`Uthmaniyya wa-hata al-Sulta al-Filastiniyya.* (Education in Palestine since the Ottoman State to the Palestinian National Authority). Ramallah: 2003[Arabic].

Nuseibeh, Sari. *'Islam's Jerusalem,' in Jerusalem, Religious Aspect.* Jerusalem: PASSIA, 1995, PP. 23- 34.

OR Commission Report: *Commission of Inquiry into the Clashes between Security Force and Israeli Citizens in October 2000 Report* (Jerusalem: Government Press, September 2003) [Hebrew].

Palestinian Encyclopedia, (Arabic) Vol. 4, 1st printing, (Damascus: Association of the Palestinian Encyclopedia, 1984), 216.

Palestinian Legislative Council-Ramallah. *The Representatives.* www.pal-plc.org. Retrieved June, 6th 2013.

PASSIA. *Palestinian Facts and Info* . Palestinian Academic Society for International Affairs. www.passia.org Retrieved November, 7th 2011.

Peteet, Julie. *Gender in Crisis: Women and the Palestinian Resistance Movement.* New York: Columbia University Press, 1991.

Pullan, Wendy, Maximilian Sternberg, Lefkos Kyriacou, Craig Larkin, and Michael Dumper. *The Struggle for Jerusalem's Holy Places.* Oxon: Routledge, 2013.

Al-Qadumi, Issa. *Al-Masjid al-Aqsa, al-Haqiqa wal-Tareekh* (al-Aqsa Mosque Truth and History). Beirut: Markaz Beit al-Makdis lildirasat al-Tawthiqiya, 2008[Arabic]

Al-Qaradawi, Yusuf. *Al-Quds, Qadiyyat Kul Muslim* (Jerusalem is the Problem of Every Muslim). Beirut, Damascus, and Amman: Al-Maktab al-Islami, 2002. Also available on al-Qaradawi's Web site: http//:www.qaradawi.net [Arabic].

Al- Ramahi, Maysoun. *Al-Islam wal-Muslimin wa-Qadaya al-Mara'a* (Islam and Muslim Women's Issues: Islam in Contemporary Palestine). Ramallah:2014 [Arabic].

Ramon, Amnon. *The Jerusalem Lexicon. Jerusalem*: The Jerusalem Institute for Israel Studies, 2003.

Ramon, Amnon. "Beyond the Western Wall: Official Israeli and Jewish Public Attitudes toward the Temple Mount, 1967-1999," in Yitzhak Reiter (ed), *Sovereignty of God and Man: Sanctity and Political Centrality on the Temple Mount.* Jerusalem: Jerusalem Institute for Israel Studies, 2001, pp. 113- 142 [Hebrew].

Reiter, Yitzhak. "The Eroding Status-Quo: Power Struggles on the Temple Mount." *Jerusalem Institute for Policy Research,* 2017.

Reiter (ed), *Sovereignty of God and Man: Sanctity and Political Centrality on the Temple Mount* (Jerusalem; Jerusalem Institute for Israel Studies, 2001), pp. 5-20 [Hebrew].

Reiter, Yitzhak. *Jerusalem and Its role in Islamic Solidarity.* New York: Palgrave MacMillan, 2008.

Reiter, Yitzhak. Status Que Change: *The Struggle for Control on the Temple Mount. Jerusalem:* The Jerusalem Institute for Israel Studies, 2016[Hebrew].

Reiter, Yitzhak. *Islamic Endowment in Jerusalem under British Mandate.* London and Portland Or: Frank Cass, 1996.

Roded, Ruth. *Women in Islam and the Middle East: A Reader.* London: I. B Tauris, 1999.

Sala'ah, Ra'ed. (2007). *Al-Masjid Al-Aqsa: Arba'un 'A man min al-Ihtilal.* (Al-Aqsa Mosque: Forty Years under Occupation). AL-Qahera: Markaz al-I'lam al-Arabi,2007 [Arabic].

Shaham (ed). *Law, Custom, and Statue in the Muslim World, Studies in Honor of Professor Aharon Layish.* Leiden: E.J. Brill, 2007, pp. 172- 197.

Shragai, Nadav. *The Temple Mount Conflict: Jews and Muslims, Religion and Politics since 1967* [Harha- Merivah: ha-Ma'avak al Har-ha-Bayit: Yehudim u- Muslemim, Dat u-Politikah Me-az 1967]. Jerusalem: Keter, 1995 [Hebrew].

Shragai, Nadav. "The Breach of the Temple Mount: a Swift Kick at Jewish History." Ha'aretz, 12 February 1999.

Shragai, Nadav. *Har ha-Merivah: Ha-Ma'avak al Har ha-Bayit: Yehudim u-Muslemim, Dat u-Politikah me-az 1967* (The Temple Mount Conflict: Jews and Muslims, Religion and Politics since 1967). Jerusalem: Keter, 1995 [Hebrew].

Shragai, Nadav. *Al-Aqsa in Danger Libel: A Profile of a Lie.* Tel Aviv: Maariv, 2012 (Hebrew).

Shurab, Muhammad. And Muhammad Hasan. *Bayt al- Maqdis wal- Masjid al- Aqsa, Dirasa Ta'rikhiyya Muwaththaqa* (Jerusalem and the al- Aqsa Mosque, a Reliable Historical Study). Damascus and Beirut: Dar al- Qalam and Dar al-Shamia, 1994 [Arabic].

Silwdi, Hasan. "Al- Mustashrikun al- Yahud Yuhawilun al-Tahwin min Qudsiyyat al- Quds wa- Makanatiha fi al-Islam." (The Jewish Orientalists Attempt to Belittle the Sacredness of Jerusalem and its Important Status in Islam), published on www.alqudsgate.com/studies/studies7.htm. [Arabic].

Stuart, Hall. "The Question of Cultural Identity." Edited by S. Hall, D. Held, and T. McGrew. Modernity and its Futures. London: Polity Press and Open University, (1992) .PP. 274- 325.

Tal, Inbal. *Women's Activism in Islamic Movement in Israel 1983-2007: Influence, Characteristics and Implications* (*PhD dissertation,* University of Haifa), 2011 [Hebrew].

Talhami, Ghada. "The History of Jerusalem: A Muslim Prespective," in Hans Ucko (ed), *The Spiritual Significance of Jerusalem for Jews,* Christians and Muslims. Geneva: world Council of Churches, 1994, pp. 21- 31.

Taraki, Lisa. *Islam Is the Solution: Jordanian Islamists and the Dilemma of the "Modern Women."* The British Journal of Sociology, Vol.46, No. 4(Dec., 1995), 643-661.

Taraki, lisa. "Mass Organizations in the West Bank," in N. Aruri (ed.), *Occupation: Israel Over Palestine,* Massachusetts, Belmont,1989.

"The Arab Woman and the Palestine Problem, the Eastern Women's Conference Held at the House of the Egyptian Women's Union in Cairo, from 15 to 18 October, 1938," Cairo, 1938. Conference publication. (Arabic), 170-172.

The Jerusalem Waqf administration's website, www.alaqsa-online.net, cites Qardawi's fatwa in response to a question from October 13, 2002.

The northern branch of the Islamic Movement's weekly newspaper is titled *Sawt al-Haqq wal-Hurriyya* (Voice of Truth and Freedom) and its official website is www.islamic-aqsa.com

The Status of the Status Quo at Jerusalem's Holy Esplanade. International Crisis Group, Belgium: Middle East Report N°159 | 30 June 2015

The Supreme Muslim Council. *Brief Guide to al- Haram al-Sharif Jerusalem.* Jerusalem: Supreme Muslim council, 1929.

Al-W'haidi, Maisoon. *Al-Mar'a al- al-Filastiniyya wa-ilihtilal al-Israeli*_(Palestinian Women and the Israeli Occupation). Al-Quds: Jamiyat al-Dirasat al-Arabiya, 1986[Arabic]

Union of Palestinian Women Committees (2013). About Us. www. UPWC.org.ps.

Women Rights Doctrine. (2006). General Union for Palestinian Women Publications

www.GUPW.net Retrieved October 17, 2013.

Yawm al-Quds, Abhath al-Nadwa al- Sadisa (al- Quds Day, Proceedings of the Sixth Convention, November 2-5, 1991). Amman: Mu'asasat al- Abhath al- 'Arabiya, 1996 [Arabic].

Yusuf, Ahmad. *Harakat al-Muqawama al-Islamiyya (Hamas): Hadathun`Aber am Badilun Da'im*(The Islamic Resistance Movement (Hamas): An Ephemeral Event or a Permanent). Chicago: The International Center for Studies and Research, 1990[Arabic].

Ra'id Sallah, "*Li'annahnu al-Aqsa al-Mubarak*" *Sawt al-Haqq wal-Hurriya*, September 15, 2000, p. 5.

Ikrama, Sabri. (Mufti Jerusalem and Palestine) (Interview 2-11-2015)-

'Azam, al-Khateb. General Director of Awqaf(Interview on September 15,2015)

Islamic and Arabic Internet Sites:

http://www.aqsaonline.org/news.aspx?id=401)
www.aqsaonline.org
www.jewishpress.com
http://mfa.gov.il/MFA/ForeignPolicy/MFADocuments
http://simania.co.il/bookdetails
www.al-multaqa.net
www.qaradawi.net
http://avalon.law.yale.edu/20th_century/hamas.asp
(Hamas Charter 1988)
www.geocities.com
www.aicpmultimedia.org
www.alqudsgate.com
www.bma-alqods.org
www.jr.co.il
www.raoulwallenberg.net
www.jerusalem.muni.il
www.kinghussein.gov.jo
www.bma-alqods.org/arabic
www.timesofisrael.com
www.mfa.gov.il
www. gulfnews.com
www.haaretz.co.il
www.binbaz.org.sa
www.almaany.com
www.islamic-aqsa.com

www.eshraka.com
www.fatawah.com
www.fatwaonline.com
www.haaretz.co.il
www.ikhwanonline.com
www.ikhwanweb.com
www.islammov.net
www.islamtoday.com
www.methak.org
www.panet.co.il
www.pls48.net
www.qaradawi.net
www.salafipublication.com
www.sawt-alhaq.com
www.ir-amim.org.il
www.tawheedmovement.com/2012
http://legacy.Qurʾan.com/
www.ma'annews.net
www.http://edition.cnn.com/
www.ibnbaz.org.sa/node
https://tawheedmovement.com
http://archive.aawsat.com
www.aljazeera.net
MOWA.gov.ps, 2013; MOWA.pna.ps, 2013
Algiers, November 15, 1988
UNRWA.org. 2013

PASSIA.org, 2013

(www.conflictincities.org)

http://www.islamic-aqsa.com

http://www.haaretz.com/hasen/spages/1072208.html/.

http://www.icpri.org/files/qadi.html

http://www.islamic-aqsa.com

http://www.aqsa-mubarak.net.

www.MOWA.pna.ps.

www.ingramcontent.com/pod-product-compliance
Lightning Source LLC
Chambersburg PA
CBHW071636270326
41928CB00010B/1948

* 9 7 8 1 9 9 9 0 9 8 2 2 3 *